BLOCKCHAIN
PROPHECIES

Edited by Liz Whelan

Book concept, art, illustrations crafted by the team at Geletka+. Austin Bond, Sadie Van Wie, Amanie Safadi, Joe Wangler, Clint May, Christina Downey.

First Edition 2023

BLOCKCHAIN PROPHECIES

PROLOGUE

THE THING ABOUT PROPHECIES...

They hold an air of mystery, a glimpse into the future, a divine connection to knowledge beyond our grasp. As I embarked on my journey of writing about the blockchain and tokenization ecosystem, little did I know that I would become a witness to the unfolding of its promises, its complexity, and its rapid growth shaping a new era in human potential.

That may seem a bit overdramatic but allow me to explain.

When I first encountered blockchain technology in 2016, the world was ablaze with ICOs and the allure of crypto. Coming from a background entrenched in the complexities of financial institutions like Capital One and Bank of America, I couldn't help but notice two things that struck me to my core.

First, I knew deep down that the days of ICOs were numbered. As exhilarating as they were, they bypassed the necessary regulations for capital raising, and I could sense the party would soon come to an end. Second, blockchain held within it an incredible infrastructure—a framework that could simplify the convoluted nature of many industries that have been struggling to handle the ever-increasing complexity of business transactions and regulations and unlock new possibilities that were previously deemed impractical.

These realizations set me on a path of exploration and experimentation. In 2017, along with my co-founders, I embarked on the creation of SPiCE VC. At that time, the idea of digital securities seemed like a distant and somewhat vague pipedream. But our intuition was that blockchain and tokenization, in full compliance with securities and fundraising regulations, had the power to revolutionize the world of securities transactions, including venture capital fundraising.

We sought to prove our theory by tokenizing the LP interests in SPiCE VC, and we even reached out to companies involved in tokenizing ICOs, providing them with the specifications required for full compliance with securities regulations. Yet, they hesitated, shying away from the complexity and insisting it couldn't be done.

As serial entrepreneurs, my co-founders and I had grown accustomed to hearing the phrase "can't be done." And as any entrepreneur worth their salt would keenly understand "can't be done" immediately becomes, "it will be done." And so, we decided to take matters into our own hands, forging our own path. We became the pioneers we were looking for, creating the legal and regulatory structures that would eventually shape the digital securities industry. Late in 2017, we birthed Securitize, now recognized as a leading player in the digital securities space.

This journey gave me a window into the world of blockchain & tokenization and opened my eyes to the power and vast potential of tokenization in every industry it would touch, including global finance. At the same time, it revealed the immense ecosystem required to support this burgeoning technology. Inspired by this revelation, we directed our investment efforts towards nurturing the blockchain ecosystem and supporting visionary companies building the future.

But make no mistake, investing in early stage companies in such a transformational and rapidly evolving movement, is no simple feat. It demands an unwavering focus, a deep understanding of the technology, its applications across industries, and the ever-shifting regulatory landscape. Navigating this terrain successfully, our first fund, SPiCE I, earned the title of "Top Tokenized Venture Capital Fund Globally," solidifying our dedication to the blockchain revolution.

This is the exact moment I realized that I had a front-row seat to witness and participate in one of the most profound technological revolutions in history, a revolution that would unfold over the next 10-15 years (and longer).

This was also the moment that I began writing.

It was an exhilarating realization that I was living through one of the most transformational periods in the development and adoption of a particular technology in history. It inspired me to document the journey in real-time.

Blockchain technology was not new when I started documenting my insights and predictions. In fact, it originated more than a decade prior. However, the renaissance of thought and ideation related to new use-cases in multiple industries, was in its early stages and I wanted to capture the evolving thought process, the adoption waves, the successes and failures, the "booms" and "busts" of each component, and the ever-changing landscape of blockchain's evolution. In a sense, I aimed to create a "starship log" that chronicled a critical and transformative period in the development and adoption of this groundbreaking technology.

Throughout this period, we witnessed the organic adoption of blockchain technology across multiple industries and verticals. Capital markets were among the first to be transformed, embracing the potential of blockchain. Venture capital investments in the ecosystem skyrocketed, ETFs and mutual funds began focusing on blockchain, and the emergence of crypto futures ETFs signaled a new phase of acceptance. At the same time, mainstream adoption of cryptocurrencies started gaining momentum, and the blockchain ecosystem expanded exponentially.

We can't talk about this fascinating period of Decentralized Finance (DeFi) discovery without mentioning NFTs (Non-

Fungible Tokens) or the Metaverse. No one could top the hype around NFTs and the Metaverse in 2021. From digital art to digital albums (throw in some celebrity-backed trading cards and one notable "tweet",) the NFT market blew up. Research platform Dune Analytics noted the total sales volume of NFTs increased to $2.5 billion in the first half of 2021 compared to $13.7 million in the first half of 2020.

The Metaverse got so big that Facebook was actually renamed Meta in its pursuit for this AR/VR/AI/blockchain–driven state of being. While both were over-hyped and over-funded, the possibilities of each were, and still are, endless.

The Decentralized Finance (DeFi) market, which includes global tokenization, blockchain, Metaverse, digital securities, Non-Fungible Tokens (NFTs), Central Bank Digital Currencies (CBDCs), crypto, and more, touches every industry—from entertainment to healthcare to financial markets. If you bring into account the addressable traditional finance (TradFi), which includes all consumer and commercial banking, insurance, and capital markets, the total addressable market is well over $100 trillion.

If you break the blockchain-based market down by verticals, the growth trajectory becomes even more clear. The blockchain-based supply-chain market is expected to grow to over $14 billion in revenue by 2028, while the healthcare market transitioning to blockchain technology (a rapidly growing trend), is expected to reach more than $126 billion by 2030. Those are just two verticals in the blockchain-only portion of the greater DeFi landscape.

If you compare that to the market cap of all cryptocurrencies at its value in August 2022, which stood at just over $1 trillion, you can see that of the entire DeFi pie, crypto is only a small slice, less than 0.1% of the total addressable market. This is particularly important as, during the course of writing this

It's about the transforma-tional power of the underlying technology driving the new era.

book, cryptocurrencies saw a historic rise, and a subsequent nose-dive, its value grabbing all of the headlines and sucking a significant amount of air out of the entire blockchain category.

In fact, the total capital inflows from investments made by venture capitalists the blockchain space in 2021 were $30.5 billion, with this amount increasing to $31.5 billion in just the first half of 2022. But, by the second half of 2022, when the crypto chaos began, those VC investments began retracting, with investors conflating crypto with all of blockchain. An April 11 report from Galaxy Research, the research arm of crypto investment firm Galaxy Digital, said the $2.4 billion invested by VCs throughout Q1 2023 was the lowest sum invested since the last quarter of 2020.

The period of time now known as "Crypto Winter," which saw well over a 70% drop in Bitcoin price between Q3 2022 and Q2 2023, had reverberating effects throughout the blockchain and tokenization ecosystem. From a decrease in investments and adoption to increases in regulatory uncertainty, the evolution of digital finance was most certainly experiencing its fair share of growing pains.

Whether or not massive and life-changing geopolitical events during this time played a hand in the boom and bust of crypto or the ebbs and flows of blockchain and DeFi adoption is still in question. I'm a venture capitalist and entrepreneur, not a political scientist or an epidemiologist. However, I'm fairly confident that experiencing the most devastating pandemic to afflict the human race in 100 years (COVID-19 Pandemic) along with the largest land war since WWII (Russia's invasion of Ukraine) occurring during this period is more than significant. I think it had a seismic impact on the trajectory of not only blockchain and digital finance, but also the new economic world order that has subsequently taken hold.

However, as "Crypto Winter" continued and geopolitical instability persisted, loyal blockchain pioneers, enthusiasts, and technologists, along with a slow but steady increase in interest and money from banks and institutional investors, the blockchain market continued to grow. In fact, the blockchain market size is currently still rising globally at a CAGR of 56.3% during the forecast period 2022 to 2029.

Even as global regulatory and legislative bodies grapple with how to handle the uses of this technology, which includes managing the companies (and fortunes) that are built on its back, blockchain will still persist and its use-cases still proliferate.

The thing is, when a once-in-generation human advancement comes along, it can handle the early stages of "Darwinism." Because it's not about the hype or even the companies. It's about the transformational power of the underlying technology driving the new era. This is Distributed Ledger Technology (DLT). This is blockchain. And while I probably won't live to see all of the innovations, ideas, and solutions created because of it, I will have been around long enough for it to take hold and alter the way we live, work and play in the most profound and pervasive of ways.

Blockchain is greater than one industry, product, asset, or technology solution. It's an entirely new framework that enables novel approaches to solve today's most complex problems, while simultaneously providing the tools and infrastructure to tackle the challenges we don't even realize are yet to come. Simply put, blockchain isn't the atomic bomb, it's nuclear fission. It's not the light bulb, it's the alternating current.

As I reflect on my journey, I am humbled by the opportunities I have been afforded. To witness and participate in the birth of a transformational advancement is a rare gift. It is a privilege to be able to share my thoughts, insights, and prophecies in real time, capturing the essence of a period marked by rapid change and relentless innovation.

The Blockchain Prophecies is an honest account of the blockchain era unfolding in front of me. It's from a variety of perspectives on an even greater number of topics all of which tethered to important moments in the ecosystem's evolution. And, while I tried to be as objective as possible, my insights and "take are woven throughout. I got some of it right and I got some it wrong, but my hope for the readers is that through digesting all of it in its imperfect and somewhat shambolic glory, they're able to gain knowledge, spark interest, and even imagine some of the wonder yet to come.

BLOCKCHAIN PROPHECIES

TABLE OF CONTENTS

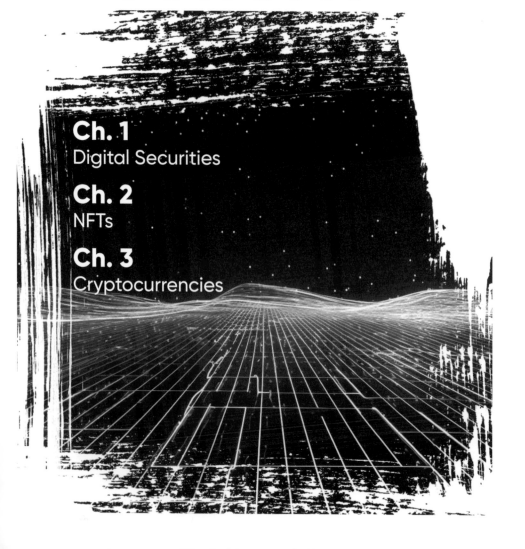

INTRODUCTION

The nuts and bolts of the traditional economy include things like stocks, bonds, commodities, options, derivatives...you get it. They've been the bedrock and the investable universe of our centuries old economy and without them, the financial engines don't run. The same is true with the new financial kids on the block, only in a digital economy, are these tools possible with blockchain technology. The tokenization of assets is constructing the brave new world of the digital economy, which include digital securities, cryptocurrencies, Non-Fungible Tokens (NFTs), Central Bank Digital Currencies (CBDCs), and the often overlooked stablecoins.

Now, let's wind back a little. The timeline during which these articles were published is something of a rollercoaster. NFTs had their Warhol-esque fifteen minutes of fame. Crypto was like a Katy Perry song, hot and cold, with multiple rallies and then its inevitable crashes. Then, like a steady locomotive, digital securities kept moving forward at a slow but steady pace, gaining traction and attention from mainstream financial bigwigs. Even CBDCs made major strides. Almost everywhere except the US.

Real estate tokenization was briefly the buzzword du jour, though as I predicted, it didn't quite seal the deal in terms of implementation. However, this is a space to continue to keep an eye on, because once blockchain secures its place as the de facto ledger for real estate ownership, I expect a sea change in how this business operates.

I also discuss tokenization as a mechanism for raising capital. It started modestly with smaller, mostly blockchain-centric companies, and now powerhouses like KKR, Hamilton Lane, and BlackRock are jumping aboard. And this is the moral of the digital economy story: hype cycles,

The building blocks of the digital economy are here just waiting to realize their full potential. Each component has its place and its function and all are powered by blockchain technology.

followed by a few small but noisy "busts," but all the while, the industry evolving, growing, and maturing.

The digital economy is still young, still evolving. New components and frameworks will inevitably sprout up over the coming years, but they'll be offshoots, cousins, of the building blocks we're discussing in the following articles. The building blocks of the digital economy are here just waiting to realize their full potential. Each component has its place and its function and all are powered by blockchain technology.

The following articles are in no way meant to be a how-to or step-by-step guide to digital finance. Rather, they are a compilation that captures the zeitgeist, the events, developments, and trends that were shaping the landscape as they happened. Buckle up, because the ride is bumpy, but the view can help you understand this emerging ecosystem on a whole new level.

DIGITAL SECURITIES

DIGITAL SECURITIES

Article #1   *09.22.2021, The Street*

Why is no one talking about the digital security explosion?

Digital Securities continue their impressive growth track with more and more investors and institutional players entering into the market.

Blockchain-based digital assets are poised for exponential growth in the next year and beyond as more and more investors and institutional players enter into the market. With the majority of the $6.5 trillion private securities market remaining inefficient and illiquid, many are looking to digital securities to unlock liquidity, digitize the ownership of trillions of dollars in assets, and create a brand new global ecosystem.

Thanks to Distributed Ledger Technology (DLT) the trend of digitalization has accelerated, with investors participating in the rapid growth of blockchain-based Decentralized Finance (DeFi), non-fungible tokens (NFTs), Central Bank Digital Currency (CBDCs), and of course, digital securities. The growing pervasiveness of digital finance has prompted even the most traditional players in the securities industry (banks, institutional players, security exchanges, etc.) to experiment with, and work towards, adopting the technology.

The digitalization and simplification of the world securities together with the promise of borderless liquidity are the most valuable features of digital securities. Also, thanks to fractionalization, digital securities can represent even the most illiquid assets, such as real estate and art. They can be traded on global digital security exchanges and marketplaces, which has been unachievable for privately held traditional securities. While we're just now understanding the power of DLT to create new types of digital assets, the potential of the technology to improve the speed, efficiency, and transparency of some of "our old financial plumbing" deserves more attention. As awareness increases, so does digital security market acceleration modernizing the world's financial system.

To date, we can distinguish three main types of digital securities:

- 24% of the digital security market comprises digital funds/stocks, which are digital forms of funds, stocks and other traditional financial assets, like SPICE (SPiCE VC) and BCAP (Blockchain Capital).

- The largest portion of the digital security market at 44%, Real Estate Equity Digital Securities, includes real estate as the underlying asset.

- Platform Equity Digital Securities, which account for 32% of the market, are shares issued during corporate fundraising, like INX (INX LTD), TZROP (tZERO) and EXDT (Exodus), reaching 84.24% market value.

GLOBAL DIGITAL SECURITY GROWTH

Every meaningful country around the globe, with the exception of Austria, has regulated secondary trading of security tokens creating a boom in the growth of digital finance infrastructure namely exchanges. In fact, 44.4% of the countries now have more than ten service providers offering custody services (including the US, United Kingdom, Switzerland, Singapore, Malta, Liechtenstein, Hong Kong, Germany, Canada, and Australia).

THE STATE OF DIGITAL SECURITY ISSUANCE

From Europe Investment Bank (EIB) launching its inaugural digital bond issuance on a blockchain platform, to Normura Research Institute (NRI) offering the first Japanese blockchain-based digital bonds, the pure number of new digital security issuances (as bonds) is indicating a long-term trend. Major capital market players are moving to digital securities because it's just a better technology. Firms stand to lower costs for both the issuers and their customers by offering easier access to a variety of assets by way of digital securities. In fact, using this technology reduces, on average, 40% of the cost of issuance, post-trade settlement and asset servicing.

In addition to efficiency and cost savings, the growth of digital securities in corporate fundraising will open up opportunities for participation by a variety of retail investors and not just accredited investors. This democratization of finance was highlighted by the recent news of the SEC approving the Exodus wallet and the subsequent fundraising of $75 million, marking a move to Reg A+ crowdfunding based on digital securities. We expect to see much more of this activity in the near term.

With every new technology, regulation typically lags.

REGULATORS STEPPING UP

With every new technology, regulation typically lags. This is true also with digital securities and the overall DLT space. However, there were some significant regulatory movements made this year that indicate regulators' willingness to provide much needed clarity on a variety of issues. Specifically in the US, the Securities and Exchange Commission (SEC) has made several decisions, including the update to the Token Safe Harbor Proposal, which would provide a three year exemption for token-based projects that seek to raise capital to develop decentralized networks. Additionally, the SEC approved INX to raise funds through a tokenized IPO. This marks the first SEC-registered (reg F) security token trading in the digital securities industry. The regulators also elevated the size of Reg CF offerings from $1.07 million to $5 million, adjusted that of the Reg A+ offerings to $75 million, and modified the definition of eligible investors. Overall, these moves create a positive impact by lowering the barriers of entry and adding liquidity for digital securities investments.

Global regulatory bodies are also moving forward with needed reforms. Recently, Japanese regulators officially launched their STO market via amendments to the country's current securities regulations. The new amendments put new requirements on exchanges and legally define STOs and ICOs.

OVERALL MARKET MOVEMENT

Access to liquidity has been a key milestone (and somewhat of a disappointment) in the development of the digital securities ecosystem. The first two promising stars emerged in the digital security secondary trading segment with Securitize acquiring DTM and relaunching as Securitize Markets, as well as INX, with their acquisition of Openfinance Network (OFN). The launch of Securitize Markets and the change of ownership of OFN mark a potential structural change in the ecosystem and reveal a new potential for the realization of the liquidity promise.

WHAT'S NEXT?

We can bank on the fact that digital securities will continue to be used in more ways and by more people, from fundraising to traditional workflows. The industry is ripe with innovation. We also know an increasing amount of mainstream assets will be securitized and issued as digital securities, allowing for increased access to global liquidity. Simultaneously, traditional exchanges will seek to reinvent themselves, much like the Swiss SIX just did, as interest in digital asset trading from both retail and institutional investors grow, with custodians seeking to address client demand and develop digital securities custody service offerings, much like CoinBase. Finally, regulated digital exchanges will continue to launch with an increase in vertical integration among players within the ecosystem.

DIGITAL SECURITIES

Article #2   *10.09.2023, The Street*

Tokenizing Real Estate Assets – the Purpose, the Promise and the Path Ahead

*Many are looking to digital securities to unlock
the liquidity that has long been missing from
the commercial real estate market.*

Digital securities address many of the barriers that have long plagued investing in assets like commercial real estate. Historically, investments in private and non-listed REITs have had virtually no liquidity because of complex regulations, a fragmented marketplace and inherent market inefficiencies. Tokenizing these investments allows for fractional ownership, widening the base of potential investors and improving liquidity in the secondary market. The tokenized format also harnesses distributed ledger technology to eliminate manual, redundant trading processes, reducing settlement times and capital costs while automatically enforcing relevant regulations.

These blockchain-based digital assets are poised for exponential growth in the next year and beyond as more and more investors and institutional players enter into the market. With huge untapped potential in the multi-trillion-dollar alternative asset space, many are looking to digital securities to unlock the liquidity that has long been missing from the commercial real estate market.

However, despite all these potential benefits, and that fact that the digital securities ecosystem has been evolving since 2017, we have not seen significant growth in tokenized real estate assets to date. The obvious question is: why is that, and will it change?

To answer these questions, we must first look at some of the potential benefits of tokenizing real estate assets:

IF YOU BUILD IT, THEY WILL COME

UNLOCKING LIQUIDITY WHERE THERE WAS NONE:

Real estate assets are illiquid. Tokenizing real estate (together with fractional ownership) allows for much easier trading of investors' holdings, as well as ownership exchanging hands without liquidation of the real estate asset. Through lowering the entry barrier for investors tokenizing has the potential to make real estate investments more attractive for a broader spectrum of participants. All of this results in an increase in liquidity allowing the reallocation of investment capital by asset managers. Where real estate investments traditionally are part of the portfolio marked for illiquid assets, with tokenization, funds can potentially shift to a liquid part of the portfolio.

IMPROVING MARKET SECURITY AND TRANSPARENCY:

Employing distributed ledger technology eliminates complexities and paper, simplifies transactions, and ensures compliance and security with every transaction. It also provides simpler and irrefutable proof of ownership.

AUTOMATION SIMPLIFIES AND STREAMLINES INFRASTRUCTURE:

Blockchain based technology can automate and streamline the complex, laborious processes that has defined private investment in real estate for decades, still ensuring full regulatory compliance of every transaction. Tokenization through embedding and automating local regulations also simplifies cross border deals, which in turn significantly expands the target universe of these deals.

REAL ESTATE TOKENIZATION REQUIRES A SOLID FOUNDATION:

While the benefits are promising and obtainable, real estate tokenization still faces a number of challenges within the industry. Yes, these barriers present an uphill battle.

These blockchain-based digital assets are poised for exponential growth.

However, industry leaders, regulators, and technologists are creating opportunities and discovering solutions to the following challenges at a rapid pace bringing us even closer to realizing the full potential of real estate tokenization.

THE TANGIBLE WORLD OF REAL ESTATE MUST EXIST IN THE VIRTUAL SPACE:

Unlike many other popular digital assets that are more "virtual" in nature, real estate assets are about as tangible as an asset class can get. Thus, the process to trade a tokenized real estate asset requires the right technology, platforms, and regulations tying the "real world" to the virtual world. For example, verifying that the asset does exist, and ownership is as stated, documenting what investors need to know about the asset and its valuation, as well as investor rights as a security holder (i.e. updated disclosures, secure, privacy-enabled, and immutable, etc.) are all needed to be clear.

**A DEDICATED REAL ESTATE-FOCUSED
TRADING INFRASTRUCTURE IS KEY:**

The industry has yet to sorted out how this particular type of digital security will be traded. Real estate assets and deals are complex in nature. From residential to commercial and agricultural assets to development and rentals, each of these assets is unique and requires a keen understanding of the various nuances of each deal. Investors in these assets depend on multiple variations and factors to extract value. These assets cannot effectively exist on a "vanilla" digital securities marketplace—suggesting the need for more dedicated marketplaces for tokenized real estate assets.

The infrastructure and standards required to identify, compare, gain insights, and then simply and safely trade tokenized real estate assets is still in its early stages. However, many firms realize the potential and are making significant progress.

Blockchain-based technology can automate and streamline the complex, laborious processes.

TAL'S TAKE ON WHAT TO EXPECT

FURTHER DIGITAL SECURITIES ECOSYSTEM GROWTH:

Further acceleration in the development of the digital securities ecosystem in general, more ecosystem providers, increased liquidity in secondary markets, and growing number of assets being tokenized.

EMERGENCE OF DEDICATED REAL ESTATE TOKENIZATION PLATFORMS:

We will witness the emergence of dedicated platforms for tokenized real estate projects. Some end-to-end platforms for issuance, fundraising, and secondary trading. Some more dedicated to a specific phase.

SUCCESSFUL REAL ESTATE TOKENIZATION PROJECTS:

Initially, we will likely see more financing and REIT type deals, as they seem to be the easiest to implement and bridge the gap between the physical asset and the virtual digital world. We will also likely see initially a bifurcation between institutional and more retail focused deals. And, as more institutional focus shifts to this ecosystem, we will have several successful prime (in quality and size) real estate tokenization projects.

The continued emergence of new regulated platforms and digital securities exchanges, that are dedicated to the real estate asset class, will allow investors to browse, sell, and buy property shares at more attainable and much lower amounts. The digital securities marketplace is entering a new phase of maturation, with growing numbers of ecosystem players emerging, increased institutional interest and involvement, along with strong positive regulatory moves.

DIGITAL SECURITIES

Article #3 *01.26.2022, The Street*

Q&A Session with INX's Shy Datika on Recent Wins and the Future of Digital Assets

Tal and Shy discuss THE INX DIGITAL COMPANY (NEO:INXD) digital securities and cryptocurrencies trading platform, its recent SEC-registered token IPO, and how it continues to push the industry forward.

Before we dive into the details, for those who don't know THE INX DIGITAL COMPANY (NEO:INXD), it is a blockchain-based platform for trading digital securities and cryptocurrencies and is also one of SPiCE VCs' portfolio companies. INX is one of the three companies within SPiCE's portfolio that have gone public in the last 12 months becoming the first company to complete an SEC-registered token IPO. Adding to its impressive accomplishments, INX shares began trading on the Neo Exchange in Canada just two days ago—a true milestone for INX and the entire digital finance ecosystem.

INX has taken a particularly unique path with two separate IPOs: One digital, one traditional, one equity based, and the other not. Why did you take this path? Was it worth it? Do you see more companies following this path?

We see INX as a bridge between the legacy capital markets and their future. The move into blockchain-based trading is no longer a question. It is happening where both governments and investment institutions have been preparing and legislating for this transformation for the past 18 months. While they all agree this is where the capital market is going, some have the ability to invest in digital assets while others cannot due to slower regulation. By choosing this path of having both an INX token and INX equity shares listed, we enable both worlds to join the INX future through any of the investment methods. We believe this will provide a gateway for many institutions to join the blockchain evolution via the equity routes until internal protocols and regulation will allow them to migrate to blockchain capital markets.

What is your vision for the future of digital assets and how do you see it evolve in the short and long-terms?

We believe digital assets are the next logical step in the evolution of capital markets. We call it internally "Capital Markets 2.0." It takes away many of the challenges of the legacy world such as T+ settlements, cross-border trading, cap-table management, and many other issues while providing more transparency and control to avoid crime and money laundering. In the short term, we see rapid growth of permissive legislation spreading across the globe enabling the big institutions and banks to legally join the new way of trading in the longer term and migrate into Capital Markets 2.0 within two decades time.

What trends in the Digital Securities and Crypto ecosystems do you see on the horizon in the next couple of years?

We see more companies raising capital via security tokens that are regulated under a prospectus and customary financial reporting protocols, while crypto trading will become more mainstream for investment banks to trade under regulated platforms. This evolution of the market will enable these assets to be deposited and transferred via the traditional banking routes with all taxation and cross-border aspects resolved.

As a director for a large institutional player, when do you see institutional investors really participating in a significant and impactful way?

I believe institutional participation will grow gradually over the next five years, which is a continuation of what we have already seen in the market. We need basic facilitations to be established such as custodianship, security registration, banking deposits, etc., before institutions will feel comfortable to jump in. All of this is happening and progressing as we speak.

What does the future hold for liquidity in Digital Securities?

The future is very similar to the equity market in its early days of the 18th century, but faster. It will grow in liquidity as the trade becomes more regulated, and more and more retail and institutions can legally and safely trade.

What's the "next big thing" in the Digital Securities ecosystem? How do you think INX will play a role in the evolution of this digital asset?

The next big thing on the horizon is "Regulated ICOs." ICO is the wrong term, but it drives the point. In 2017, token offerings became all the rave as companies raised billions in ICOs. It was an amazing new instrument but illegal as it was not regulated. The instrument is still amazing and groundbreaking, and once regulated, it will become the new way to raise capital. It is a new asset class that is neither dilutive as equity or non-repayable as debt. As such, it bears huge promise for both small companies and Fortune 500 giants.

I believe that Regulated Token Offerings (or regulated token IPOs) are the next explosion in this world. INX has the experience and know how to help many enterprises and startups alike to start using this route for capital raises. As such, we believe our achievements and positioning will be pivotal for this industry's emergence.

How do you see the Crypto ecosystem changing/ evolving over the coming year?

I believe there will be a natural selection into quality. Many of the "shit coins" will be driven to the sidelines while a few quality coins will migrate to regulated platforms and will attract institutional investors as well as retail. This will be a massive boost to the evolution in capital markets.

Do you see an increase in regulatory clarity in the digital finance sector as a major catalyst to mainstream adoption and greater institutional participation?

Absolutely. We have seen over the last months increased activity of the regulators especially related to Crypto, DeFi, and Stablecoins, as well as a call to legislators to advance digital finance related legislation. I am convinced the more clarity provided through these activities, more institutions will participate in the market, and the adoption circle will grow among the retail investment community.

What are the next major moves for INX and how will you get there?

We are extremely aggressive and working hard to bring amazing developments to the regulated blockchain arena and our community. Stay tuned.

A FINAL THOUGHT ON MY Q&A SESSION WITH SHY:

I always enjoy my discussions with Shy Datika, an industry disruptor and a friend. It's especially a pleasure to publish this article in the first week of INX shares trading, a major triumph for INX, the digital securities market and the entire digital asset ecosystem. Along with SPiCE VC, of course, INX is a company you will definitely be hearing more about in the coming months and years. As an early pioneer, they are among a select few organizations well positioned for success as the blockchain-based digital economy evolves.

DIGITAL SECURITIES

Article #4   *12.15.2021, The Street*

Interview with Securitize's Carlos Domingo on Digital Assets, Tokenization and the Exciting Journey Ahead

As the digital finance ecosystem—specifically the digital security market—continues to expand rapidly, I thought it was the perfect time to sit down for a chat with friend, fellow co-founder and CEO of Securitize, Carlos Domingo.

Since Securitize launched in 2017, the market has evolved tremendously and so has Securitize's role in leading the movement to make all of the world's assets digital using blockchain technology. In the following Q&A session I had with Carlos, we discuss the major milestones achieved this past year for not only Securitize, but also the entire digital finance and digital securities markets. We also opine on the opportunities and challenges still ahead.

TAL:

How has the digital asset security market matured in 2021? What are the most exciting developments as we look to 2022?

CARLOS:

At the start of 2021, we said that this would be the year that digital asset securities would start to take off, and it has. But, if you compare where we are today to the internet, we are in 1998.

We are still in the days of the dial-up modem, but competition, innovation, and movement of capital into digital assets is happening so rapidly that I think the growth we will see in the next four years will be exponentially faster than the last four since the industry really started.

The most exciting development in 2021, which will accelerate into 2022, is the speed of institutional adoption of blockchain. There is a major headline almost every day. Morgan Stanley co-led our Series B, and there have been major investments from Visa, JP Morgan, and virtually all of the other major firms. Blockdata has a very good chart about this.

We just announced a partnership with S&P to create two tokenized funds that track their indices, including their cryptocurrency large cap index and the Kensho New Economies index, as our inaugural S&P funds. We expect a wave of tokenized funds that track indices over the next year.

TAL:

Why is tokenization a better way of raising capital than the old way?

CARLOS:

My co-founder, Jamie Finn, has a simple way of answering this question I like: he says tokenization is just "fundamentally better" than the old way. And that is correct.

In the old way of dealing with company investors, shares, and ownership are actually recorded on paper or very simple ledgers. It is very hard to prove who owns what shares at any moment, when transactions are tracked on paper and in Excel spreadsheets. This is all very expensive and slow.

When we tokenize an asset on the blockchain, everything is automated. The digital transfer agent, such as Securitize, always knows who owns what shares, because it's transparently recorded on the blockchain. Settlement is immediate, so you are not waiting days for transactions to clear and funds to become available and you don't have to deal with counterparty risk. Proving ownership of your shares is very simple, just connect your wallet.

One of the good things about the public markets is that shares are typically the same class, and anybody can own them. This is not the case in the private markets, where offerings occur under different regulations, and ownership may be limited to accredited investors, or US investors, or non-US investors, or have holding periods, or other limitations. This complexity contributes to illiquidity which turns people away from private markets. But, when assets are digitized, all of these rules are applied automatically, so in a marketplace like Securitize Markets, it's very easy to see what you can invest in, what you can trade, and when you make a transaction. It occurs immediately.

I should also say because tokenization is a more efficient way of raising capital, and makes fractional ownership very easy to track, it allows retail investors to participate in private business capital raises, which were previously restricted to institutional ones. And this is very important in democratizing

ADDITIONAL PREDICTIONS FROM TAL ELYASHIV:

Carlos had some insightful and eye-opening responses to my questions, and I agree with his observations about where the industry is now and where he sees it heading. To add to his thoughts, I believe in the short-term, five key developments will shape the trajectory of digital securities:

1. **CROWDFUNDING:**
   Significant increase in use of digital securities for crowdfunding fundraises (Reg CF) and Reg A+ that are open to retail investors.

2. **DLT INSTITUTIONAL ADOPTION:**
   Acceleration in DLT and digital securities technology adoption by traditional capital markets players, leading to greater institutional involvement in the digital securities ecosystem.

access to wealth creation because most of a business' value is generated when it's private, and businesses are remaining private longer than ever. We call this process a Mini-IPO.

A good example is the $75 million capital raise in May, 2021 by Exodus, a digital wallet company, using Securitize. Through our Mini-IPO process, Exodus was able to complete its capital raise in only six weeks, from over 6,000 of its own customers. This is good for Exodus, good for the customer, and it also helps Exodus' leaders focus on running the business instead of flying around the country meeting with VCs. So, this is a very good example for other businesses to consider.

TAL:

What is the current 'lay of the land' in terms of digital asset security trading?

CARLOS:

The market for alternative assets has been very fragmented until now. There are many websites or brokers, each has its own process, and people do not have the time for multiple sign ups, to monitor multiple sites, and so on. The result is there are just not enough investors in each place for liquidity to occur.

So, the goal of Securitize Markets is by bringing more opportunities under one roof, an investor with a Securitize iD can see many kinds of opportunities in one marketplace where trading takes just a few clicks, similar to Robinhood or E-Trade. Then, the advantages of digital asset securities, such as 24/7 trading, instant settlement, or incentives for customers who become shareholders, become even clearer.

It's also important to note that what we are doing is within the existing regulatory framework. This is important because businesses and investors want to know they are participating in a legal market, that they are not participating in scams or money laundering or funding terrorism, and this is what the regulations are intended to help prevent. As investors understand that this is a regulated space, not the Wild West, we will see adoption increase.

TAL:

How is Securitize Markets different from the other alternative trading systems out there? How do you see it driving innovation, adoption and the ultimate goal, liquidity?

CARLOS:

The promise of digital asset securities is the potential to provide liquidity to the private capital markets in a regulated venue. This is only beginning because the industry is so new and there has not been enough competition to create the innovations that will attract more investors. Securitize Markets is an important step forward.

ADDITIONAL PREDICTIONS FROM TAL ELYASHIV:

3. **ASSET TYPES:**
   Increase in the number of digital security asset types driven by further ecosystem innovation.

4. **ECOSYSTEM CONSOLIDATION:**
   As the industry continues maturing there will be some consolidation through M&A and collaboration, driving more market depth and de-facto standardization.

5. **ADAPTATION TRADITIONAL INVESTING SERVICES:**
   Market analytics tools and investment portals will be created to better support investors in the digital securities space.

There are other businesses that do part of what we do—raising capital, or transfer agency services, or are an ATS—but Securitize is the only solution that has everything the private market requires under one roof. This is very attractive to businesses who want to raise capital, to fund managers, and to investors who want exposure to the maximum number of investment opportunities.

Securitize Markets is the new standard competitors will need to meet. It's akin to when web browsers started; you had Netscape, then Internet Explorer took over the market, and there was a lack of innovation for a while. When Firefox arrived, then Safari, and then Chrome, the competition drove innovation and adoption, and it was good for everyone.

This is also important in creating liquidity. Liquidity requires three things: more opportunities for investment, more investors in the market, and current shareholders who want to sell. Securitize Markets provides the structure for this to occur.

This will take time, but we are very excited by the progress we are seeing. On its second day of business, Securitize Markets processed 30% of all digital asset security trades. We now have six investments trading, eight more opportunities available for primary investment, and we are seeing trading activity increase as investors become aware of assets that may be under-valued. So, we are seeing the beginnings of a more liquid market, and we expect the market to continue to see strong growth.

TAL:

Securitize has made a big move into funds. Tell me more about that.

CARLOS:

We launched Securitize Capital in May, 2021 because we recognized the increasing interest in tokenized assets by institutional and accredited investors, particularly family offices, who are hearing a lot about crypto, and increasingly understand its value as a hedge against inflation and as being uncorrelated with the traditional markets.

Our first two funds offered exposure to Bitcoin and USDC plus yield, which are generating above 9% in the case of the USDC Yield fund, and above 3% APY in the case of the BTC Yield fund, since their inception at the end of July.

We made even bigger news this week with our partnership with S&P to tokenize two of its most innovative indices.

Through the new Securitize S&P Tokenized Cryptocurrency Index Fund, investors can access a diverse blend of top performing cryptocurrencies by tracking an index that has realized year-to-date returns of over 300% as of today. And the Securitize S&P Kensho New Economies Tokenized Fund, will provide investors exposure to emerging markets and technology globally, including fintechs, AI, virtual reality, nanotechnology, and more.

We anticipate strong demand for funds, and tokenized funds can be offered more efficiently, with lower fees, than traditional funds. I can promise you will see more funds from us soon.

TAL:

What are the advantages of investing in a tokenized VC versus a traditional VC?

CARLOS:

We have a few blockchain-focused VCs available on Securitize Markets. Aside from the efficiency and cost benefits we've already discussed, the main advantage is when a VC fund is tokenized and available for trading, it creates the ability for shareholders to find potential liquidity when they desire, opposed to a traditional VC fund, where shareholders have less access to liquidity events.

Additional predictions from Tal Elyashiv:

As for the longer-term outlook, Carlos and I are in sync in our view that more mainstream asset types will be tokenized and more traditional capital market players will participate and reinvent themselves in the process. Finally, ecosystem consolidation will continue through vertical integration and interoperability, and institutional-grade support in the areas of compliance, regulation and standards will emerge.

We are seeing the beginnings of a more liquid market, and we expect the market to continue to see strong growth.

SECTION 1 • CH. 2

NFTs

Article #1   *10.21.2021, The Street*

Tal's NFT Take:
Discovery and Search is Key to NFT Growth

*NFTs continue to explode in growth, but
the market won't reach critical mass until
average consumers have access to it*

There's no doubt that the NFT market continues to experience
massive tailwinds. Research platform Dune Analytics noted
the total sales volume of NFTs increased to $2.5 billion in
the first half of 2021 compared to $13.7 million in the first
half of 2020. However, while NFTs continue to represent
the "shiny new object" of the digital finance ecosystem,
its utility and market cap is far from being realized.

I've always stated that if NFTs are ever going to live up to their
potential for mainstream consumers, they need to be represented
and available in mid-market landscapes and not just in luxury,
top-of-the-line opportunities. The average consumer needs access
and the ability to search, compare, and shop. The discovery phase
in a person's buyer journey is critical. And let's not underestimate

the power of impulse purchases. This will likely also drive specialization of NFT marketplaces based on specific use-cases.

One of the first NFT marketplaces, OpenSea, is experiencing impressive growth. Trading volumes on OpenSea surged by more than 12,000% in 2021, with a record $150 million in NFT sales just in June. If that wasn't enough positive data, their user count increased from 315 to 14,520 in just 6 months, pushing the company to officially surpass $3 billion in monthly NFT volume this August.

This is all great news for the NFT and the digital finance space as a whole, but a niche marketplace can't move the market forward the way an internationally-known behemoth like Alibaba can. That's why Alibaba's recent news is just so exciting.

ALIBABA AND THE 40 NFTS

Earlier in August, Chinese e-commerce giant Alibaba Group Holding (BABA) launched a new NFT marketplace with the approval of the Sichuan provincial government. The marketplace was launched as part of Alibaba Auction, the Alibaba's online auctioning platform. Appropriately named "Blockchain Digital Copyright and Asset Trade," the service enables writers, musicians, and other artists to sell the rights to their content via blockchain. The NFTs will be issued by a platform run by the Sichuan Blockchain Association Copyright Committee, the New Copyright Blockchain.

Alibaba's move is significant on a number of levels. First, it seems to contrast with the latest crackdown on Bitcoin Mining and cryptocurrencies, which may indicate that while the Chinese administration may have an issue with private cryptocurrencies in order to advance the Digital Yuan, they also want to lead the world in blockchain technology and become the most advanced blockchain power in the world by 2025. By allowing Alibaba to sell NFTs, Chinese authorities are facilitating the integration of blockchain technology into key industries as part of this blockchain arms race.

Second, it shows that China is recognizing the NFT paradigm as much greater than just its utility for digital art, virtual gaming assets, and collectibles. They seem to be recognizing that there is significant utility to using NFTs for replacing and automating old systems like public registries (and in this case copyrights registry), but also applying the technology to property, patents and so much more.

The NFT market is one that I keep a very close eye on and will continue to write and comment about this ever changing market. As major players like Alibaba, Visa, and so many others participate in this exciting sector of the digital finance ecosystem, its utility, and versatility will only expand.

The average consumer needs access and the ability to search, compare, and shop.

NFTs

Article #2   *10.28.2021, The Street*

Tal's NFT Take:
From Crafts to Concerts, NFT
Possibilities Expand

NFT use-cases go well beyond art to solve everyday problems and create new opportunities for innovation in a variety of consumer markets.

In the last few months, the NFT market has seen significant moves that are not only notable but are also clear indicators of where things are headed.

However, in order for the NFT's potential to be truly realized, the industry as a whole needs to shake off the perception that its use-cases are only for luxury items like art and expensive collectibles. If the market ever has a chance to reach mainstream adoption and critical mass, NFTs need to become pervasive in mid-market goods and services.

This is why I decided to dedicate this piece to some recent sample moves in the NFT market out of a slew of creative and intelligent ways to leverage the power of NFTs which are increasingly popping up. This is promising in a variety of ways.

NFT GAMIFICATION GOES BEYOND GAMING ASSETS

Genopets, a Solana-based NFT "move-to-earn" game, where players are rewarded for the steps they take in real life is doing something new and very exciting in the world of NFTs. For the first time, a gamified NFT is combining free-to-play and play-to-earn style gameplay attracting crypto junkies and a mainstream non-crypto audience alike.

Because Genopets is a "move-to-earn" experience, the NFT ecosystem may be ripe to disrupt the world of wearable tech, as the game pulls data from users' phones and wearable fitness devices to convert steps into rewards within the game.

Once again, a forward-looking, innovative company in the blockchain universe is opening up new possibilities for the uses of NFTs and other blockchain-based tools, while also engaging with users who otherwise wouldn't be interacting with NFTs.

IF MARTHA'S INTO IT, YOU KNOW IT'S GOOD

Moving from games to gourmets, when you think of a NFT enthusiast, I don't think anyone would've guessed Martha Stewart. However, the 80-year-old queen of cooking and crafting plans to unveil a collection of NFTs on her e-commerce site this week. Alongside her typical dining, drinking, and decorating offerings, Ms. Stewart will be launching her first line of digital collectibles, Halloween-themed NFTs featuring images of her costumes carved into pumpkins.

You may find this a bit humorous, but it's not the NFTs that are important here. What's interesting is the fact that a Boomer (and a cooking and crafting Boomer at that) has entered the NFT ecosystem with the real potential of introducing this new technology to a new, very large audience—one with plenty of expendable income.

FASHION WELCOMES TOKENIZATION TO THE RUNWAY

While brands like Chanel and Gucci are prime examples of luxury items, these storied companies offer us a glimpse into how all levels of textile brands can and will leverage NFTs to attract a younger, more tech-savvy audience.

Most recently, Gucci announced that they were offering one-of-a-kind sneakers as NFTs, while luxury watch brands are creating NFT auctions and promoting them on social media.

Additionally, LVMH Moët Hennessy Louis Vuitton, owner of some of the world's most desirable and influential fashion brands, such as Dior and Givenchy became the first company to use blockchain-based tokens as a record of authenticity.

NFTS AS THE STAR OF THE SHOW...LITERALLY

In recent news, the app YellowHeart and its "YellowHeart Wallet" announced that it will begin to store tickets to events and shows as NFTs. NFT-based ticket purchasers will become ticket holders for the events and acts they see and have access to exclusive content and perks without any additional cost.

This makes incredible sense in its application in the resale ticket market as tracking tickets with blockchain could altogether squash illegal scalping, bulk sales with marked-up prices and even help with lost or stolen tickets. Going beyond e-tickets, NFT-based tickets protect buyers, create added-value and are an obvious solution to another antiquated market.

FINDING MEANING IN THESE MOVES

When NFTs first showed up on the scene, there were limited use-case scenarios, even if blockchain/crypto-savvy market participants were dreaming of more. Well, those dreams are becoming reality as new companies, investors, and users enter the market and bring with them new ideas and possibilities. That funnel of innovative ways to leverage NFTs will continue to widen creating rapid growth opportunities. Who will the next Martha Stewart be for NFTs?

All art has value in the end. The difference in the NFT market is whether or not the artist has the knowledge, support, and drive to turn his or her creation into the next "darling of the digital age."

NFTs

Article #3   *06.17.2022, Newsweek*

The Anatomy of a Successful NFT: Value, Brand, Community

*It takes time and sound strategy to create
an audience of loyalists and believers.*

NFTs offer artists new opportunities to create and sell their
pieces in our evolving Web3 world. But, what actually makes
a successful NFT? Is it all about the art, or is there more to
the story surrounding the market's winners and losers? As
the founder and managing partner of a VC fund specializing
in the blockchain/tokenization ecosystem, I've developed an
understanding of what can help make an NFT successful.

As the NFT market matures, it offers new insight into what actually
makes an NFT a success. You can draw conclusions as to why,
for example, Bored Ape Yacht Club (BAYC) is one of the most
successful NFT projects to date, selling for $3.5 million (769 ETH),
and owned by big names such as Jimmy Fallon and Stephen Curry.

The same attributes that made BAYC an NFT star also
played a significant role in the success of other NFT winners
like The Kings of Leon's NFT released album, or even
UkraineDAO's Ukrainian flag NFT, which raised more than
$6.5 million for the Ukrainian people. These success stories
tell us a lot about what fuels interest and value in an NFT.

On the contrary, the greatest NFT flops can tell us a great deal as
well. From Jack Dorsey's first tweet to The Indifferent Duck (and
let's not even discuss the Fart Jars), these NFT projects failed
miserably. When hype and novelty wear out, what's left? Can artists
create an NFT that can perform well initially, and then sustains
momentum long term? The answer is yes, but it's not always easy.

CREATE VALUE

Many artists only focus on creating the actual NFTs, which includes a somewhat cumbersome process of creating and listing an NFT on one of the many marketplaces like OpenSea (a marketplace I have used before) or Crypto.com. While the technical aspect is complicated, most marketplaces help shield users from complexities making the NFT creation the easiest part of the journey.

The more difficult task is how to create an NFT that people find valuable and actually want to buy. Every artist should be asking themselves a few simple but essential questions before they dive into NFT creation:

- Is my NFT perceived to be rare or exclusive?

- What will make my NFT desirable now, as well as in years to come?

- What are the benefits of owning my NFT?

- By owning my NFT, does it offer the owner joy, status, nostalgia, humor and so on?

- Does the NFT create a personalized and unique connection to its owner (offering personal value)?

- Who is my audience and what is unique about the NFT that appeals specifically to them?

For any NFT to become a success, these questions should not only be answered by the artist prior to creating the NFT, but should be clearly communicated to their audience to ensure they understand the value propositions even if that value is targeted and subjective.

BUILD A BRAND

It's imperative for artists to create, articulate, and manage a distinctive brand. An NFT isn't just a digital interpretation of a piece of art. It's actually more like a living organism that must be nurtured for it to thrive. This only happens when a unique and authentic brand surrounding the NFT is established and maintained.

Artists should consider capitalizing on their own unique voice and style to help differentiate their NFT from others. Consistency is also key so awareness and loyalty grow over time. It's equally important to continuously innovate to keep the brand fresh and the audience engaged.

ARTIST MUST-HAVES FOR NFT BRAND BUILDING:

Create on-chain identity: On-chain IDs are stored on a public Blockchain (like Ethereum), in a decentralized way, which establishes a smart contract for the artist and a certification of authenticity for the piece of art.

CREATE A ROBUST ONLINE IDENTITY:

Creating brand awareness in our digital world means being visible, accessible and active online. Building an engaging website and being present on social media sites like TikTok and Instagram all add to your brand visibility.

BE A LEADER, NOT A FOLLOWER:

Avoid following current trends and hype. While being relevant is important, building a lasting brand with loyal followers requires novelty, innovation, and continuous creative evolution.

BUILD A COMMUNITY

It takes time and sound strategy to create an audience of loyalists and believers. NFT creators can start by understanding which audiences will be most enthusiastic about the NFT. By identifying that group early, artists can tap into established communities and expand from there.

The most successful NFTs have amplified their community-building efforts by doing the following:

- Connecting with NFT influencers

- Engaging with the community where they are (social media sites like Discord and others)

- Offering exclusive giveaways and presale registration

- Understanding the audience and pricing accordingly (if the NFT is targeted to Gen Z buyers, it has to be affordable)

- Presenting the possibility of scarcity to drive interest

- Offering new experiences that are only available to the community of buyers

MARKET AND MANAGE

Even after the NFT has been successfully created, branded, and targeted to a particular audience, the work is never complete. NFTs must be nurtured and managed. Simply launching an NFT is not enough. In fact, the difficult work begins after the NFT launch, when the artist must find ways to continue to engage and excite. This is no easy task. However, in order to play the NFT long game, creators can't afford to take their eyes off the prize.

Investing in ongoing digital marketing efforts can take a grassroots influencer effort to the next level. An effective campaign should include some FOMO with a dash of hype. Smart and strategic storytelling and even compelling video content can get the job done effectively. And, one must never underestimate the power of "the new drop." Keeping owners wanting more is a surefire way to keep them invested in the creative process of the NFT.

ARTISTS AT THE CORE

All art has value in the end. The difference in the NFT market is whether or not the artist has the knowledge, support, and drive to turn his or her creation into the next "darling of the digital age."

NFTs

Article #4   *11.13.2021, The Street*

Tal's NFT take:
Healthcare is the Newest Frontier for NFTs

From patient data access and privacy to blood donation tracking, the healthcare industry stands to benefit significantly from NFTs.

In previous articles in my series covering all things NFTs (Tal's NFT Take), I discussed some of the more commonly used NFT use-cases, including digital art, collectibles, gaming, events, and ticketing, as well as the Metaverse. However, one vertical that stands to benefit significantly from NFTs is the healthcare industry.

While we know that the healthcare space has experienced an aggressive period of digital transformation, it still has a way to go. But, with the growth of blockchain-based solutions that include NFTs, that digital acceleration could be both more effective and efficient.

NFTs can be huge in the Healthcare industry, with multiple potential use cases.

KEY NFT USE-CASES IN HEALTHCARE

NFTs can be huge in the Healthcare industry, with multiple potential use cases. Here are a few examples:

LIFETIME MEDICAL RECORD

Although multiple attempts were made in the past, due to the fragmented nature of the US healthcare ecosystem, we've never had the technology to consolidate a person's slew of medical records into a master document safely and efficiently and shared between the relevant caregivers. Nor were we able to figure out a solution for such record's custody, updating, and maintenance.

Sensitive patient health data is scattered across platforms and is notoriously difficult for operators and patients to access. In fact, over $1.2 billion clinical documents are produced in the US every year, yet 80% of that data is unstructured or locked away. Additionally, Americans spend over $750 billion each year on unnecessary treatments, many of which stem from misdiagnosis, or redundant treatment due to poor data management. NFTs have the potential to solve these various problems giving the power of medical records back to the patient and streamlining the healthcare experience.

Think about what could be possible if primary care physicians can exchange real-time updates with other healthcare specialists, allowing for easier collaboration and more patient-centric care. NFTs could allow patients to access medical tests results as soon as they're available, along with access to their complicated (and many times disparate) medical histories instantly and easily, without having to spend time and energy explaining their history to doctor after doctor. With NFTs, this sensitive and critical information would all exist in one place—a patient medical "passport" that's secure and accurate.

The possibilities to revolutionize patient data ownership and access are endless, all of which offer the industry the opportunity to increase efficiencies and lower costs.

PHARMACEUTICAL MANUFACTURING

NFTs and blockchain can support the fight against counterfeit pharmaceuticals by streamlining the authentication process. NFTs create digital footprints or a "token ID" that attaches to a particular item throughout its lifespan. The uniqueness of each NFT is specifically defined by the information stored within the NFT's metadata pointing to valuable digital resources that are updated in real-time on the blockchain. NFTs provide an immutable record on the ledger reducing, and potentially eliminating, discrepancies, and outright fraud.

In the case of pharmaceuticals, NFTs have the ability to secure and streamline the tracking process enabling the immediate identification of issues. That means problems can be resolved much more rapidly, including the identification of black-market prescriptions and eliminating them from the system.

BLOOD DONATIONS

Much like a patients' unique health history and data, NFTs can be used for the tracking and management of blood donations. Blood donors are given a unique token that is then tracked throughout the system. From the time the blood is drawn, to its travels to the blood bank, and to its eventual recipient, NFTs can be an integral part of the tracking process. The technology can also be used to register it in a digital "blood bank," where the demand for specific blood types may be tracked via a blockchain system and distributed to where it is most required.

FITNESS AND HEALTH DATA

As wearables, at-home workout equipment and other tracking devices gain popularity and mass adoption, many question how to harness health data efficiently while managing it responsibly. Seeing an opportunity, entrepreneurs are leveraging NFTs as a way to decentralize data collection, optimize access, and give patients back control of their health records.

As with other industries ripe for blockchain disruption, healthcare could be the one that benefits the patients the most. The proliferation of personal and health information is creating an immediate need to manage it effectively, while also maintaining autonomy and security. And, as the globalization of healthcare continues to explode, the need to track and manage medical and pharmaceutical devices becomes more critical. All of these factors and more create the perfect opportunity for NFTs to solve problems and improve experiences across the healthcare industry.

AIMEDIS

an in-house NFT marketplace, allows patients to process their data as NFTs and easily forward it to their doctor, dentist, or physiotherapist.

ENJIN

partnered with digital platform Health Hero in June to create Go!, where users can create a "Well-being NFT", or W-NFT, unique to their health and activity characteristics.

RIGHTSHASH

a decentralized software engine, aims to track and manage patient consent for clinical trials.

NFTs

Article #5   *12.07.2021, The Street*

Tal's NFT take:
Can NFTs Take the Headache Out
of Real Estate Transactions?

NFTs can be an effective solution and a versatile tool in an industry that needs less middlemen and more efficiency.

By now, you've probably heard about (or read about in one of my Tal's Takes Series) Non-Fungible Tokens (NFTs) are the "Little engine that could." From art sales to supply chain hiccups, NFTs are proving they are versatile and effective. Therefore, why not put them to use in an industry that needs less middlemen, more efficiency—the completely illiquid real estate market.

Real estate transactions are mired in a sea of bureaucracy involving layers of intermediaries from real estate agents and banks to notaries and lawyers, all inflating the cost and complexity of what should be a simple transaction between two parties. And, just think about all that paperwork!

NFTs can significantly impact the way the real estate business is transacted. Since NFTs create digital footprints or a "token ID" that attaches to a particular item throughout its lifespan, each NFT is specifically defined by the information stored within its metadata pointing to valuable digital resources that are updated in real-time on the blockchain. This immutable record on the ledger can revolutionize how real estate is bought, sold and everything in between.

Just by replacing intermediaries with smart contracts that allow for the safe and simple transfer of ownership, NFTs could greatly expedite the property-buying process. A real estate NFT can include all history of ownership of the property, and rights can be recorded and committed to the blockchain and instantly and easily verifiable. It can also include all relevant documents like title and ownership deeds, neighborhood association rules and membership, land surveyance documents, floor plans, history of modifications, etc. And, because all of this relevant data is updated in real-time, buyers and sellers can trust the single source of truth that NFTs offer.

Take title insurance for example. When you buy real estate in the US, a title search is required to understand the property's history of ownership. This can be the most time-consuming aspect of a closing. A clean title means that you can get title insurance to safeguard from future disputes and related issues. This is exactly where NFTs on the blockchain can help. They have the ability to provide an indestructible chain of ownership for the buyer and seller that remain intact and updated in real-time—eliminating discrepancies, disputes, and increasing security and ease-of-use.

FROM RESIDENTIAL TO CORPORATE

For corporate real-estate, the same holds true. NFTs have the opportunity to address many of the barriers that have long plagued investing in assets like commercial real estate. Tokenizing private and non-listed REITs allows for fractional ownership widening the base of potential investors and improving liquidity in the secondary market. The NFT format also DLT to eliminate manual, redundant trading processes, reducing settlement times, and capital costs while automatically enforcing relevant regulations.

NFT USE-CASES IN REAL ESTATE ALREADY EXIST TODAY

Connecting an NFT with a physical property allows for straightforward usage and easy collateral, an idea Europe-based start-up, Propy, is already exploring. Propy offers a transaction platform with which each NFT comes with access to ownership transferred paperwork. The first Propy-hosted NFT auction sold TechCrunch founder Michael Arrington's apartment for 36 ETH, or $93k at the time of sale.

New digital-first players entering the real estate market is a good thing for its evolution. It highlights the benefits that NFTs can bring to the real estate sales experience, from beginning to end. As in other vertical markets where NFTs are emerging and making positive change, I'm excited to see what's next.

NFTs have the opportunity to address many of the barriers that have long plagued investing in assets like commercial real estate.

NFTs

Article #6   *11.10.2021, The Street*

Tal's NFT take:
NFTs are a Supply Chain's New Best Friend

NFTs have the opportunity to completely disrupt the supply chain industry by eliminating decades old pain points.

In previous articles in the NFT series, I already covered the commonly used NFT use-cases like digital art, collectibles, gaming, events, and ticketing, and of course, the Metaverse. However, where the NFT can have the most lasting and powerful impact is not with personal ownership, but with its digital footprint and data tracking capabilities.

While 2021 will be remembered as the year of the supply chain disaster, supply chain hiccups actually happen quite often and cost companies millions each year. From onboarding to production to transportation, NFTs and blockchain can reduce costs, eliminate bottlenecks, create greater transparency into supply networks, and help to prevent the chaos that we've experienced this year.

WHY ARE NFTS A SUPPLY CHAIN SOLUTION?

Instead of long, extensive, and complex paper trails that go along with transactional ownership and activity of a variety of items, NFTs create digital footprints or a "token ID" that attaches to that item throughout its lifespan. The uniqueness of each NFT is specifically defined by the information stored within the NFT's metadata pointing to valuable digital resources that are updated in real-time on the blockchain.

For the supply chain, NFTs enable participants to access the same immutable record on the ledger reducing and potentially eliminating discrepancies in information flow between parties.

That transparency and immutability traits of blockchain ensure the reliability and authenticity of the supply chain data. As such, NFTs can increase efficiencies, and reduce costs incurred in the process of sourcing and acquiring goods and services a company needs. NFTs also produce an end-to-end view of a parts location, quantity, and other useful information.

AVOIDING TODAY'S SUPPLY CHAIN WOES USING NFTS

A delay in just one section of the supply chain can result in the complete meltdown of the entire journey. For example, in the auto manufacturing industry, cars have hundreds if not thousands of parts that come from all over the world. If one of those items, be it an oil filter or a complex dashboard touchscreen, the vehicle can't be completed, and the production facility grinds to a halt.

Because NFTs create a digital identity to any item (from chips to car batteries), the item's real-world metadata—such as its identity, current physical location, responsible party, possession, container temperature, and other metrics—is attached to that item garnering useful insights about its condition, location, etc. This data is automatically updated as conditions change (via time-stamping to the geolocation of a transported good), which presents an accurate and timely view of the physical object to all involved parties.

Therefore, if a part in China is delayed, the manufacturer will know well in advance and have options to source from another location like India keeping the supply chain working.

Many organizations such as Amazon have already started using blockchain for tracing their product's journey through the supply chain from point of origin to the customer. MAERSK's TradeLens system and IBM's Foot Trust are two other examples of large blockchain logistics solutions—both use Hyperledger Fabric, an IBM blockchain that supports the use of NFTs.

Supply chain operators are tapping into the NFT framework, leveraging the uniqueness, and traceability of the assets to help demonstrate provenance and prevent counterfeited products from entering the market.

One example of this technology already getting put to good use is in the luxury goods market, where operators like Cartier, Prada, and LVMH have teamed up to launch a blockchain platform called Aura. When consumers buy a high-end watch, handbag, or piece of jewelry, they'll be provided with a corresponding unique NFT, which shows the origins of their product, including information about the materials and manufacturing process. This means all such products can be individually authenticated. The NFTs can be used to identify and trace the complete supply chain.

Moving from fashion and into Pharma, NFTs traits of transparency and immutability are still appealing and effective. Take pharmaceutical manufacturing. NFTs and blockchains

A delay in just one section of the supply chain can result in the complete meltdown of the entire journey.

When all parties involved in a particular supply chain are operating off a "single source of truth," discrepancies, mismanagement, and miscommunication can all be avoided.

can support the fight against counterfeit pharmaceuticals by streamlining the authentication process. Also, tracking the process via the system will enable the immediate identification of issues allowing problems to be resolved much more rapidly.

While the technology can be used to identify fake prescriptions, it also can be deployed as an extremely effective solution to pharmaceutical viability. When using this technology, customers have visibility into the conditions of each product on its supply chain journey, including storage locations, environmental factors (temperatures and humidity), and duration of storage. An NFT attached to a pharmaceutical product has the potential to protect consumers from some seriously bad medicine.

A "SINGLE SOURCE OF TRUTH" IN SUPPLY CHAINS

When all parties involved in a particular supply chain are operating off a "single source of truth," discrepancies, mismanagement, and miscommunication can all be avoided. The secure sharing of data and, along with seamless coordination within the supply chain (all enabled by NFT technology), is already being deployed by forward-thinking companies that understand what's at stake. Further deployment of NFTs (coupled with AI technology) in this industry will only help us avoid catastrophes like "The Great Disruption" of 2021.

CRYPTOCURRENCY

CRYPTOCURRENCY

Article #1   *03.26.2021*

The Solution is in the Problem

*How Bitcoin's Hacks, Heists and Lost Treasures
All Could Have Been Avoided*

Bitcoin recently eclipsed $60,000 in value, and the digital currency has passed $1 trillion of market cap, larger than Facebook's market cap. One of the biggest benefits of Bitcoin is that any person in the world can open a digital bank account and hold the tokens, such that no government can regulate it, since Bitcoin is governed by a network of computers that agrees to follow software containing all cryptocurrency rules.

Bitcoin, like other cryptocurrencies, was created based on a set of basic principles, two of which are anonymity and decentralization. In essence, the market's lack of trust in centralized entities like financial institutions and governments, and the desire for complete privacy of one's financial transactions are reasons for crypto's ongoing popularity. So, instead of bank account, bitcoin holders have wallets that are completely anonymous, but still provide protection for ownership. A win-win, right? Not so fast.

The software that enables the creation of wallets and passwords is complex and virtually unregulated. Anyone can create a Bitcoin wallet without standard identity checks and paper trails. Not a single person or institution, other than the crypto owner, has access or knowledge of a wallet. This anonymity and privacy is great until a common mistake is made: you lose or forget your password.

In fact, according to recent estimates, about 20% of the Bitcoin supply might be permanently lost, and about $40.6 billion worth of Bitcoin (3.7 million BTC) has not been touched for over five years, due to issues like forgetting passwords and sending Bitcoin to the incorrect address.

Bitcoin is all about rejecting the traditional financial system and replacing it with something that is not centralized, regulated, and intermediated. The autonomous and trustless nature of owning cryptocurrency and the ability to transact directly through the blockchain, obviates the need for central control and intermediaries. However, this decentralization also means that there are no real checks and balances and no back stop— someone you can call in an emergency if you lose a password—to prevent human error or malicious activity. Fraudulent Bitcoin-related activity more than tripled in 2019 over the year before, with about $3.5 billion taken from millions of victims.

BITCOIN'S DESIGN FLAWS MAY ALSO BE THE SOLUTION

Cryptocurrencies have a few design flaws, including a user interface that leaves much to be desired, compounded by complicated transitions, long passwords and wallets, and the software that facilitate the sending and receiving of crypto.

Unfortunately, for those reasons and others, crypto hasn't been welcomed with open arms into the traditional financial world. About 80% of all financial investments come through institutional players, so the lack of institutional investment has certainly slowed down the growth of Bitcoin. However, everything is about to change.

THE DIGITAL FINANCE TRANSFORMATION

The blockchain-based digital finance revolution, which includes cryptocurrency, along with Central Bank Digital Currency (CBDC), digital securities, stable coins, and more, continues to permeate the global financial system creating positive change and exciting opportunities. Traditional players like Tesla, PayPal, MasterCard, BNY Mellon, and many more are fully aware of this changing landscape and are on board. For example, Tesla recently bought $1.5 billion in Bitcoin, and the company announced that it would begin accepting Bitcoin as a payment method. And PayPal now allows its users to buy and spend Bitcoin and other cryptocurrencies through the platform.

As big-name investors understand and embrace digital finance, the "grey areas" of crypto investing and ownership will need to be solved, including questions surrounding Know Your Customer (KYC) and Anti-Money Laundering (AML) checks to help protect against identity theft and fraud. Ironically, the technology that crypto was built on, is also the technology that will save it.

THE BLOCKCHAIN SOLUTION

Blockchain can solve a number of challenges with digital transactions, including data security, frauds, double spending, chargebacks, cross-border transactions, currency reproductions, and of course, the Lost Treasure issue. Blockchain can also improve the overall user experience for owners and investors. Take the blockchain-based smart contract.

About 80% of all financial investments come through institutional players.

Additionally, investing and improving the "blockchain infrastructure" will be key. KYC/AML will become a universal requirement, and the link between the investor and the wallet will become supported through blockchain infrastructure. Brokers, banks, and investment platforms will begin providing cryptocurrency custody, freeing investors from the responsibility of directly dealing with wallets and other blockchain complexities.

Furthermore, services will be built to make automatic transactions more secure against fraud. And crypto EFFs and futures will be provided to allow those interested to invest in cryptocurrency by trading traditional securities through their IRAs and brokerage accounts.

Finally, if Bitcoin is to become part of the mainstream financial system, then it must lose a bit of that anti-establishment anonymity and be regulated in a way that creates a favorable and secure environment for all investors. Along with clarifying regulations and an increase in mainstream adoption, improved blockchain-based technology could mean a new age for ownership of cryptocurrency and help cryptocurrency owners avoid security problems and maintain autonomy at the same time.

WINNERS, LOSERS, AND THE LOST

As with any market, there are winners and losers in the digital finance space. In this instance, the biggest losers have been those who've had bad luck with passwords.

Whether or not all of the unclaimed Bitcoins are found, the story is less about the actual currency and more about the dramatic increase in attention and investment of digital finance, including cryptocurrency.

The lure of private islands and brand-new Tesla's may be inflating the market and driving those with lost Bitcoin treasures crazy. However, serious Wall Street experts know that digital finance is not fluke or fad, it's the inevitable evolution of a market ripe for disruption. Blockchain technology will not only solve the problems of the past, but lead us all to a place where the possibilities (and the treasures) are endless.

Blockchain can solve a number of challenges with digital transactions.

CRYPTOCURRENCY

Article #2   *08.31.2022, Medium*

Is Crypto Giving Blockchain and Decentralized Finance a Bad Name?

Cryptocurrencies are only a sliver of the massive Decentralized Finance ecosystem— one which has blockchain at the center of a rapidly growing digital economy.

If 2021 was the "Year of the Cryptocurrency," then 2022 was the year it collapsed. Millions were made and lost by crypto investors, while crypto companies were built and folded. For those with significant positions in the crypto market, it's been volatile and uncertain to say the least.

Let's be clear on one thing: cryptocurrencies are different from, and are a small portion of, the blockchain technology and tokenization ecosystem. So, while much of the "hype" has been focused on crypto, there has been an entire universe built on blockchain technology that is experiencing incredible growth as we speak with exponentially more to come. In fact, the blockchain market size is rising globally at a CAGR of 56.3% during the forecast period 2022 to 2029.

TradFi, which is a new way of referring to the entirety of the traditional finance (capital markets) is completely unrelated to blockchain. However, TradFi market is beginning to use blockchain more and more but having absolutely nothing to do with crypto. Take the Depository Trust & Clearing Corp. (DTCC). According to a recent article in CoinDesk, DTCC's use of blockchain in TradFi, has been growing so quickly (and successfully) that they're now processing almost every trade in the more than $40 trillion USUS stock market.

The former president of the New York Stock Exchange told The Wall Street Journal in a story published Aug. 22, 2022, that "blockchain technology is going to rewire all financial services."

NARRATIVES VS. FACTS: CRYPTO'S NAME IS MUCH LARGER THAN ITS MARKET IMPACT

While the media continues to focus on the "crypto crash," they're emphasizing and prolonging a narrative regarding the entire blockchain industry, which is both inaccurate and misleading. The roots of this "false narrative" comes from widespread naivety and continued misunderstanding about what the digital economy, built on blockchain technology, really is.

The facts are clear. The Decentralized Finance (DeFi) market in its current form—which includes global tokenization, blockchain, Metaverse, digital securities, Non-Fungible Tokens (NFTs), Central Bank Digital Currencies (CBDCs), crypto and more—touches every industry from entertainment to healthcare to financial markets. If you bring into account the addressable traditional finance (TradFi), which includes all consumer and commercial banking, insurance, and capital markets, the total addressable market is well over $100 trillion. Crypto represents less than 1% of the overall market's potential size.

To put 1% in even greater perspective, the recent dip in the US stock market, a jarring but not an abnormal fluctuation for today's market, turned out to be the equivalent of the entire crypto market cap.

As for the current tokenized assets market—again, just a portion of the greater DeFi ecosystem—the size is relatively small (estimated at around $350B), but the total addressable market (TAM) of asset tokenization, including gold, real-estate, commodities and currency, is around $46 trillion.

If you break the blockchain-based market down by verticals, the growth trajectory becomes even more clear. The blockchain-based supply-chain market is expected to grow to over $14 billion in revenue by 2028, while the healthcare market transitioning to blockchain technology (a rapidly growing trend), is expected to reach more than $126 billion by 2030. Those are just two verticals in the blockchain-only portion of the greater DeFi landscape. If you compare that to the current market cap of all cryptocurrencies, which stands at just under $1 trillion, you can see that of the entire DeFi pie, crypto is about as small of a slice as you can stomach.

DON'T JUDGE AN ENTIRE MARKET BY ITS COVER

As the crypto market continues its pattern of volatility, the other critical components of the DeFi ecosystem are holding strong and continue to grow their share of the market. The underpinnings and the engine of the DeFi market, distributed ledger technology (DLT) is here to stay and will continue to fuel the digital economy for decades to come. Whether or not crypto will survive is neither here nor there (I happen to believe it will). The point is that crypto's size, power, and worth within the greater DeFi universe is irrelevant. The technology, innovation, and usefulness of blockchain and digitization is where the world economy is headed and a down day for Bitcoin will never stop that forward progression.

CRYPTOCURRENCY

Article #3   *1.16.2021, The Street*

Welcome to Miami:
The New Crypto Capital of the US?

Is it just a PR stunt or is there real substance and a future vision to Miami's move to integrate cryptocurrency into its local economy?

Miami implemented MiamiCoin cryptocurrency a few months ago, but the real news came late last week when the city's charismatic mayor, Francis Suarez, announced that the yield from MiamiCoin would be redistributed to its citizens. This sounds ground-breaking, but is the mayor a true visionary, or is he just a part of creative PR stunt?

LET'S TAKE A CLOSER LOOK

MiamiCoin launched in August through CityCoins, an open-source protocol that allocates 30% of its reward to cites when their coins are bought or mined. So far, the cryptocurrency has generated over $21 million in the past three months for the city. "If annualized, it would amount to roughly $80 million, which is already one-fifth of the city's total annual tax revenue of $400 million," Mayor Suarez said.

Miami will share with its residents some of the gains from the city's new cryptocurrency and will distribute payments through digital wallets, but while Suarez called the payment "a Bitcoin yield," the dividend will come from staking MiamiCoin, a separate digital currency.

The high income from the mining and staking, is related to the attractiveness of the coin and also the current discrepancy between the market interest rate and the interest income from staking the coin. It will be interesting to see if MiamiCoin will continue to generate the same level (or greater) of income for the city as it did the first three months of operation. If so, it may be an interesting alternative to bank deposits for Miamians. More importantly, this may be a strong message to traditional banks—figure out alternative model to the current deposit system or potentially face the loss of savings revenue in cities that implement similar concepts.

For implementing the plan, Miami will have to create crypto wallets to all [eligible] Miami residents based on eligibility criteria the city sets. This is novel considering that it will make the concept of cryptocurrencies and the practice of interacting with the crypto economy more of a mainstream activity in Miami. People who otherwise may not have been comfortable directly holding cryptocurrencies may be more receptive and more knowledgeable. This move may also inspire more innovation in the areas of UX/UI within the crypto ecosystem, something that it has lacked since its inception.

Miami will share with its residents some of the gains from the city's new cryptocurrency.

MIAMI EYES CRYPTO AS A DEFINING CITY FEATURE

It's clear that along with Mayor Suarez's goals of supporting city residents without taxes, becoming a creative funding source for the city, he also wants to put the stake in the ground that Miami is the King of Crypto. Crypto and Bitcoin are not new to the city. Miami has a long history with crypto and Bitcoin, including hosting the annual Bitcoin conference. The Mayor has also stated multiple times that he wants to turn Miami into the most crypto-friendly US city proclaiming that he'll receive his next salary in Bitcoin.

While New York is known as the Big Apple and Chicago is still the city of Big Shoulders, will Miami be forever referred to the city of Big Coin? We certainly can't make any determinations at this point, but Miami's move may be part of a larger trend with municipalities turning to alternative funding sources in an evolving digital economy.

Will Miami be forever referred to the city of Big Coin?

CRYPTOCURRENCY

Article #4   *09.02.2021, The Street*

Bitcoin is the currency of choice for global ransomware attacks

Why has Bitcoin become so popular in ransomware attacks? Bitcoin is still the "King of Crypto" and with its decentralized nature, irreversible transactions, and lack of any oversight, it's clear why it is easier to hide and move around ransom money in crypto.

Earlier this summer, the world's largest meat processor, JBS, announced that it paid $11 million in Bitcoin after a cyber attack forced the shutdown of its plants in the US, Canada, and Australia. This attack was followed by the news that the Justice Department recovered some $2.3 million in cryptocurrency ransom paid by Colonial Pipeline Co, cracking down on hackers who launched the most disruptive US cyberattack on record.

So, why has Bitcoin become so popular in ransomware attacks?

BITCOIN IS STILL THE "KING OF CRYPTO"

In terms of market cap and number of users Bitcoin reigns supreme in the cryptocurrency ecosystem. For right now, crypto is also the digital equivalent of a "suitcase of unmarked $100 bills."

The traditional financial system is a walled garden. To enter one needs to have their identity verified by a regulated financial institution, a process known as Know Your Customer (KYC), and pass checks related to exclusion lists (terror, drugs, money laundry, etc).

Additionally, most jurisdictions have also been clamping down on cash transactions, which makes it extremely difficult for bad actors to move large sums of ransom money and then make it disappear without trace.

Crypto, on the other hand, was created originally as an alternative to the financial system and one of the principles to its creation was anonymity. Crypto transactions are executed between blockchain addresses and they are not linked originally 1:1 to the identity of a specific entity and/ or person. Despite the fact that many jurisdictions started requiring providers (like exchanges) to require KYC checks, some still don't, and enforcement is still fairly weak. The result is that many user wallets are still anonymous.

Additionally, the fact that crypto transactions are irreversible and much faster than "traditional money" transactions, and there are no intermediaries in the crypto system to stop a transaction, or to lock an account, it becomes clear why it is easier to hide and move around ransom money in crypto.

CRYPTO REGULATION COULD MAKE A DIFFERENCE

More and more regulators are requiring KYC and AML (Anti Money Laundering) checks and balances, and most financial institutions today require verification of "cleanliness" of money originating from Crypto (checking the crypto path from origination to destination).

As a result, it's getting harder and harder to get rid of dirty money, even if it originates in cryptocurrency. In addition, as the volume of institutional money and investment in crypto continues to increase, legitimate use and wallets will also grow.

The more KYC/AML checks are required and enforced, the magnitude of problems will decrease.

However, legislation will not solve the inherent issue of lack of intermediaries in the crypto environment (at least for existing blockchains), as they are based on decentralized blockchains. So, even when law enforcement identifies a suspected address, it is nearly impossible (baring very special situations) to seize these funds or prevent their movement elsewhere.

Crypto, on the other hand, was created originally as an alternative to the financial system and one of the principles to its creation was anonymity.

The decoupling of Bitcoin and stocks could revive one of the historic promises of cryptocurrencies, they can serve as hedge portfolios against equity market sell offs.

CRYPTOCURRENCY

Article #5   *10.13.2021, The Street*

What Bitcoin's Non-Reaction to the Pandora Papers Tells Us About Crypto Behavior

Pandora Paper revelations validated Crypto's anti-elite, anti-establishment views, yet Bitcoin held steady

A few days ago, the secret deals and hidden assets of some of the world's richest and most powerful people were revealed in the biggest trove of leaked offshore data in history, dubbed "The Pandora Papers."

While still appalling, most of us were not completely shocked with the revelations. The Pandora Papers reminded us what many of us already knew; power corrupts and people at the top of the pyramid have many opportunities to abuse our trust, manipulate the system, and put personal gain over anything else.

In addition to the widespread corruption of the world's most elite, The Pandora Papers also taught us something about Bitcoin.

As far as financial assets go, Bitcoin and other cryptocurrencies are still very new with relatively little history, so we're slowly trying to learn their behavior as an asset. Every major market event, including The Pandora Papers, is a learning opportunity to discover what correlations matter and how digital currencies react to both micro and macro events.

One of Bitcoin's (and other cryptocurrencies) key purpose and principle was originally to anchor an alternative financial system that is decentralized and anti-establishment. Crypto's power is in its ability to exist and thrive without centralized authority. This vision comes from the underlying belief of founders and early crypto adopters that power corrupts, and people can't trust those who are in positions of power. Many investors believed that events like the Pandora Papers, proving one of the key drivers for the creation of Bitcoin, would result in a significant price appreciation, with investors flocking to the digital currency after such a validating moment. However, that did not happen. The crypto market pretty much shrugged off the Pandora Papers, just like the market has shrugged off other critical macro events over the course of the last few months (i.e. China's ban on crypto transactions, etc).

WHAT DOES THE REACTION TO THE PANDORA PAPERS TELL US ABOUT BITCOIN?

Why is Bitcoin and its price movements, both the upside and downside, still so difficult to predict? Is it because a significant part of Bitcoin ownership still resides with "Whales," which are driven by a different agenda and strategy than the rest of the market? Or, is it because Bitcoin has matured and has a more complex set of drivers than originally thought? Maybe it's because Bitcoin is different than all other traditional financial assets, an uncorrelated asset that is moved not by events, but rather by people and their demand.

Let's attempt to try to get to the bottom of the "crypto question:"

WHALES' IMPACT ON BITCOIN'S PRICE MOVEMENT

Large Bitcoin holders are called Whales. The 20/80 rule applies in "Bitcoinland:" the top 20% of Bitcoin holders have more than 80% of Bitcoin value in US dollars. According to BitInfoCharts, as of Q2 2021, the top 100 Bitcoin wallets held around 18% of all Bitcoin. Whales tend to be long-term holders, and according to Chainalysis, Whales tend to retain at least 75% of the Bitcoin they buy.

This market domination greatly impacts Bitcoin price movement in multiple ways. When the concentration of wealth sits unmoved in an account, liquidity decreases, which in turn, increases price volatility. Volatility is further increased if a Whale sells a large quantity of Bitcoin all at once. This lack of liquidity, combined with a large transaction size, puts downward pressure on the price of Bitcoin. Additionally, as other market participants watch the Whales' actions (courtesy of the crypto full transparency principle), they may be inclined to try to sell, creating fire sales and more volatility.

Finally, Whales may try to sell their assets in smaller amounts over a longer period of time to avoid drawing attention, thus producing market distortions and sending the price up or down unexpectedly. Whales drive speculation among the "little fish," which can result in a vicious cycle where prices become untethered to underlying fundamentals.

IS BITCOIN TRULY AN 'UNCORRELATED ASSET'?

A 2020 report from Fidelity Digital Assets claimed that Bitcoin has a very low correlation with mainstream assets such as stocks or gold. Starting in 2020, however, we have seen a growing correlation to gold and stocks.

September 2021 analysis showed that Bitcoin and stocks were moving in the same direction (downward) when that correlation quickly reversed in October. One could argue that the correlation seems to be mostly during a crisis. However, Bitcoin recovers at a different rate than other assets recovering faster post-crisis and returning to its uncorrelated nature.

The decoupling of Bitcoin and stocks could revive one of the historic promises of cryptocurrencies, they can serve as hedge portfolios against equity market sell offs. This function is currently in high demand, with many worrying that treasuries can't be relied upon to perform that role during a period of ultra-low yields and accelerating inflation. More

WHAT TO WATCH FOR NOW

As time progresses and Bitcoin investors experience more meaningful financial events, the understanding of Bitcoin behavior as a financial asset will continue to evolve.

THREE OBVIOUS DRIVERS ARE OF PARTICULAR INTEREST TO WATCH:

1. **The increase in institutional and corporate investment in Bitcoin.**

2. **The potential approval of Bitcoin ETFs by the SEC (there are 20 in review).**

3. **Potential regulatory actions to create clarity and guardrails in the crypto market.**

The number of Bitcoin holders is growing dramatically and so is institutional holding of Bitcoin.

importantly, Bitcoin's correlation with inflation expectations may signify its adoption as an inflation hedge over gold.

IS BITCOIN MATURING AS AN ASSET?

The number of Bitcoin holders is growing dramatically and so is institutional holding of Bitcoin. Corporate holding of Bitcoin (e.g. MicroStrategy, Tesla) is increasing as well. With larger players participating in the crypto market, distribution of Bitcoin may shift from its current structure, with institutional and corporate behavior likely to differ from "small fish" behavior. Time and experience will also guide the market, especially as investors become more aware of crypto behavior and develop strategies to handle the volatility.

All three of these drivers are imminent and have a potential impact on Bitcoin/crypto behavior. Let's also remember to keep our eye on the "inflation" ball. How will Bitcoin and the crypto market as a whole react to a predicted and expected period of inflation? Could the market consider Bitcoin as an inflation hedge? Only time will tell.

CRYPTOCURRENCY

Article #6   *12.01.2022, The Street*

Crypto Exchange Proof of Reserves – A Real Solution or Just a Band Aid?

There's a lot of talk about Proof of Reserves as a way to solve crypto's woes, but it only provides information about investors' funds, and not how the exchange is using them.

Following the FTX collapse, many are advocating for crypto exchanges to prove they have enough assets in reserve to back investors' deposits and cover their liabilities. The concept of Proof of Reserves (PoR) emerged as a favored way to try to solve problems and prevent another FTX. As chatter about reserves has ramped up, the crypto industry's largest organizations are racing to prove they have plenty of cash to cover deposits.

In fact, Binance, the world's largest cryptocurrency exchange by volume, has already shared its wallet balances and says it plans to conduct a PoR snapshot in the next few weeks. The delay in proof has led to questions about transparency and validity, but at the very least, they plan to share their data. Other exchanges like Huobi, OKX, KuCoin, Poloniex, Bitget, and Bybit have made similar commitments. Furthermore, CoinMarketCap, a web service that provides aggregated cryptocurrency market data, started to share crypto exchanges' PoR on their ranking pages a week ago.

All of these latest moves have triggered loud industry debate about the effectiveness of the concept. For example, the claim that the PoR CoinMarketCap displays is not as sophisticated as the market requires, or Kraken's CEO questioning the integrity of the proof of reserve posted by Binance as it does not include Binance's liabilities.

Regardless of the finger pointing, what is PoR and could having it prevented FTX's collapse? Most importantly, is it really the solution to crypto world's problems or just smoke and mirrors?

WHAT IS PROOF OF RESERVES (POR)?

According to Investopedia, PoR is a transparent auditing practice for cryptocurrency companies that provides an unbiased report of the companies' assets in reserve. Third-party auditors access cryptographic signatures representing the total balance of customer assets and ensure that the custodian of these assets has an equal (or greater) amount of reserve assets in place to cover all potential customer withdrawals.

Proof of Reserves uses blockchain technology, often a structure called a Merkle tree, like Binance's BTC PoR, to provide a secure way to audit a crypto company without exposing any private user data. PoR can be published by crypto companies periodically or through a real time reserves tracker.

The thinking behind all of this is that in theory, this will help prevent a "run on the bank." By providing transparency to users about whether there are sufficient funds backing all deposits (presumably reassuring them that their deposited funds are safe,) investors are likely to be less skittish during downturns, like the one we've seen this year.

COULD PROOF OF RESERVES HAVE PREVENTED FTX'S COLLAPSE?

There are plenty of "expert" commentary and opinions about what could have prevented FTX and others from their tailspin downwards. However, there's no single mistake or an accompanying solution that could have stopped FTX and its leader, Sam Bankman-Fried, from committing outright fraud. Regulation, audits, compliance, and an actual accounting firm (not one built in the Metaverse) would be a better start to solving FTX's myriad of debacles.

Merkle tree-based PoR cannot prevent the misappropriation of customer funds completely. It tracks holdings but would never stop an exchange from lending money to dodgy borrowers who have no hope of repaying or keeping the reserves in currency, which don't hold their value in case of a "run on the money" all of which FTX has done and more. Additionally, if a company intentionally engages in practices of fraud, incompetence, negligence, reckless risk-taking, and lack of transparency, PoR is not the "Superman" of the digital economy to swoop in and save the day.

It is simply not a realistic expectation regarding PoR. While it doesn't solve every problem, it does accomplish what it was created for, providing more information to investors about their funds. But what PoR doesn't do is monitor or control how the company handles those funds. Even if FTX had implemented PoR, a customer would have been able to watch their crypto evaporate, but with no ability to prevent it from happening.

Lastly, PoR is only as good as its verifier. A crypto exchange could lie outright, and a third-party auditor may miss it, upholding the lie for many reasons including: incompetence, overlooking or missing wallets, or failing to understand how the exchange had structured customer holdings.

IS PROOF OF RESERVES THE SOLUTION TO CRYPTO'S PROBLEMS?

PoR is a good start, if implemented honestly and thoroughly, but it's certainly not enough. While it's well-intentioned for the remaining crypto organizations to disclose their PoR, it may be too little too late. Too much trust has been eroded and skepticism infused into the crypto ecosystem.

The truth is the crypto industry has grown too fast without suitable regulation and has unfortunately attracted some bad eggs that have damaged the reputation of even the good players in the market. In light of the slew of catastrophic failures, which occurred this year, and given the apparent inability of the current US government to pass any meaningful legislation given the balance of power, perhaps it is time for the crypto industry to get serious about self-regulation.

LET'S LEARN FROM TRADFI MISTAKES TO MAKE DEFI BETTER

Traditional finance institutions learned lessons written in blood over decades on issues like how to manage risk, how to match short term price volatility and interest rates with long term interest on loans, and how to guard deposits and how to provide consumer/investor protections, etc. Although the technology and the asset may be different, the financial services provided to clients/investors are similar in the crypto space and similar processes and guardrails should be adopted.

The Utopian dreams of having a system that is completely decentralized, self-governed, and "off-grid" is unrealistic at the very best, and dangerous at the worst. This holistic mindset is preventing the digital economy from moving forward in a meaningful way alienating the institutional money and investors it wants and needs. The sooner the industry realizes that a healthy balance of decentralization with regulation can actually co-exist, the sooner it will evolve and further innovate.

THE POSSIBILITIES OF BLOCKCHAIN

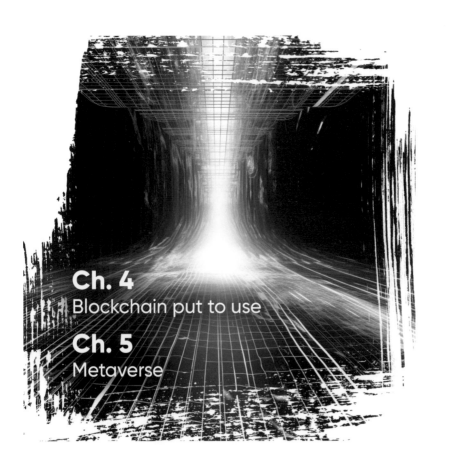

Ch. 4
Blockchain put to use

Ch. 5
Metaverse

INTRODUCTION

In the collective consciousness, the mention of blockchain typically evokes images of cryptocurrency: Bitcoin and the likes. This perception, albeit widespread, couldn't be farther from the nuanced reality of this revolutionary technology. Over the past half-decade, blockchain has dramatically evolved, breaking away from its crypto-centric cocoon to emerge as a transformative force across various industries, from finance and healthcare to gaming and more.

Even as the world's gaze remained fixed on the feverish activity in the crypto and ICO markets, my extensive experience with large transactional industries—banking, payments, securities, healthcare, and gaming—allowed me to peer into the immense potential of blockchain beyond the bitcoin frenzy. However, I was acutely aware that such potential couldn't be unlocked overnight; it demanded vision, innovation, legislative advancements, sustained investments, and the development of a robust ecosystem of standards, protocols, blockchains, layers, and other integral components.

Now, if we glance across industries, we find a fascinating dichotomy in their adoption of blockchain technology. Certain sectors, like the finance and gaming industries, are historically swift in harnessing new technologies, evident in their wide-scale application of blockchain in areas such as payments, securities, banking, fundraising, and insurance. On the other hand, traditionally slower-moving industries like healthcare and manufacturing have taken a more gradual approach to integrating blockchain.

Despite the varied pace of adoption, the ubiquity of blockchain across multiple sectors and its implementation on a significant scale affirms its capacity to instigate transformative change.

In the context of blockchain, the technology frameworks or token types such as NFTs, Security Tokens/Digital Securities, stablecoins, and utility tokens have become increasingly prominent. Moreover, DLT platforms like Ethereum, Avalanche, Algorand, Cardano, Cosmos, and R3 are rapidly gaining traction.

Indeed, as we've witnessed, the pioneers of this field are relentlessly pushing the envelope, devising new blockchain use-cases, protocols, and building blocks, and here's what we can anticipate:

All in all, this section intends to guide you through the labyrinth of blockchain, beyond its traditional crypto association, shedding light on its pervasive influence across industries (many we don't yet know) and its profound potential to reshape our world.

- Robust adoption of blockchain across various sectors, exemplified by impressive growth figures in different industries.

- A paradigm shift in the financial industry, with blockchain serving as its backbone, particularly in payments, capital markets, and fundraising.

- An exponential surge in the adoption of blockchain for supply chain management and manufacturing.

- Monumental growth in retail, synergistically powered by blockchain and AI.

- NFTs finally realizing their true potential as a significant component in healthcare, supply chain management, gaming, and entertainment solutions.

Despite the varied pace of adoption, the ubiquity of blockchain across multiple sectors and its implementation on a significant scale affirms its capacity to instigate transformative change.

BLOCKCHAIN PUT TO USE

BLOCKCHAIN PUT TO USE

Article #1:   *03.16.2023, The Street*

Cha-Ching on the Chain - Why DLT-Powered Payments are Here to Stay

The future of payments is here and it's seamless, secure, and borderless

Blockchain technology isn't new and over the past decade of its existence has proven, time and time again, its unique ability to drive operational efficiencies and modernize global industries from finance to healthcare. Specifically, the Distributed Ledger Technology (DLT) powering blockchain networks provides a transparent, secure, and immutable ledger that has revolutionized payment systems globally. And while most of the blockchain-based payment innovations have been incremental and fairly discreet, the sum of these consumer and enterprise payment developments have created the foundation for the next era in digital financial transactions.

A whitepaper from the US Faster Payments Council and blockchain-based payments powerhouse Ripple finds that

97% of industry leaders across multiple sectors believe in the power of blockchain and digital assets to speed up payments within the next three years. This universal support of blockchain-powered digital payments by some of the largest payment organizations in the word is remarkable.

But to understand why there is wide support, one must first understand why blockchain-based payments are so desirable. A payment involves much more than a simple transfer of funds from one account to another. It encompasses a variety of processes that are often overlooked, such as managing transaction disputes, detecting and preventing fraud, processing chargebacks and bank reversals, integrating with accounting systems, and handling taxes and financial reporting.

Blockchain technology offers many advantages over traditional payment systems, and it has the potential to revolutionize the world of finance, including speed, security, and transparency. Blockchain-based payments can also reduce transaction costs and eliminate the need for intermediaries.

CONSUMER ADOPTION OF BLOCKCHAIN PAYMENTS

The "holy grail" of digital payment growth and adoption is to simplify the complexities for both consumers and businesses. Companies like PayPal, Visa, and Mastercard have all embraced blockchain technology in an effort to achieve more simplicity, while offering enhanced consumer experiences. Well-known names like Mastercard, and its partnership with Web3 payment protocol Immersve, are allowing users to make crypto payments on digital, physical, and the Metaverse worlds. But lesser-known names like Ripple and Stellar are also doing some incredibly interesting things. Specifically, Stellar makes it possible to create, send, and trade digital representations of all forms of money (dollars, pesos, bitcoin, etc.) so that the world's financial systems can work together.

Each of these efforts by digital and traditional payment companies have the following similar objectives:

- **FINANCIAL INCLUSION**
  blockchain technology provides more affordable and scalable solutions to help increase financial inclusion, democratizing the global banking ecosystem.

- **PAYMENT SETTLEMENT AND CLEARANCE:**
  blockchain can enable banks to settle transactions directly and keep track of them better than traditional methods, facilitating immediate and low-cost transaction settlement.

- **LENDING:**
  DLT can simplify business processes and reduce risk and costs in learning, with automation through smart contracts.

- **IDENTITY SERVICES AND ENHANCED SECURITY:**
  DLT allows permitted parties to share data securely and in real-time, which could address challenges of Know Your Customer (KYC), Anti-Money Laundering (AML) and provide enhanced security through immutability of distributed ledgers.

ENTERPRISE ADOPTION OF BLOCKCHAIN PAYMENTS

In order to remain competitive in today's digital landscape, banks must prioritize process automation and delivering a top-notch digital experience for their customers. Blockchain technology has the potential to transform the banking industry and improve services while enhancing the customer experience. Furthermore, blockchain can help banks save costs and reduce risk from fraud, data loss, and more.

A research report from Bank of America shows that over a quarter of the banks they cover have already incorporated blockchain technology into their businesses in some form. JPMorgan, Citi, Wells Fargo, US Bancorp, PNC, and Fifth Third Bank are among the many banks already using DLT/blockchain, while many more intend to implement in the coming months. Here's why:

- **Recording transactions:** blockchain automates back-office operations, reducing errors and saving businesses money.

- **Trade finance:** blockchain manages trade documents, reducing fraud risk, and providing real-time information sharing.

- **Syndicated loans:** blockchain simplifies loans with standard contracts and automated processes.

- **Automating processes:** blockchain's smart contracts automate business relationships, eliminating middlemen and saving money.

- **Global payments:** blockchain enables fast, low-cost, and secure cross-border payments.

For international payments, it's clear that the trend is moving towards borderless, digital payments. In fact, 90% of the payments leaders surveyed by US Faster Payments

Council say that blockchain technology will deliver cost improvements for international transactions and 75% anticipate cost benefits for domestic payments.

Ripple, an early pioneer in enterprise DLT payment systems, continues to gain significant traction in the banking and financial industry by enabling cross-border payments, but even legacy payments companies like Visa are getting in on the action. Visa's B2B Connect enables secure and transparent cross-border payments for businesses.

SECURE, BORDERLESS PAYMENTS WITH CBDCS

International, cross-border payments cannot be discussed without the recognition and mention of universal stable instruments of exchange, such as stablecoins and Central Bank Digital Currencies (CBDC). CBDCs are the digital form of a country's fiat currency built and managed on-chain and appropriately regulated and optimized for payments.

The main goal of CBDCs is to provide businesses and consumers with privacy, transferability, convenience, accessibility, and financial security. CBDCs could also decrease the maintenance a complex financial system requires, reduce cross-border transaction costs, and provide those who currently use alternative money transfer methods with lower-cost options.

The move towards CBDCs continues to gain momentum, especially now as Central Banks look to bolster their economy in uncertain times. All told, around 100 countries are exploring CBDCs at one level or another, with Europe and Asia making huge steps forward in the process. Many of these efforts are in partnership with major banking institutions like Goldman Sachs and JP Morgan in an effort to leverage the versatility of CBCDs as international payment tools.

THE FUTURE OF PAYMENTS IS BLOCKCHAIN

While crypto seemed to explode onto the scene all at once, the journey for blockchain-based payments has been slow and steady, purposeful, and careful. The efforts have been collaborative and pioneering all at the same time, with startups working alongside legacy banks, governments and regulators. This is all a good sign that the world knows the future of money is digital and blockchain is the foundation it will all be built on.

Blockchain technology offers many advantages over traditional payment systems, and it has the potential to revolutionize the world of finance.

BLOCKCHAIN PUT TO USE

Article #2 *04.10.2023, The Street*

From Life to Health: Blockchain is Transforming the Insurance Industry

The adoption of blockchain technology in the complex world of insurance and re-insurance will streamline processes, increase transparency, and reduce costs.

Blockchain technology is just breaking the surface in the immense potential to revolutionize nearly every industry in the global economy, including finance, healthcare, supply chain management, and more. One industry that's definitely worth our time exploring is the world of insurance and re-insurance.

Why is it worth review? Well, according to a report by MarketsandMarkets, the global blockchain in insurance market size is expected to reach $1.4 billion in 2023 up from $64 million in 2018. Plus, a report by Deloitte found that 74% of insurers are either researching or piloting blockchain technology, and 14% have already implemented blockchain-based solutions.

The insurance and reinsurance industries are complex, with numerous stakeholders involved, including policyholders, insurers, reinsurers, brokers, and regulators. The adoption of blockchain technology in these industries could potentially streamline processes, increase transparency, and reduce costs.

One of the most significant use-cases of blockchain in insurance is the creation of smart contracts. These self-executing contracts can be programmed to trigger specific actions based on predefined conditions, such as the occurrence of an event or the fulfillment of a particular obligation. In insurance, smart contracts can automate claims processing and reducing the time and costs associated with manual processing. For example, a smart contract can automatically release a payment to a policyholder when a predefined event occurs, such as a flight delay or a car accident.

This technology is critical now more than ever due to the growing climate change crisis and the catastrophic weather events that have resulted. For example, if there is a flood or high wind event, a policy could be triggered via a smart contract without any human involvement. And, if the policy holder meets all the parameters, then they could be paid immediately through the blockchain, eliminating much of the current claim pain points during these types of events that are becoming all too common.

Blockchain can also facilitate the sharing of information among different stakeholders, increasing transparency and reducing the potential for fraud. Insurance companies can use blockchain to store policy information, claims data, and other relevant information in a secure and transparent manner. This can help prevent fraudulent claims, as insurers can quickly verify the authenticity of a claim by accessing the relevant information stored on the blockchain.

The benefits of blockchain in insurance are too significant to ignore across all insurance types.

Re-insurance companies can also benefit from blockchain technology. Re-insurance is the practice of insuring insurance companies themselves against catastrophic losses. Blockchain can help streamline the re-insurance process by enabling faster and more accurate tracking of data related to the underlying insurance policies. Re-insurance companies can use blockchain to track policy information, premiums, and claims data, enabling them to make more informed decisions about which risks to take on and at what price.

Moreover, blockchain can help improve the customer experience in the insurance industry by providing policyholders with more control over their data. Blockchain-based insurance solutions can give policyholders the ability to manage their policies and claims data securely and transparently. This can lead to increased trust in the insurance industry and improved customer satisfaction.

The adoption of blockchain technology in the insurance and re-insurance industries has the potential to streamline processes, reduce costs, increase transparency, and improve the customer experience. Companies like Lemonade, which combines AI and blockchain technology to offer home, car, pet, and more insurance are leveraging the power of blockchain's smart contract technology to simplify and modernize the insurance ecosystem. Yet, while there is plenty of innovation, there are still some challenges to overcome, such as regulatory hurdles and the need for interoperability between different blockchain solutions. That being said, the benefits of blockchain in insurance are too significant to ignore across all insurance types.

HEALTH INSURANCE

In health insurance, blockchain can be used to improve the accuracy and security of medical records. Patients can have their medical data stored on a blockchain network, which can be accessed by doctors and other healthcare providers. The blockchain-based system ensures that the medical data is secure, tamper-proof, and easily accessible to the authorized parties.

A company named Medicalchain is already offering a blockchain-based platform for storing and sharing medical records, while Blue Cross Blue Shield's (BCBS) digital solutions arm created a blockchain consortium called Coalesce Health Alliance. The partnership is evaluating blockchain as a means of streamlining healthcare data exchanges among BCBS players.

Additionally, Avaneer Health, which designed a blockchain-based architecture to enable secure and streamlined transactions for its participants, is now being backed by blue chip insurance behemoths Aetna, Anthem, Cleveland Clinic, Health Care Service Corporation, PNC Financial, and Sentara Healthcare, solidifying blockchain's staying power in the vertical.

CAR INSURANCE

Blockchain can help streamline the claims process in car insurance. For example, when a car accident occurs, the blockchain can be used to store and share information such as the accident report, photos of the damage, and police reports. This can speed up the claims process, reducing the time it takes to settle a claim. Moreover, blockchain can also help prevent insurance fraud by verifying the authenticity of the claim data. A company named Insurwave is already offering a blockchain-based platform for marine insurance, which can also be extended to car insurance.

HOMEOWNERS INSURANCE

In homeowners insurance, blockchain can be used to improve the transparency and security of property records. By storing property records on a blockchain network, homeowners can have a tamper-proof and transparent way of verifying their property ownership. This can help prevent disputes and fraud related to property ownership. Moreover, blockchain can also be used to automate the claims process in homeowners insurance. For example, if a natural disaster damages a property, a smart contract can automatically initiate the claims process, reducing the time and costs associated with manual processing.

Let's not forget about one of the most complex forms of insurance: Life Insurance. From fraud to family disputes, blockchain technology has the opportunity to right the wrongs that have riddled this form of insurance for decades.

Blockchain can also be used in this corner of the insurance ecosystem to enhance several ways. Here are some examples:

- **CLAIMS PROCESSING:**

  Blockchain can automate the claims process in life insurance, reducing the time and costs associated with manual processing. Smart contracts can be programmed to automatically execute payouts to beneficiaries when the policyholder passes away. This can eliminate the need for fraud. transparency, security, and efficiency in intermediaries, reducing the chances of errors and

- **FRAUD PREVENTION:**

  Life insurance fraud is a significant problem that costs the industry billions of dollars every year. Blockchain can help prevent fraud by creating a secure and transparent way of storing and sharing policyholder data. Insurers can use blockchain to verify the authenticity of policyholder data and identify any fraudulent activity.

- **UNDERWRITING:**

  Blockchain can be used to streamline the underwriting process in life insurance. By using a blockchain-based platform, insurers can have a secure and transparent way of collecting and verifying policyholder data, such as medical records, lifestyle habits, and other risk factors. This can help insurers make more accurate underwriting decisions and reduce the chances of disputes.

- **BENEFICIARY MANAGEMENT:**

  Blockchain can help simplify beneficiary management in life insurance. By storing beneficiary information on a blockchain network, policyholders can have a secure and transparent way of managing their beneficiaries. This can help ensure the right people receive the payouts in the event of the policyholder's death.

Insurance is the Big Business that everyone loves to hate but needs especially in the worst of times. What if blockchain could remove much of what insurance customers hate the most creating massive efficiencies and offering a better customer experience? It's possible and it's happening. Companies like State Farm, Allstate, and USAA are all working to incorporate DLT as part of their overall operations. And, much like legacy organizations from other industries, these giants are finding that blockchain isn't just a "nice to try," but rather a "need to have."

BLOCKCHAIN PUT TO USE

Article #3   *05.05.2023, The Street*

Is it Really A Smart Factory Without Blockchain?

How the fusion of IoT and blockchain is transforming US and global manufacturing.

Manufacturing has come a long way since the days of assembly lines and conveyor belts. With the combination of IoT (Internet of Things) and blockchain, it's about to go through another revolution. However, unlike the stretch of automation and outsourcing that desecrated the US manufacturing market, American manufacturers are adding jobs and capacity, leading to a need for better (and smarter) management and operations. The "Smart Factory" is now the driving force behind manufacturing, with a hybrid synergy with IoT and blockchain leading the way.

It's no surprise that IoT is a key component of smart factory and Industry 4.0 initiatives, with IoT in manufacturing driving unprecedented disruption helping make factories safer for frontline workers, increasing productivity and efficiency, and reducing costs drastically. In fact, the data to back this up is staggering. Global industrial IoT market size was estimated at $326.1 billion in 2021 and is expected to hit around $1.7 trillion by 2030 with a registered CAGR of 20.47% during the forecast period 2022 to 2030. Discrete manufacturing and process manufacturing alone are expected to account this year for over $200 billion in IoT services spending. Companies that are driving this IoT boom are ABB, General Electric, IBM, Intel, Rockwell Automation, Siemens, Microsoft, Cisco, and NEC, among others.

But there are still challenges to overcome, particularly in terms of security and privacy. That's where blockchain comes in. By decentralizing IoT networks, blockchain technology can add a layer of security that traditional centralized models can't match. Hybrid blockchain and IoT applications offer a range of benefits specifically when it comes to the power of "smart contracts."

Smart contracts are self-executing programs built on the blockchain that automatically enforce the terms of an agreement between parties without the need for intermediaries. Because of their on-chain existence, smart contracts are decentralized, immutable, and secure. IoT technology enables automation but, coupled with smart contracts, automated responses can be authorized through the network more efficiently.

The potential role of blockchain within the manufacturing ecosystem is immense, so attempting to touch upon every single use-case would have the reader tied up for days. That's why, for this particular piece, I've chosen to focus on some key areas that DLT can really make a difference and is doing so now.

PROACTIVE MAINTENANCE AND QUALITY CONTROL MANAGEMENT:

In a smart factory, smart contracts can be used to automate and streamline various processes, such as production scheduling, proactive maintenance, and quality control.

By using sensors and other IoT devices connected to a blockchain network, data about the performance and health of equipment can be collected in real-time and stored securely on the blockchain. This data can then be analyzed using machine learning algorithms to identify patterns and predict potential failures before they occur. This enables proactive maintenance and repairs, minimizing downtime, and increasing productivity.

Additionally, blockchain technology can be used to create smart contracts that enforce quality control standards throughout the supply chain. They can be put to use between the manufacturer and suppliers for specifying quality standards for the raw materials used in production. When the materials are delivered, they can be scanned and verified using sensors, and the data can be stored on the blockchain. If the materials do not meet the required standards, the smart contract can automatically trigger a process to reject the materials or send them back to the supplier.

SUPPLY CHAIN MANAGEMENT:

One area where blockchain can revolutionize the manufacturing industry is in supply chain management. Counterfeiting, supply chain failures, inventory management, and supply chain fraud have plagued the industry for years. But with the creation of a shared digital ledger, along with smart contracts, blockchain technology can tackle these issues head-on.

By enabling suppliers to access a shared, secure, and permissioned database, blockchain technology can prevent fraudulent data manipulation and mitigate the risk of certain suppliers altering data. It also enables manufacturers to verify where their materials have come from, preventing counterfeit materials from entering the ecosystem.

With everyone involved in the process connected and able to access information in real-time, manufacturers can better manage and plan inventory, ensuring a smooth supply chain and preventing hiccups that can slow down production. And with the immutable audit trail created by blockchain technology, manufacturers can prove the origin of materials and reduce the risk of fraud.

WARRANTY AND RECALL MANAGEMENT:

The ecosystem of manufactures, supply chain participants, warranty providers, and consumers is vast and complex. What happens when something goes wrong and a part is recalled? Furthermore, what if a false claim is made? Blockchain can help to bridge the information gap within that vast ecosystem, so warranty and recall lifecycles are streamlined and shortened. With the immutability of DLT, the chain of custody can be securely maintained to prevent counterfeits from entering the supply chain and fraudulent claims from being filed. Blockchain also offers excellent traceability. Companies can quickly and accurately trace products through the supply chain, identify affected items in the event of a recall, and notify consumers in a timely manner significantly decreasing negative fallout by orders of magnitude.

WORKPLACE SAFETY MANAGEMENT:

Blockchain technology can also transform workplace safety management and monitoring. Despite the Occupational Safety and Health Administration's (OSHA) requirement for employers to provide a safe work environment, ensuring compliance and real-time incident tracking can be difficult. Blockchain technology offers increase transparency by creating a permanent record of safety incidents, simplifying auditing and verification of safety protocols, and enabling workers to report incidents quickly and accurately via digital interfaces. It also enhances data security and facilitates predictive analytics, allowing employers to identify and prevent safety hazards before they occur.

MANUFACTURERS ALREADY PUTTING BLOCKCHAIN TO WORK:

According to Gartner, the business value-add of blockchain is expected to exceed $3.1 trillion by 2030, with close to 30% manufacturers (with more than $5 billion in revenue) implementing industry 4.0 projects leveraging blockchain by 2023.

Some interesting examples of blockchain in motion include Ford. The auto behemoth has been exploring the use of blockchain technology to track the origin and authenticity of critical parts in its vehicles. By using a blockchain-based system, Ford can create an immutable record of each part's journey from the factory to the vehicle. Additionally, the company partnered with blockchain company Everledger to launch a battery passport pilot. The battery passport will use technologies including auto ID, blockchain, and artificial intelligence to support the responsible recycling of electric vehicle (EV) batteries.

Additionally, Bosch, a major manufacturer of automotive and industrial technology, developed a blockchain-based platform called "Trusted IoT Alliance" to help improve the security and transparency of IoT devices. The alliance includes several major companies, including Cisco, Gemalto, and Huawei. Additionally, the company has partnered with Fetch.ai to fund the development of Web3, artificial intelligence (AI) and decentralized technologies.

POTENTIAL COST SAVINGS:

According to a report by the World Economic Forum and Accenture, blockchain technology could potentially save supply chain management costs by up to $100 billion per year by 2025. This includes savings in areas such as inventory management, product tracking, and supply chain finance.

In a case study conducted by DNV GL, a global assurance and risk management company, a blockchain-based solution was used to digitize the management and tracking of marine equipment. The solution resulted in a 30% reduction in administrative costs and a 50% reduction in equipment downtime.

Another example is Provenance, a UK-based company that uses blockchain technology to track and verify the sustainability and ethical standards of supply chains. Their solution has helped companies like Co-op Food and Unilever reduce compliance and management costs, while also improving their sustainability and ethical credentials.

GREEN FACTORY MANAGEMENT:

The use of blockchain can help manufacturers achieve more sustainable operations in a number of innovative ways, including tracing the origin of materials and products, tracking energy consumption and carbon emissions, and identifying areas where efficiency can be improved. From creating more efficient and green supply chains, to identifying renewable energy sources, reducing waste and more, the technology can significantly improve a variety of production processes that align with an organizations' ESG objectives. Additionally, blockchain-based solutions can be used to support green financing, carbon trading, and a variety of carbon offset initiatives.

BLOCKCHAIN PUTS THE SMART IN SMART FACTORY:

Achieving a true "smart factory" just isn't possible without the use of blockchain technology, period. What we do know about US and global manufacturing is that it's not afraid of evolution nor innovation. Now, as we embark on a Fourth Industrial Revolution and the Web3 Era, I believe, and the data is proving this out, the industrial sector stands to significantly benefit from its ability to digitize and modernize quickly and efficiently with implementation of blockchain technology across all aspects of the ecosystem. In fact, manufacturing may become the industry to watch as other sectors look to innovate and evolve with similar successful outcomes.

BLOCKCHAIN PUT TO USE

Article #4: *06.25.23, Newsweek*

The Carbon Credit Problem Finds a Trustworthy Solution

Climate once again was thrust onto the national and international scene when US President Joe Biden vetoed "a Republican proposal to prevent pension fund managers from basing investment decisions on factors like climate change." The bill, which cleared Congress earlier in the year, overturned a previous Labor Department rule that actually would make it easier for fund managers and investors to participate in the widely-known world of ESG—environmental, social, and governance.

While Biden's veto has little to do with the blockchain and tokenization ecosystem, it does emphasize the hard truth: unless we make it easier and more financially desirable, a majority of the US and global voting block won't take climate matters seriously.

It's possible, however, that all we need to make a global, coordinated, enterprise-based climate approach a reality is one thing—trust.

PUT YOUR TRUST IN CARBON CREDITS

Carbon credits are "a way for companies to support activities, such as protecting and restoring irrecoverable natural carbon sinks, like forests or marine ecosystems, and scaling nascent carbon removal technology, that keep global climate goals within reach."

Companies like Delta, Alphabet, and Disney are among the biggest buyers of carbon credits. According to a recent Forbes article, those companies purchased $7.8 million, $3.5 million, and $2.5 million, respectively, metric tons of CO_2 equivalent between 2017 and 2019.

From a global perspective, the Citizens' Climate Lobby states, "Of all the world's developed economies, only the US and Australia do not have some form of nationwide carbon pricing in place. Alternatively, of the 20 biggest economies, the only holdouts are India and a few Persian Gulf states."

While getting governments and major corporations involved in climate balance initiatives is good, there's still much to be done. That's partly because managing the carbon credits economy and incentivizing it to drive down and balance global carbon emissions takes significant commitment, leadership, and resources by governments and industries. It involves significant politics, lobbying, and foreign interests, and in my opinion, can only efficiently be driven top-down and not bottom-up. It requires not only legislation and penalties and sanctions where necessary, but also supervisory mechanisms verifying the authenticity of credit sources, standards, etc. The "operating rules" of this ecosystem, as defined by the governments involved together with industries, will also enable the infrastructure, the technology, function, and systems required to support it.

The web of carbon credits is complex at face value. However, looking at it more closely, the success or failure of the entire idea is based on trust: trust of data, trust of market participants, trust of enforcement, and so on. That's where blockchain takes a leading role.

CARBON CREDITS USING BLOCKCHAIN

Blockchain and tokenization can significantly change the carbon credit market by facilitating a simpler, more efficient market for carbon credit transactions and balancing. Creating more transparency and helping ensure authenticity of the credits will also make it easier to expand the ecosystem with more standard interaction between players, and better control and reporting, making the carbon credits ecosystem more trustworthy.

A recent flurry of activity in the blockchain-for-carbon space is suggesting a new focus on disrupting the market's status quo using the trustworthiness of Distributed Ledger Technology (DLT).

As RMI, a nonprofit with a goal of a zero-carbon future, states, "while not a panacea, blockchain can ultimately enable the exchange of data in an entirely new way." DLT can bring a whole new definition of trust to a world where only a few gatekeepers control the flow of money, services, and data. If done right, trust is designed into the entire system facilitated by a technology that can enforce it, encrypt it, and maintain it." Here's how:

- Increase transparency and trust in carbon markets through a decentralized ledger that records carbon credit transactions, reducing the risk of fraud and enabling the tracking of credits from issuance to retirement.

- Enable the creation of a unified standard for carbon credit quality and accounting principles, eliminating confusion among buyers and increasing the credibility of climate benefit claims.

- Automate business processes with smart contracts that can store metadata about carbon credits securely fused into tradable units, enabling fast, reliable, and transparent information exchange among participants in the network.

- Reduce transaction costs, minimize paperwork, and streamline the carbon trading process through blockchain's ability to interact with other systems and facilitate interactions with less reliance on intermediaries.

CARBON CREDITS AS NFTS

Blockchain can also be a means to incorporate some of the most versatile of DLT innovations into the carbon credit world—NFTs. I know what you're thinking: NFTs are for trading cards and digital art. Actually, yes, but the use-cases of NFTs are so vast, it's hard to even fathom. However, in this instance they have the ability to make a real difference in making the carbon credit world just plain work better.

Investors and buyers who find themselves perplexed by the different classifications of offset types can greatly benefit from the utilization of NFTs and their associated smart contracts. These innovative technologies enable the categorization of avoidance and removal credits, providing clarity and advantages to stakeholders. Furthermore, fractionalized carbon credits offer an opportunity for ordinary consumers to assert their ownership over a carbon credit, fostering increased participation and democratization within the carbon credit marketplace.

THE FUTURE OF CARBON CREDITS

Managing the carbon credits economy and incentivizing it to drive down and balance global carbon emissions takes significant commitment, leadership, and resources by governments and industries. It involves significant politics, lobbying, and foreign interests. It will require not only legislation and penalties/ sanctions where necessary but also supervisory mechanisms verifying the authenticity of credit sources, standards, etc.

With that said, the power of blockchain-based systems of trust could facilitate greater collaboration and coordination between market participants in the carbon credit ecosystem. However, not much will happen without proper legislation, regulations, international treaties, supervisory organizations, and overall global cooperation.

While blockchain technology is not the sole solution, I believe it's a better approach than anything else we've seen to date. Shouldn't we try the best tools we have to ensure a more sustainable future?

BLOCKCHAIN PUT TO USE

Article #5   *05.02.2023, The Street*

Blockchain is Changing the Retail Industry From the Container Ship to the Closet

Nike, Louis Vuitton, Mercedes-Benz, Walmart—What do all of these brands have in common? They're leveraging the power of blockchain to optimize operations, customer experience, and their bottom line.

The Nike Air Force 1 sneaker debuted in 1982 and became an instant cultural icon worn by celebrities ranging from NBA stars to hip-hop artists. It was the must-have sneaker when it burst on to the scene and still is. Nike was ground-breaking in both shoe design and its product and customer experience marketing. The shoe wasn't just a shoe. It was marketed as a "lifestyle."

More than 40 years later, Nike is still pioneering the retail industry by combining today's most significant and transformative technology available with its iconic shoes. The company has taken the Air Force 1 to the next level by utilizing blockchain technology to create a unique and collectible digital experience for one of its iconic sneakers. Nike's Swoosh platform, launched in November 2022, has been a major focus for the company in recent months as it marks their entry into the world of NFTs. The Our Force 1 collection is the first of many offerings expected from Nike, with a range of designs inspired by the original Air Force 1.

Nike is one of many companies exploring the use of blockchain technology and how it can benefit their businesses. Luxury brands like LVMH are putting blockchain to work to ensure authenticity and eliminate fraud, while others like DeBeers are addressing supply chain and sourcing challenges with blockchain's immutable and decentralized ledger. Furthermore, the promise of a total immersive customer experience via the Metaverse is quite attractive to retail organizations that are looking beyond just brick-and-mortar and online shopping to attract and engage with a new generation of shoppers.

Blockchain isn't some hypothetical idea in retail. It's here, it's being used, and its impact will change how brands interact with their customers. Here's how:

SUPPLY CHAIN IMPLICATIONS:

One of the significant advantages of blockchain technology in retail is its ability to create a more transparent supply chain. Retailers can use blockchain ledgers to track their products from the manufacturer to the end consumer, ensuring that the products are authentic and have not been tampered with. Blockchain technology also improves supply chain operations by allowing retailers to track specific timing and location of product alerting them of merchandise delays before it ties up the entire system. This is especially key with international shipments.

CUSTOMER ENGAGEMENT ON STEROIDS:

The customer is still king even as the methods and means to reach them change over time. What makes blockchain technology so attractive to retailers is the ways in which it optimizes legacy customer incentive programs, like loyalty and rewards, simplifying the process for consumers and reducing the administrative burden. Blockchain technology also helps retailers to reduce fraud and chargebacks by creating a tamper-proof record of each transaction, making it easier to resolve disputes in real-time.

Retailers are also leveraging the potential of the Metaverse, a virtual world where users can interact with each other and with digital objects in a simulated environment, to create immersive shopping experiences for customers.

While Roblox, Decentraland, and Sandbox are some of the most popular Metaverse platforms, other consumer brands are leveraging 3D enabled digital spaces, where people can socialize and shop. Retailers are also looking to create virtual stores personalized to each customer's preferences and shopping history, offering a more personalized experience. Retailers are also hosting events and experiences in virtual spaces, reducing costs associated with physical events, and reaching a wider audience.

The Metaverse also offers retailers the opportunity to experiment with new retail concepts and products. Retailers can test new store layouts or product designs in a virtual environment before committing to a physical store or product line, reducing the risk associated with introducing new products or concepts to the market. The Metaverse can also create a sense of community among customers, bringing customers together, fostering engagement and loyalty, and building a strong brand identity.

THE WHO'S WHO OF RETAIL ARE ALL IN ON BLOCKCHAIN:

After losing an estimated $98 billion (672.4 billion RMB) in a single year due to counterfeiting, the luxury industry is embracing a tech-forward crusade to veto the imitation market. The sector may not be able to stop the production and sale of replicas, but it can make it easier for genuine luxury buyers to validate the real thing. For instance, the next time you buy a legitimate luxury handbag, chances are it will come with its very own verifiable and traceable digital identity. Blockchain technology can also help retailers to reduce fraud and chargebacks, where customers dispute transactions and request a refund. By using DLT, retailers can create a tamper-proof record of each transaction, making it easier to resolve disputes in real-time.

Several luxury brands, including LVMH, Prada, Mercedes-Benz, OTB, and Richemont, are implementing blockchain technology to track and trade luxury goods. The technology offers a database mechanism to trace authenticity, origin, warranty, repairs, and even history of ownership, reducing the production and sale of replicas in the luxury industry. The Aura Blockchain Consortium, consisting of LVMH, Prada, OTB, and Richemont, promotes a single global blockchain solution open to all luxury houses.

WHAT'S NEXT FOR THE META-SHOP?

As we move further into a digital world, it's important for brands to focus on creating emotionally appealing retail experiences. In the Metaverse, this means using sight and sound to create a space that feels as real as possible. With Nike taking some of the first steps into Metaverse retail, it's worth looking to them for guidance and tactics; attention to detail, and a focus on providing an immersive experience, will be key to brands being able to create retail experiences that are second to none even in a virtual world.

But exceptional customer experiences and retail success in a Web3 world also depends on the behind-the-scenes operations and supply management that is so critical. You can't offer a superior experience while recalling products due to spoilage. This is exactly why blockchain technology is the solution embraced by the retail industry for a variety of challenges and opportunities that the industry is grappling with.

BLOCKCHAIN PUT TO USE

Article #6   *06.02.2023 , The Tokenizer*

Unleashing Blockchain's Potential to Solve The Entertainment Industry's Toughest Challenges

From Fair Compensation to Deep Fake Menace, Blockchain's Role in Empowering Artists

The entertainment industry has undergone a massive transformation in the last decade. Digital streaming services like Netflix, Hulu, and Amazon Prime Video have revolutionized the way people consume and access media, providing more convenient and cost-effective options for watching movies and television shows. In fact, Streaming services are by far the largest sector of the US Media and Entertainment industry. In total, annual video revenue is projected to reach $316.1 billion in 2023 and is poised to reach $462.9 billion by 2027. For context, other major sectors include Music ($43 billion), Movies ($91.83 billion), Gaming ($160 billion), TV Broadcasting ($63.2 billion), and Book Publishing ($26.8 billion). Of these sectors, it would take four of them to equate to the same size as the Streaming sector.

Additionally, the rise of mobile devices have made mobile access to music and videos pervasive, while the shift towards more interactive content, like virtual reality gaming, are becoming increasingly popular. By 2025, Virtual Reality (VR) and Augmented Reality (AR) in the media and entertainment industry is expected to reach $67.6 billion.

Overall, the entertainment industry has become much more diverse, with a wider range of content available to consumers and new technologies making it possible to experience that content in new and innovative ways. But with all the positive change new industry challenges have emerged. The studio, streaming, artist, and fan relationships have become murky. Artists and creators have lost much of their ability to maintain direct relationships with fans along with commanding a much smaller share of the revenue produced. This is complemented by challenges protecting intellectual rights, ad fraud, and the latest challenge—the "deep fake."

In an era where technology constantly pushes boundaries, the music and entertainment industry finds itself grappling with numerous challenges. Enter blockchain. The distributed digital ledger that underpins cryptocurrencies like Bitcoin, that has gradually emerged as a powerful tool with the potential to disrupt various sectors. Its immutable and transparent nature, coupled with the ability to create secure, decentralized

Blockchain's potential lies in its ability to verify and authenticate content through cryptographic techniques.

ecosystems, presents a unique opportunity for the music and entertainment industry to tackle long standing issues and pave the way for a fairer and more authentic landscape.

FIGHTING FRAUD AND THE DEEP FAKE DEBACLE:

The "deep fake" (literally) heard round the world, was recently produced anonymously using generative AI that featured the shockingly realistic voices of Drake and the Weeknd. At first, listeners rejoiced as this never-before but always-desired collaboration spread like wildfire online. Little did they know that they (and the artists) were being duped. When all was said and done, the track called "Heart on My Sleeve," reached more than 15 million views on TikTok, 275,000 views on YouTube, and over 600,000 streams on Spotify in just under five days.

Deep fakes have emerged as a significant concern for the entertainment industry because these deceptive creations pose a range of problems, from eroding trust and authenticity to damaging artists' reputations. However, blockchain technology, with its ability to verify and authenticate content, holds the key to detecting and preventing the proliferation of deep fakes, safeguarding the industry's integrity.

The scourge of ad fraud continues to plague the advertising industry, costing consumers and brands an estimated $100 billion by 2023. From bot traffic to deceptive ads, the current system is riddled with inefficiencies and wasted resources. Blockchain technology presents an opportunity to combat this issue head-on. By leveraging its transparency and trust mechanisms, blockchain can eliminate click fraud, reward ad viewers for their attention, and provide a verifiable trail for tracking ad spending.

One of the ways blockchain achieves this is through digital fingerprints, or "hashes," that uniquely identify an artist's original work. These hashes can be stored on the blockchain, acting as a tamper-proof signature that verifies the authenticity of content. As a result, when a deep fake emerges, the blockchain can quickly expose it as a fraudulent creation, protecting artists from reputational damage, and fostering a more trustworthy ecosystem.

Blockchain's potential lies in its ability to verify and authenticate content through cryptographic techniques. By establishing a decentralized network for verifying the authenticity of artists' work, blockchain can create an immutable record that distinguishes genuine performances from deep fakes. This ensures that audiences can trust the content they consume, safeguarding artists' reputations and preserving the integrity of their craft. Moreover, blockchain applications can empower creators to verify identities, control content sharing, and retain ownership of their digital assets, addressing the rampant issue of digital content piracy.

Several initiatives are already exploring blockchain-based solutions to tackle deep fakes, which comes as a relief as artists grapple with what to do next.

RIGHTS, ROYALTIES, AND THE RETHINK OF ARTISTS IN A WEB3 ERA

The entertainment industry has long been fraught with tension between writers and studios, resulting in periodic writers' strikes that disrupt the production of television shows, films, and other creative works. The current system of rights and royalties management is rife with complexities and inefficiencies, leaving artists with only a fraction of their potential earnings.

Blockchain, with its smart contract capabilities, can revolutionize this landscape. By automating royalty payments through immediate, accountable transactions, artists can receive fair compensation for each view, stream, or download of their work. Moreover, smart contracts can streamline content tracking across complex workflows, ensuring transparency and accuracy in the distribution of royalties. Notably, the rise of Non-Fungible Tokens (NFTs) on platforms like OpenSea has provided a new avenue for artists to earn royalties each time their art is resold, creating a sustainable revenue stream.

Blockchain can facilitate the implementation of rights management systems, enabling writers to retain control over their work and negotiate fair deals. By recording and enforcing ownership rights through blockchain, writers can protect their creations from unauthorized use and exploitation. This gives them the ability to negotiate contracts with studios on more equitable terms, fostering a healthier relationship between writers and the entertainment industry.

To fully realize the potential of blockchain in resolving writers' strike concerns, collaboration among industry stakeholders is crucial. Studios, writers' guilds, and technology innovators need to work together to establish standardized practices and protocols for blockchain implementation. This includes defining digital rights management frameworks, resolving copyright issues, and developing user-friendly interfaces that cater to the needs of writers.

NFTS AND CREATING DIRECT-TO-FAN RELATIONSHIPS

Non-Fungible Tokens (NFTs) are revolutionizing the entertainment industry, unlocking new possibilities for artists and creators. With NFTs, artists can establish direct relationships with fans, bypassing intermediaries. This shift in power disrupts the dominance of platform providers and empowers artists to regain control over their work.

NFTs also enable unique fan experiences fostering deeper connections. Artists can offer limited-edition collectibles or exclusive interactions, allowing fans to own digital memorabilia and participate in virtual events. NFTs facilitate unprecedented fan engagement and strengthen artist-audience relationships.

Take Kings of Leon, who embraced the engaging fan experience that NFTs offer earlier than most. The band released its 2021 album When You See Yourself as an NFT, which offered fans exclusive content and experiences like a digital download, limited-edition vinyl and "enhanced media."

Beyond NFTs, the blockchain-based Metaverse is playing a major role in fan-to-artist connections. Harry Connick, Jr. leveraged the power of digital fan experiences with NFTs and the Metaverse by launching The Neutral Ground. The goal of the platform is to create a community of music lovers that can engage on a deeper level and, in turn, get access to content and experiences that they otherwise have never been able to get, including piano lessons from Connick Jr. himself.

NFTs also enable unique fan experiences fostering deeper connections.

But the impact of NFTs goes beyond engagement:

- **AUTHENTICITY AND OWNERSHIP:**

  NFTs provide verifiable proof of ownership for digital assets. Artists can tokenize their work, establishing ownership on the blockchain, enhancing authenticity, and increasing the value of rare digital assets.

- **CONTENT MONETIZATION:**

  NFTs create new revenue streams for creators by enabling direct sales of digital content. Artists can sell NFTs representing music, artwork, or exclusive experiences, reaching a global audience without intermediaries. NFT sales generate ongoing royalties for artists, even on the secondary market.

- **ENHANCED LICENSING AND ROYALTY MANAGEMENT:**

  NFT platforms streamline licensing processes and automate royalty distribution through embedded smart contracts. Creators receive fair shares of revenue from NFT sales and usage, ensuring transparency, reducing disputes, and simplifying tracking.

- **INTELLECTUAL PROPERTY PROTECTION:**

  NFTs offer a secure mechanism for protecting intellectual property rights. By tokenizing and timestamping works on the blockchain, creators establish permanent ownership records, enabling copyright enforcement and safeguarding against plagiarism.

Over the past few years, early artist adopters of blockchain-based NFT technology jumped on the trend and reaped the benefits in a major way. Since 2021, independent artists have earned millions from primary NFT sales, including Beeple who sold his Days of Our Life NFT for $69 million, the most expensive digital art ever. Additionally, musicians like 3LAU and Snoop Dogg have embraced NFTs, offering unique perks and experiences to fans. NFT marketplaces like OpenSea, Blur, and SuperRare are gaining popularity, along with specialized platforms like Audius and Catalog for music NFTs. This shift toward NFTs has the potential to benefit all industry participants, marking a tokenized revolution in entertainment.

PROMISING BLOCKCHAIN PROJECTS IN ENTERTAINMENT ALREADY UNDERWAY

Built on Ethereum, SingularDTV uses smart contracts for transparent revenue distribution, providing a reliable system for creators to earn from their creations. There's also the TaTaTu streaming platform, which rewards viewers with TTU tokens for engagement. Viewers can use tokens to access premium content or exchange them for fiat currency, creating a more engaging streaming experience and offering creators an alternative revenue stream. Additionally, MovieBloc, connects filmmakers directly with audiences and ensures fair revenue distribution using smart contracts. Creators can also secure funding through the token-based crowdfunding platform, granting them more control and fair compensation.

For gaming, a well-known brand from the 1980's is back and has totally reinvented itself. Atari is teaming up with Enjin to develop blockchain-based versions of its classic games. Players can earn and trade digital assets within the games, creating new revenue streams for both players and creators. Ubisoft is leveraging blockchain to amplify its creating immersive gaming experiences. Their upcoming game, Rabbids Token, allows players to collect and trade NFTs, giving players true ownership of in-game assets. Ubisoft is also introducing mechanisms for players to earn in-game currency by contributing to the game's ecosystem, enhancing gameplay experiences.

THE NEXT GREAT ERA EVOLUTION OF IN ENTERTAINMENT IS HERE

Blockchain technology and Web3 are driving a transformative shift in the entertainment industry, comparable to the pivotal moments when silent movies gained sound and films transitioned from black and white to color. Similarly, for the music industry, this moment is as disruptive as the arrival of the MP3 and the complete digitization of recorded music.

This technological revolution is ushering in a new era of possibilities, empowering creators, and revolutionizing the way content is created, distributed, and consumed. Blockchain's decentralized nature ensures transparency, security, and immutability, providing a trusted foundation for artists, filmmakers, musicians, and other creators to protect their intellectual property, establish ownership rights, and receive fair compensation for their work. With the integration of smart contracts and NFTs, artists can unlock new revenue streams, engage directly with fans, and offer unique, limited-edition digital collectibles and experiences. Blockchain and Web3 are democratizing the entertainment landscape, fostering innovation, creativity, and collaboration, and enabling fans to play an active role in shaping the future of the industry.

This technological revolution is ushering in a new era of possibilities, empowering creators, and revolutionizing the way content is created, distributed, and consumed.

METAVERSE

METAVERSE

Article #1 *01.06.2022 , The Street*

The Dawn of the Metaverse: A New Series on The Street/DeFi

2022 may be "the year of the Metaverse," but in reality, the journey has just begun. In this ongoing series, we'll dive into the road ahead and the possibilities abound.

2021 ended with major Metaverse hype. Facebook rebranding as Meta, while multiple other organizations like Epic Games, Microsoft, Coinbase, and Tencent joined the Metaverse "universe" setting the stage for 2022 becoming "the year of the Metaverse." This is all great news for techies, investors, and regular "Joes" alike. However, the current problem is despite the declarations and funds committed, much infrastructure, hardware, software, and capabilities still need to be developed and made more widely accessible in order to support mainstream Metaverse experiences. This will take years and billions of dollars to accomplish.

However, even with the challenges ahead, the work has begun and the Metaverse is being built as we speak. While not much will come to fruition in 2022, the building

blocks will be established. This is exciting news, so
let's dive into why this is so game-changing.

WHAT EXACTLY IS THE METAVERSE?

Facebook CEO Mark Zuckerberg defines it like this: "You
can think about the Metaverse as an embodied internet,
where instead of just viewing content, you are in it."

Advancements and convergence in 3D, AR, VR, AI and 5G will
enable the creation of a digital twin of the physical world, fully
rendered in lifelike virtual environments, while at the same
time allowing us to superimpose a digital layer onto the real
world. In this way, every object, store, conversation, image, has
the potential to be integrated seamlessly into the Metaverse
and overlaid with additional data, enhanced with 3D/AR, or
expanded, explored, and personalized in a digital environment.

THE METAVERSE VISION AND
DIGITAL FINANCE'S ROLE

As with every new ecosystem that comes into existence, the
successful functioning of it will depend on how easy it is for
people to engage and transact. This is especially true for the
Metaverse. Digital finance, including cryptocurrencies, will
play a starring role with the conversion of fiat currencies
to cryptocurrencies, allowing people to switch between the
physical world and the Metaverse with relative ease. These
frictionless experiences will facilitate real-world and digital
transactions rapidly expanding the global economy.

Think about it: Consumers will purchase digital avatars and
virtual land and even throw a party for loved ones by using
crypto tokens that are issued by entities facilitating these virtual
interactions. Artists will perform in the Metaverse, get paid in
cryptocurrencies, and exchange those earnings for real-world

revenue. Workers will purchase virtual workspaces that put Zoom to shame. All in all, we haven't even scratched the surface of possibilities, along with the immense challenges ahead of us.

A DEEPER DIVE INTO THE METAVERSE: ONE BABY STEP AND ARTICLE AT A TIME

As it stands now, the Metaverse is much like the Internet was in the late 80's and early 90's, social networks of the mid-90's, and the Cloud in the early 2000s. It's mysterious and a bit elusive. However, much like the massive disruptive technology revolutions that came before, the Metaverse will change the way we interact, transact, and behave. In that vein, I'll be publishing a series of articles about a variety of topics dealing with the Metaverse with a heavy focus on Decentralized Finance (DeFi) and investing.

From industries ripe for disruption like education, gaming, and retail, to companies that are building the foundation upon which the Metaverse will exist, grow, and thrive, the entire ecosystem is up for discussion and debate. For investors, there's never been a better time than now to understand this new market and learn about which players are making a real difference. I for one am excited about what's to come and I invite my followers and readers to join me as I explore the road ahead as we approach the "Dawn of the Metaverse."

METAVERSE

Article #2 *11.02.2021, The Street*

Making Sense of the Metaverse and the Role of Decentralized Finance (DeFi)

Facebook's "Meta" rebrand underscores global focus on the Metaverse where physical and virtual worlds collide and the DeFi ecosystem, including NFTs, plays a starring role.

The mega announcement last week of Facebook rebranding as "Meta" and its commitment to leading the development of the Metaverse, couldn't be ignored even in our current two-dimensional mobile world.

For some of us, the notion of the Metaverse may bring up visions of The Matrix or maybe of Pink Floyd's immortal Welcome to The Machine. Yet, regardless of your associations with the Metaverse, there are several questions everyone should be asking now: What is the Metaverse? Why is Facebook so aggressive with their goal to lead Metaverse development? What is NFT's role in the Metaverse? And, why on earth should we care?

THE METAVERSE EXPLAINED

The term "Metaverse" generally refers to shared interconnected virtual world environments that let people interact with digital objects and avatars, all of which can be accessed via the Internet.

Metaverse can also refer to digital spaces which are made more lifelike by the use of virtual reality (VR) and/or augmented reality (AR). As such, many use the word Metaverse to describe gaming worlds, in which users have a character that can walk around and interact with other players.

In more technical terms, the Metaverse represents the sum of all processes and protocols that power the emerging Web 3.0 and are coalescing into a fluid and interoperable space. In this realm, communications, finances, game worlds, personal profiles, NFTs, and more, where the physical world is bridged to these virtual worlds, uniting them to one continuous experience space.

IS IT A PR STUNT OR A REAL AVENUE FOR GROWTH FOR FACEBOOK?

The cynics will say that Facebook (FB) is changing its name to Meta in order to divert attention from its whistle blower and leaked "Facebook Papers" trouble. Though there may be some truth to this, I believe FB is sincere in its focus on the Metaverse. This focus is not new, given some of its past acquisitions, like Meta's $2.3 billion acquisition of Oculus, back in 2014. Oculus produces virtual reality headsets, including the Oculus Rift and Oculus Quest lines.

As the world's largest social media network, Facebook's user-base currently sits at around 2.89 billion, more than a quarter of the world's population. As such, Meta is seeking avenues for growth, especially since Facebook has seen steady declines in its young user base since 2019.

Leading the creation of an entirely new and exciting (and possibly even addictive) experience as part of a social network may be a solution to this growth issue the company has been longing for.

AS THE METAVERSE TAKES OFF, SO WILL NFTS

The Metaverse and NFTs have become almost analogous because of the explosion of NFTs in blockchain gaming. For many, the Metaverse will materialize through virtual worlds, and interoperable games are an obvious vehicle.

Real-life identities tied to digital avatars are just one way the NFTs provide access to the Metaverse.

Many gamification projects are moving to capitalize on the intersection between the Metaverse and NFTs promising to transform the way we interact online. NFTs may come to serve as the deed to a "virtual" property, as well as a digital key that allows the owner exclusive access to enter a particular location in the Metaverse, grant access to others, as well as sell the property to another inhabitant of the Metaverse.

Taking this notion even further, NFT-controlled access could span a range of use-cases, including VIP access to real-life events such as conventions and festivals (see my previous NFT article), as well as those occurring within the Metaverse.

NFT-based augmented experiences are likely to become a cornerstone of social media experience. However, the Metaverse has much further reach than just social experiences. The development of blockchain-based ID systems may accelerate the adoption of financial services in the Metaverse.

All in all, NFTs can and will serve as a great bridge between the physical world and the Metaverse providing a frictionless experience for users.

WEB 3.0 IS THE COLLISION OF THE METAVERSE AND BLOCKCHAIN

The Metaverse is the next evolution of our connected world combining social, gaming, digital finance, search, and so much more. The transition for a Metaverse existence is happening now, whether we like it or not.

While Facebook may have been the first major tech giant to make the Metaverse move, we will likely see more social networks and ecosystem players heading in this direction. TikTok for example, already started flirting with NFTs last month with its TikTok Moments.

Unlike the explosion of NFTs in the digital art and collectibles arena, the Metaverse evolution will take time as it involves connecting multiple worlds, an undertaking that will require evolution, maturation, commercial accessibility, and seamless integration of many technologies, like VR, AR, blockchain/NFTs, etc. While this transition into a fully functional Metaverse experience may take years, with smaller incremental advancements over time, there's no doubt that the entire world is heading in this direction impacting our lives in noticeable ways.

NFTs can and will serve as a great bridge between the physical world and the Metaverse providing a frictionless experience.

METAVERSE

Article #3   *02.08.2022, The Street*

Metawork Is On Its Way To A Company Near You

The Metaverse in the workplace is being developed now impacting the way we work forever.

In the third installment of the Metaverse series for The Street/ DeFi, and the first piece focusing on various Metaverse use-cases, I'd like to take the opportunity to spotlight the impact Metaverse will have on the workplace. This particular use-case is not as fun and glamorous as gaming and concerts but will be an important catalyst for Metaverse mass adoption in the coming years.

Thinking about a world where many of our meetings and collaboration will be in a digital realm is not that far off. After so many of us were forced to switch to digital-only or hybrid modes of work due to COVID, we've become accustomed to a reality where many of our everyday tasks are already in some virtual form. Therefore, the leap to a Metaverse landscape in the workforce isn't that large and is actually a natural iteration of where we are today.

Working in the Metaverse takes working remotely to the next level bringing you all the capabilities and interactions of the real world, with very little of its challenges or limitations.

VIRTUAL OFFICE SPACE REBOOTED

In his annual year in review blog, Bill Gates wrote, "within the next two or three years, I predict most virtual meetings will move from 2D camera image grids to the Metaverse, a 3D space with digital avatars."

Throughout the pandemic, we have become accustomed to Zoom, Skype, Microsoft Teams, and other communication tools to provide us with virtual communication. However, the Metaverse will enhance the remote collaboration experience by providing participants with a virtual office space so realistic that everyone will feel like they're in the same room together.

We're already seeing companies like Virtuworx create avatar-based hybrid of virtual reality and mixed reality environments that turn remote work into a meaningful and productive experience. With a fully customizable solution for virtual training, offices, events, trade shows, and conferences, instead of staring at a screen all day, participants get to explore and engage in a number of ways.

When telecommuting, employees often complain that they lack the ability to read body language and communicate effectively. Managers struggle to maintain visibility over productivity of teams and individuals. And, due to the prolonged absence of in-person interactions, there is risk of disengagement. The Metaverse can create an immersive virtual "in office" workplace where avatars of employees can work together just like in the real world and alleviate some of the elements of isolation associated with remote work.

SIMPLIFYING COMPLEX TRAINING

By creating an industrial plant in the Metaverse a whole new world has the opportunity to unfold for industrial trainees. A trainee entering that world would appear to be right in the plant, surrounded by other trainees in the same Metaverse. Trainees could interact inside the Metaverse, training together on complex tasks, and in this way learning from shared successes and mistakes that may be injurious. The cost savings for this virtual training experience is dramatic, along with an organization's ability to better assess and provide real-time feedback to trainees.

The same concept can apply to training teams that need to operate in a complex, scarce, or dangerous environment. A version of this exists in the form of flight simulators in the military and airline industry. However, the Metaverse experience in these types of intense training environments will stunningly simulate real life scenarios without exposing trainees to danger. Think firefighters, astronauts, rescue personnel, and even automobile crash testing. On top of all of this, the applications for the Metaverse in the medical field are equally impactful (i.e., training brain surgeons, trauma doctors, and ICU nurses, etc).

USING 3D VISUALIZATION FOR PROBLEM-SOLVING

Some tasks and business problems are better tackled visually, in a way that is not practical in the real world. For example, architects might want to design and draw up multiple detailed mock-ups before finalizing a concept. However, there are time and cost constraints, and often errors are overlooked due to the lack of precision. The Metaverse gives you a space where you can 3D-model virtually anything, and real-world specifications can be replicated via digital twin technology. This enables smarter problem-solving in industries like construction, architecture, healthcare, life sciences, and more.

WHO IS BUILDING THE VIRTUAL WORKPLACE?

Now that we've established some of the motivation for moving at least some of our work life into the Metaverse, who is actually building the virtual workplace?

It seems like everyone, from large tech players to new startups, have identified the opportunity. Microsoft plans to integrate its VR/AR platform Mesh with Teams, while Meta has built Horizon Workrooms to hold meetings with Oculus headsets. While this is excellent progress, it may actually be the companies we've never heard of that are likely to make the "Metawork" happen.

Virtual office companies were getting a lot of traction already before the word "Metaverse" entered our lexicon. With mass adoption of remote work, startups saw an opportunity and pounced. Some have raised serious funding from big-name investors. Gather, founded in May 2020, raised $77 million, and Teamflow has raised $50 million since its launch in 2021. Virbela, a virtual world-builder since 2012, saw a 260% increase in revenue in the second quarter of 2020. SoWork, is a digital office company that grew out of the mega shift to remote work in 2020. In SoWork, avatars representing employees populate the virtual halls, bumping into each other for spontaneous conversations, as they would in a traditional workplace. Two hundred companies moved to the platform in the first week SoWork was open to the public.

From the perspective of the companies planning to use digital offices, there's only an upside. Corporations will be able to save on ever-increasing real estate costs, while employees reap the benefits of living where they want, saving time on commuting, and still have the collaborative social engagements and interaction they love at work.

WHAT'S NEXT FOR METAWORK?

As exciting as it may seem, it's important to remember that the Metaverse as an embodied, interconnected network doesn't exist yet. For today, companies are building the next best thing: worlds you can move around in as a digital stand-in. The look and feel significantly vary. Gather looks like an old-school video game, with pixelated characters in a 2D world. Teamflow lets you move around a modern-looking office as a floating circle of video. Virbela has a 3D design, allowing you to navigate through an office campus behind a full-bodied avatar.

When will "Metawork" actually be fully realized and become part of the mainstream workday experience? Some aspects of it, as Bill Gates suggests, may be only two or three years out. However, fully immersive corporate environments are more like a decade into the future, as they require significant progress on hardware, accessibility, security, social interaction, and of course, standards and regulation.

Similarly, to the evolution of digital finance, many questions will need to be answered and some regulations will need to adapt before the mainstream, mass corporate adoption takes hold. In the meantime, I like to think about how I would decorate my "virtual conference room."

Some tasks and business problems are better tackled visually, in a way that is not practical in the real world.

METAVERSE

Article #4   *06.12.2023, The Street*

7 Stats That Prove the Metaverse is Definitely Not Dead

The hype bubble has collapsed, but don't be fooled.
The Metaverse is quietly and consistently growing.

The Metaverse, often touted as the next phase of the internet and thought to be the darling of the Web3 era, has faced considerable skepticism due to the gap between its visionary potential and the current reality of cartoony avatars and expensive headsets. However, recent discussions surrounding the Metaverse and its demise may be premature.

This trend of overestimating the short-term impact of a new technology, while simultaneously underestimating it in the long-term, is common. In fact, Roy Amara, a Stanford University computer scientist and head of the Institute for the Future, coined a "law" for this tendency, referred to as Amara's Law.

In the case of the Metaverse, Amara's Law is in full effect. However, a closer look at the data reveals that while challenges persist, the Metaverse is far from dead and its long-term impact and staying power is undeniable.

Let's examine the top statistics that prove the Metaverse's ongoing development and potential.

The hype bubble has collapsed. But the Metaverse is growing.

1. Metaverse platforms grew by 15 million users year-over-year in the first quarter of 2023 to 520 million monthly active users (MAUs), according to a report

from the analyst firm Metaversed. That includes 149 platforms either live or in development.

2. Some 120 companies are working on Metaverse technologies, which include digital twin (a virtual model designed to accurately reflect a physical object), and Internet of Things (IoT) data integration, avatars and identity, interface hardware such as haptics, holography, spatial audio, and augmented reality, according to a report by S&P Global Market Intelligence. While the hype surrounding the Metaverse has subsided, the underlying technologies continue to develop and mature. Hardware and software improvements are gradually bridging the gap between the Metaverse's vision and its current state. The establishment of organizations like the Metaverse Standards Forum indicates the growing consensus on standards.

3. Metaverse investment transactions topped $24 billion, with the biggest investments going to Meta Platforms, Epic Games, Infinite Reality, and Roblox Corp., according to S&P Capital IQ Pro.

   As mentioned in the full S&P Report, "For the consumer, we expect 3D virtual worlds to more fully embrace advertising, social networking, live sports, video exhibitions, and e-commerce functions in the years ahead, in addition to the more gaming-focused applications that are popular today. The Metaverse also is a place for less commercially focused social uses, art, education, sharing of experiences, and just plain fun things to do. The use-case of an industrial manufacturing plant improving efficiency, safety, and energy use—instrumented through IoT creating a digital twin and supported by AI predictive maintenance and shopfloor tools such as autonomous robots and augmented reality (AR) headsets—is very different from a collaborative community art project."

4. A survey conducted by Protiviti and the University of Oxford found that two-thirds of respondents believed the Metaverse would have a substantial influence on global business.

   Almost half (45%) have already begun to use the Metaverse to engage with customers, and a further 20% plan to start doing so in the next two to three years. Marketing and advertising are the most common use-case (79%), followed by immersive shopping and product simulations (43%).

   Games such as Roblox, Fortnite, and Minecraft Marketplace have been viewed as one way for businesses to engage in an early form of the Metaverse. Blockchain-based digital worlds such as Decentraland and Sandbox have a strong focus on commerce. Nike, Lego, Walmart, H&M, Coca-Cola, and Burberry are among the brands that have established a presence in these types of shared 3D worlds in recent years.

   The Metaverse also offers retailers the opportunity to experiment with new retail concepts and products. Retailers can test new store layouts or product designs in a virtual environment before committing to a physical store or product line, reducing the risk associated with introducing new products or concepts to the market. The Metaverse can also create a sense of community among customers, bringing customers together, fostering engagement and loyalty, and building a strong brand identity.

5. Almost three quarters (73%) of business leaders surveyed believe Metaverse technologies will impact employee engagement in the next decade, with immersive training and learning most widely cited (54%), followed by collaboration (45%), recruitment (41%), and internal company events (35%).

   The Metaverse will enhance the remote collaboration experience by providing participants with a virtual office space that will be so realistic that everyone will feel like they're in the same room together. Microsoft is already building Metaverse capabilities on its Teams collaboration tool, using the company's Mesh platform on Azure, and deployed the technology at the World Economic Forum meeting in Davos in January. Additionally, companies like Virtuworx create avatar-based hybrid of virtual reality and mixed reality environments that turn remote work into a meaningful and productive experience.

With mass adoption of remote work, startups saw an opportunity and pounced. Some have raised serious funding from big-name investors. Gather, founded in May 2020, raised $77 million, and Teamflow has raised $50 million since its launch in 2021.

6. Financial services firm BlackRock recognizes the Metaverse's disruptive potential and has established an exchange-traded fund (ETF) focused on tech companies with a wide-ranging connection to the Metaverse concept, including Apple and Microsoft, Nvidia, Qualcomm, Ubisoft, and others. Moreover, according to a McKinsey report, over $120 billion was invested in Metaverse-related technologies in 2022, more than double the previous year's investment.

While BlackRock is the most recognizable participant in the Metaverse investment ecosystem, it's certainly not the only one. Roundhill Ball Metaverse ETF (METV), Fount Metaverse ETF (MTVR), Amplify Transformational Data Sharing ETF (BLOK), and the most recent, Subversive Metaverse ETF (PUNK). The Metaverse is an environment that is an amalgamation of multiple technologies and domains. It's a complex digital environment that relies on seven distinct layers, populated with companies that contribute to, or impact, each specific layer. For investors looking to enter into the investment landscape now, this means the list of relevant public companies to choose from will constantly be growing over the next few years.

Some companies, like Meta Platforms (FB), Apple (AAPL), Amazon (AMZN), Tencent (TCEHY), and IBM (IBM) impact multiple layers, which include the following: Infrastructure, Human Interface, Decentralization, Spatial Computing, Creator Economy, Discovery, and Experiences.

7. Apple Vision Pro just changed the entire Metaverse game. It's predicted that eventually 10% of Apple's revenue will come from the Vision Pro. Apple's entry into this space is crucial to mainstream adoption of the overall Metaverse revealing a combination of benefits from an entertainment and media perspective.

The launch of the Apple Vision Pro represents a momentous occasion for app developers, ushering in a realm of spatial computing filled with unbounded opportunities. It challenges them to reconsider the nature of apps, inspiring them to create richer, more immersive experiences that exist not just on a screen, but in the user's space. This, in turn, offers businesses the opportunity to engage with their customers in innovative ways and take their services to the next level.

In a note to clients last week cited by MarketWatch, Bank of America Securities analyst Wamsi Mohan commented, "Although the lackluster uptake of the AR/VR (augmented reality/virtual reality) market and the transitory enthusiasm about the Metaverse create a backdrop of challenges, it is instructive to remember that Apple invents entire new categories that have the potential to disrupt existing markets (e.g., AirPods) and create entirely new markets."

While the Metaverse may not be fully realized in its envisioned form, these statistics underscore its ongoing development and potential. Businesses are actively engaging with the concept, exploring its use-cases, and investing in the underlying technologies. The journey towards a mature Metaverse may take time, but the signs of progress and growing interest suggest that the Metaverse is far from dead.

This trend of overestimating the short-term impact of a new technology, while simultaneously underestimating it in the long-term, is common.

THE INVESTABLE UNIVERSE OF THE DIGITAL ECONOMY

Ch. 6
Investing in
Blockchain-Based Assets

Ch. 7
Venture Capital Investing

INTRODUCTION

In the last few years, the trajectory of blockchain technology, along with the enterprises that are shaping and reaping the benefits of its ecosystem, has taken an impressive upward curve. The anticipated growth rate of this sector is nothing short of astonishing, with projected figures spanning from 56% to a staggering 80% in Compounded Annual Growth Rate (CAGR).

To put this into perspective, such an explosion of growth is rare to find in our economic history books. The scale and potential implications of this surge on several key industries, and indeed, on our day-to-day lives, could be as transformative as the seismic impact of the previous three Industrial Revolutions.

The investment implications are equally compelling: sidestepping this growth could equate to missing out on the phenomenal expansion we saw with the rise of the internet, social media, and mobile connectivity. Think about the potential of Google, Amazon, Apple, Meta, or Netflix in their infancy.

Yet, investing in the landscape of blockchain technology and its expanding ecosystem isn't an easy stroll in the park. Several factors complicate the journey:

1. **Sifting through the hype:** The significant buzz around blockchain makes it tough to separate genuine, transformative initiatives from mere trends. It's like trying to find a diamond in a sandstorm.

2. **Bleeding-Edge Complexity:** Investing in cutting-edge technology always presents challenges, but blockchain takes it up a notch. As of 2023, there are over 1,000 blockchains, more than 20,000 cryptocurrencies, multiple token types, and little standardization around protocols. This dynamic, ever-evolving landscape demands a lot in order to keep pace.

3. **Regulatory Uncertainty:** An unpredictable regulatory environment, struggling to keep up with the rapid evolution of the blockchain ecosystem, adds an extra layer of risk for potential investors.

4. **Evolving and Expanding Use-Cases:** The constant emergence of new use-cases and business models for implementing blockchain technology can make it hard to identify the ones that hold water.

While this complex ecosystem is indeed challenging, the potential rewards are well worth the effort. But, where should one investment in the vast universe of digital finance? I believe the most significant value lies in platforms and infrastructure, which form the bedrock of the blockchain ecosystem. While venture capital (VC) promises the most growth, alongside obvious risk, the maturation of the industry also opens avenues for participation through mutual funds, ETFs, and public companies.

When evaluating investment opportunities, I caution against the allure of "one-trick ponies." Companies with a more extensive engagement across various use-cases, industries, and technologies—think blockchain combined with AI or AR/VR—offer a more promising prospect.

The investment implications are equally compelling: sidestepping this growth could equate to missing out on the phenomenal expansion we saw with the rise of the internet, social media, and mobile connectivity.

INVESTING IN BLOCKCHAIN-BASED ASSETS

Article #1   *09.09.2021, The Street*

Digital Finance Investing Strategies That Work

While there's no doubt that crypto and digital assets continue to grow in popularity as another way to achieve diversification and liquidity, they still remain volatile and require a combination of caution and strategy.

By all accounts, 2021 is the year of cryptocurrency. Stories of millionaires being made overnight are not uncommon causing a collective feeling of intense FOMO all over the world. But, just as the market goes up, so does the collective gasps when it suddenly drops 50%. This has all the makings of a thriller leaving the spectators and active participants in suspense and questioning if they should buy the dip or wait it out.

Before diving in, assess your risk tolerance. Once determined, mapping the market is key. The digital finance ecosystem offers a variety of investment opportunities and tools each with their own benefits and risks.

Investing directly in cryptocurrencies

- **Pure-play crypto:** The most straightforward approach, but one with arguably more risk, is to invest directly in a coin. While its recent surge to more than $60K in value may be quite enticing to even the most experienced investor, take heed. Bitcoin (and others) can fall in value as quickly as it rises.

- **Basket of coins:** If the direct investment in crypto makes you nervous, another option is to diversify by investing in a "basket of coins." This approach includes choosing some or all of the top 10 cryptocurrencies or creating a diversified mix of some of the larger cryptocurrencies, along with some up-and-coming coins experts believe may have more aggressive upside potential.

- **Exchange Traded Funds (ETFs):** A more traditional way to invest in cryptocurrencies is to use an exchange-traded fund (ETF). ETF's are easier to own as they are a standard security and can be bought through any brokerage/investment account and even through your IRAs. However, a crypto ETF has the same volatility and risk as the cryptocurrency it represents, so there's still no easy ride here.

  While there are currently no US-based crypto ETFs, thirteen are already in the approval process with the Securities and Exchange Commission (SEC), and there are several crypto ETFs abroad, including three bitcoin and three Ethereum ETFs in Canada.

- **Crypto trusts:** ETFs are not the end game. Grayscale is a successful asset manager currently offering Bitcoin and Ethereum trusts. These are traditional publicly traded securities are accessible through one's investment, brokerage, or IRA accounts.

- **Hedge funds:** A crypto hedge fund is like a mutual fund, where a person can invest in a large group of underlying securities. Unlike an ETF, hedge funds are an active asset class and are managed by a team of experts and typically focus on higher frequency trading for short term gains.

There are plenty of direct-investment options for getting in on the crypto game, but they're not the only game in town. Investing in the growing, comprehensive blockchain market could potentially have much more promise than just pure-play crypto. In fact, the digital finance ecosystem is growing exponentially including assets like Non-Fungible Tokens (NFTs), digital securities, Central Bank Digital Currencies (CBDCs) and, of course, Decentralized Finance (DeFi).

INVESTING IN DEFI

DeFi refers to peer-to-peer financial services that permit crypto trading, loans, interest accounts, algorithm-driven cross platform trading, and other services. The growth of the DeFi industry accelerated in 2020, growing from $700 million to $13 billion. It reportedly hit $40 billion this year, based on industry data across a host of sources.

- **DeFi Assets:** One of the ways to invest in DeFi is to trade DeFi assets, tokens representing DeFi networks, applications, or protocols. It's not for the faint of heart since there is also high volatility and risk involved.

- **Staking:** Staking is just one more option to achieve passive income based on DeFi. Users lock or hold their funds in a crypto wallet to participate in maintaining the operations of a proof-of-stake based blockchain system, and in return get a pre-defined interest rate. The total amount of cryptocurrency assets staked on DeFi platforms is worth around $21 to $23 billion, as of January 2021.

- **Yield Farming:** Yield farming refers to providing liquidity in the form of crypto assets to a decentralized exchange (DEX). The DEX uses this liquidity to execute orders created by token swappers who pay fees. Based on their contribution, yield farmers earn a portion of these fees, which offers additional passive income for your Crypto holdings. In the case of staking as in yield farming one needs to be aware of the potential loss of value of the crypto in a liquidity pool as a result of crypto volatility.

DEFI LENDING

DeFi Lending platforms enable users to lend their crypto to someone else and earn interest on the loan. Defi lending can benefit both lenders and borrowers. It offers margin trading options, as well as allows long-term investors to lend assets and earn higher interest rates.

INVESTING IN THE ENTIRE BLOCKCHAIN ECOSYSTEM

After auditing your own personal risk-aversion and your overall investment objectives, you may find investing in the entire blockchain ecosystem is the more "secure" route to take.

MINING STOCKS

It's important to note that crypto mining profitability is not necessarily tightly correlated to the value changes in cryptocurrencies. You can invest in mining companies' stocks or mining-related stocks, which might benefit from the increased demand for processing power for crypto mining.

BLOCKCHAIN-FOCUSED STOCKS

You can also invest in publicly traded blockchain related stocks. Since there are no pure crypto or blockchain stocks, the closest thing will be to invest in publicly traded stocks that have some digital finance exposure, like CoinBase, PayPal, Square, Microstrategy, NVIDIA, or IBM.

TO INVEST OR NOT TO INVEST?

There's no lack of investment opportunities in the digital finance world. From investing directly in cryptocurrencies, to investing in the comprehensive blockchain ecosystem, individual investors can easily find the right methods that fit their individual needs. But before jumping in, learn more about each of these investment options, understand their risks, and assess how much risk is manageable for you. Just like any investment, taking the time to talk to experts and doing your own research can help you decide the right course of action for you.

DeFi Lending platforms enable users to lend their crypto to someone else and earn interest on the loan.

INVESTING IN BLOCKCHAIN-BASED ASSETS

Article #2   *09.09.2021, The Street*

DeFi 101: Decentralized Finance and How To Invest in its Rapid Growth

As the global financial system continues to digitally transform, DeFi has incredible growth potential, catching the eye of the world's largest banks and investors, but how can you participate?

In a broad sense, DeFi refers to Decentralized Finance, the ecosystem of blockchain-based, digital financial tools which include everything from digital securities and cryptocurrency to NFTs (Non-Fungible Tokens) and CBDCs (Central Bank Digital Currency). However, DeFi also refers to a variety of peer-to-peer financial services that permit crypto trading, loans, interest accounts, algorithm-driven cross platform trading, and other services. It is reliant on public blockchains like Ethereum and cryptocurrencies. The growth of the DeFi industry accelerated in 2020, growing from $700 million to $13 billion. It reportedly hit $40 billion this year, based on industry data across a host of sources.

As the global financial system continues to digitally transform, DeFi (in both its broader and more narrow definitions) has incredible growth potential catching the eye of the world's largest banks and investors. Yet, as with any asset class, it's imperative to understand the asset, the market, and the ways to invest.

DEFI ASSETS

One of the ways to invest in DeFi is to trade DeFi assets, tokens representing DeFi networks, applications, or protocols, which typically involves buying low and selling high. It's not for the faint of heart since there is also high volatility and risk involved. However, the opportunities abound. Some examples include Uniswap (UNI), Terra (LUNA), Wrapped Bitcoin (WBTC), and Chainlink (LINK).

DEFI STAKING

Don't feel intimidated by these new financial terms. Staking is just one more option to achieve passive income based on DeFi. Users lock or hold their funds in a crypto wallet to participate in maintaining the operations of a proof-of-stake (PoS) based blockchain system, and in return get a pre-defined interest rate. In a world of negative interest rates, getting a decent interest rate on your holding (especially if you were planning to hold these digital assets anyway) is not something to sneeze at. The total amount of cryptocurrency assets staked on DeFi platforms is worth around $21 to $23 billion, as of January 2021.

DEFI YIELD FARMING

Yield Farming provides another way to gain additional passive income for your crypto holdings. Yield farmers make a living by providing liquidity in the form of crypto assets to a decentralized exchange (DEX). The DEX uses this liquidity to execute orders created by token swappers who pay fees. Based on their contribution, yield farmers earn a portion of these fees. This can be done automatically through an automated market maker (AMM) protocol that executes the transactions. There are a number of DeFi projects currently involved in Yield Farming, including Aave, a project that allows users to lend and borrow a number of cryptocurrencies. Another, Yearn Finance, enables users' funds to move between difference lending and liquidity protocols to get the best interest rate. Finally, Compound is a platform that allows people to earn money on their crypto savings.

DEFI LENDING & LENDING PROTOCOL

DeFi Lending platforms enable users to lend their crypto to someone else and earn interest on the loan. Defi lending can benefit both lenders and borrowers. It offers margin trading options, as well as allows long-term investors to lend assets and earn higher interest rates. It also enables users to access fiat currency credit to borrow loans at lower rates than DEX. Moreover, the users can sell it on a centralized exchange for a cryptocurrency and then lend it to a DEX.

DEFI FUNDS

Another way to invest in the DeFi ecosystem is through funds and trusts. This is the most, passive, "novice friendly" way to get exposure to DeFi. Some examples are Bitwise's DeFi Index Fund, Grayscale's Diversified DeFi fund, and Galaxy Digital's DeFi index tracker fund.

RISK VS. REWARD WITH DEFI

The diversity of investment opportunities, along with the continued growth of the market, makes DeFi an attractive and potentially very lucrative investment. However, as with any investment, there are risks and market participants should be informed before jumping in. Specifically, beyond the risk of the crypto volatility impact, there is also a security and fraud risk with DeFi that stems from the DeFi protocols that rely on smart contracts, which may have vulnerabilities that can be exploited.

The DeFi market, the technology that drives it, along with the needed regulations that will inevitably come, will only lower vulnerabilities and risk and increase the attractiveness of this digital finance tool. Be patient, be smart, and never miss a good opportunity.

INVESTING IN BLOCKCHAIN-BASED ASSETS

Article #3   *04.08.2022, The Street*

The Blockchain Ecosystem: Review of the Investable Publicly Traded Universe

Ripe With Investing Possibilities and Options, Here's How to Get In On the Blockchain Trade

WHY INVEST IN BLOCKCHAIN?

As a new technology with potential game-changing effects on the business world, blockchain is garnering interest across the investment community. Here are a few factors that make it attractive:

- Blockchain could help an organization become more efficient, unlocking higher profitability over time.

- Blockchain is getting high-profile attention from big tech firms.

- Because of COVID-19, the world is accelerating its shift to digital. Blockchain goes hand-in-hand with other adjacent technologies, such as cloud computing, e-commerce, and AI.

- In terms of industries using blockchain today, it goes well beyond crypto to include payments, capital markets, banking, insurance, gaming, healthcare, and retail (just to name a few).

Given all the above, the blockchain ecosystem is already on a path for dramatic growth. In fact, the blockchain market size is expected to grow from $4.93 billion in 2021 to $227.99 billion by 2028; it is estimated to grow at a CAGR of 72.9% from 2021 to 2028.

BLOCKCHAIN AT A GLANCE

While there are multiple categories of publicly traded companies in the blockchain ecosystem, for the purposes of this article, I'm focusing on a few of the most interesting offering some exciting investment potential. However, depending on the scope of definition of "blockchain investable universe," there are 50 to over a 100 publicly traded companies that make up this universe. It's also important to note that there are companies integral to multiple categories like Meta Platforms (FB), Alphabet (GOOGL), Amazon (AMZN), Tencent (TCEHY), Alibaba (BABA), and Apple (AAPL).

As with the tech giants listed above, there is a wide breadth of established companies that are in no way blockchain "pure plays, but rather seized the opportunity for growth and branched into the blockchain ecosystem." These types of investible companies provide added diversification to a blockchain-focused investment strategy.

In contrast, the space is also populated with a significant amount of private companies due to blockchain's relative newness. While these smaller organizations are not featured in this particular piece, as the ecosystem evolves and relevant public companies emerge, they will join the categories I list here.

BLOCKCHAIN CATEGORIES

Companies developing infrastructure
critical for blockchain technology

- Basic infrastructure: Companies in this category are developing
  basic infrastructure that is key for blockchain, although
  it is not necessarily blockchain-specific infrastructure. As
  blockchain usage and implementation grows, it will drive
  significant increases in market share for these particular
  companies. The most basic example is in the semiconductors
  manufacturing space. Graphics processing unit (GPU) chips
  designed by NVIDIA (NVDA) and Advance Micro Devices
  (AMD), as well as Intel's (INTC) Bitcoin mining chips, are all
  critical components to keeping the blockchain, crypto mining,
  NFTs, and the Metaverse engines running at full speed.

- Spatial computing: The following companies are developing
  essential 3D visualization and modeling frameworks, which
  are significant to building the underlying infrastructure
  to domains like Bbockchain-based gaming, NFTs, and
  the Metaverse. Some notable companies in this space:
  Hexagon AB (HXGBF) and PTC INC (PTC).

COMPANIES DEVELOPING
BLOCKCHAIN TECHNOLOGY

- IBM is heavily involved in the blockchain domain and its
  blockchain segment has already partnered with numerous
  companies to help offer real-world exposure to new
  blockchain technology. IBM developed its own distributed
  ledger technology, Hyperledger, which is used by multiple
  corporations for implementing blockchain applications.

- Salesforce is another early player in the blockchain
  infrastructure business (since 2019). Salesforce blockchain

allows companies to create low-code blockchain apps, ensure governance, and share CRM data with their network securely.

- Amazon (no surprise) is also a player in the blockchain ecosystem. Amazon Managed Blockchain is a fully managed service that makes it easy for developers to join public networks or create and manage scalable private networks using Hyperledger Fabric and Ethereum.

COMPANIES USING AND MAKING INVESTMENTS IN BLOCKCHAIN TECHNOLOGY

There are multiple industries that are already utilizing blockchain technology, including the financial industry (payments, banking, capital markets), insurance, healthcare, art, gaming, retail, and e-commerce. Therefore, this category is large and includes quite a few companies that vary in technology investment, along with the level of adoption within their businesses.

Some examples include: JPMorgan (JPM), Banco Santander (SAN), Morgan Stanley (MS), HSBC (HSBC), Swiss Re AG (SSREF), Nomura Holding (NMR), Mitsubishi Financial Group (MUFG), Intercontinental Exchange (ICE), and Louis Vuitton (LVMH).

For a more specific example, JPMorgan's Blockchain Center of Excellence actively researches, develops, and tests a variety of blockchain technology for use across lines of business within the organization. From leveraging blockchain to fuel its Interbank Information Network, to navigating the crypto landscape, JPMorgan is just one of many large financial institutions making blockchain technology a priority.

METAVERSE COMPANIES

Because of its pervasiveness and eventually universality, the Metaverse will impact every industry and almost every aspect of our lives. With a movement like that, the investment opportunities are immense. From Nike (NKE), which already indicated its intent to make and sell virtual branded sneakers and apparel, to Disney (DIS), with its plans for a Metaverse theme park, companies are already putting the Metaverse to work across business units. However, more specifically, the creators and the gamers are interesting leaders in this space, with significant investment potential.

- Creator Economy: Companies in this category provide tools and services allowing creators to develop content in blockchain based businesses. Some examples include Matterport (MTTR), Adobe Inc (ADBE), Autodesk (ADSK,) and Unity Software (U).

- Gaming Companies: The gaming industry is adopting blockchain through the use of Non Fungible Tokens (NFTs), and Metaverse participation. Some examples include game developers like Roblox (RBLX) and Krafton Inc.

DECENTRALIZATION COMPANIES

- **Pure-play crypto:** Some companies in this category are Coinbase (COIN), Galaxy Digital (BRPHF), and Silvergate Capital (SI).

- **Crypto mining companies:** In this category, companies are providing crypto mining equipment to the industry and companies specializing in crypto mining. Canaan Inc. (CAN) and Ebang International Holdings Inc (EBON) are two key suppliers to the industry that have specialized in offering bitcoin and cryptocurrency-specific mining equipment with ASIC chips.

  Marathon Digital (MARA), Riot Blockchain Inc (RIOT), Hive Blockchain Tech (HVBTF), and Hut 8 Mining Corp (HUTMF) are few of over 10 publicly traded crypto mining companies.

- **Decentralization enablers:** CME Group (CME)

operates the world's largest financial derivatives exchange allowing investors to trade futures. This includes cryptocurrency futures trade. At this stage in the regulatory landscape of the digital economy, all SEC crypto approved ETFs are based on crypto futures.

Additionally, Block (SQ), PayPal (PYPL), Visa (V), and Mastercard (MA) are all major enablers of the decentralization ecosystem, supporting crypto payments and conversion, while Shopify (SHOP), the E-commerce infrastructure and software provider, allows merchants using its platform to accept cryptocurrencies as payment.

BLOCKCHAIN BALANCE SHEETS

Companies that made a large bet on cryptocurrency and are holding significant amounts in cryptocurrency on their balance sheet. The most notable examples in this category are Tesla (TSLA) and MicroStrategy (MSTR).

BLOCKCHAIN BET OR BUY?

Blockchain is certainly a buy as the technology is still fairly new but promises to permeate every industry moving forward. From supply chain to cybersecurity, the companies deploying the technology now stand to reap significant benefits moving forward. The upside for early investors is impressive, but patience is required. Rome wasn't built in a day.

INVESTING IN BLOCKCHAIN-BASED ASSETS

Article #4   *10.26.2021, The Street*

Bitcoin Futures ETFs Are Here – Paving the Way for Spot-Based Bitcoin ETFs

Bitcoin ETFs Offer New Ways To Invest in the Growing Crypto and DeFi Ecosystem

A full eight years after the first application for a Bitcoin Exchange-Traded Fund (ETF) was filed by the Winklevoss twins, the first Bitcoin ETF in the United States (BITO, by ProShares) started trading on the NYSE. The fund had a whopping $1 billion volume in the first day of trading, the highest first-day organic volume in ETF history, prompting Bitcoin to reach an all-time high above $66K.

This past Friday, October 22, the second Bitcoin futures ETF, Valkyrie's Bitcoin Futures ETF (BTF) started trading in the US. Both BTF's and BITO's price went down on Friday by 2.8% and 3.23% respectively, same as Bitcoin's price (-2.8%).

There are more than four additional Bitcoin futures-based ETFs waiting for SEC approval that are likely to start trading in the coming weeks indicating a surge of interest and participation in the DeFi industry by mainstream investors who previously shied away from direct crypto investments.

WHAT ARE BITCOIN ETFS AND WHAT IS ALL THE NOISE ABOUT?

A Bitcoin ETF mimics the price of the digital currency, allowing any investor to buy into the ETF and get exposure to Bitcoin without trading Bitcoin itself. This makes Bitcoin exposure more accessible to institutional investors as well as to the average investor as it eliminates any issues of complex storage and security procedures required of cryptocurrency investors. It also shields investors from any potential regulatory risks.

The road to approval of a Bitcoin ETF has been long, dating back to 2013. Many applications for Bitcoin ETFs have been submitted over the years, with many rejections and some still pending SEC approval. The approval of the first few futures-based Bitcoin ETFs is cause for celebration for many who've been waiting. It also represents a significant shift in the forward-progress towards a fund based on Bitcoin spot prices.

FUTURES-BASED ETF VS. SPOT ETF

Futures based Bitcoin ETFs track Bitcoin prices through futures contracts traded at the Chicago Mercantile Exchange (CME). These contracts are settled in USD, not Bitcoin. When futures are held in an ETF, they must be rolled at the end of each month, which can result in some inefficiencies. That's the reason futures-based Bitcoin ETFs will have a difficult time tracking the spot Bitcoin price and will be an expensive way to achieve Bitcoin exposure in a portfolio.

On the flip side, spot-based ETFs (i.e., ETFs holding actual Bitcoin) are more efficient and can more accurately track Bitcoin prices. However, many analysts believe that it will be a while before spot-based Bitcoin ETFs are approved, as the SEC has been consistently leery of approving ETFs that hold actual Bitcoin. Gary Gensler, chairman of the SEC, has said, "futures-based Bitcoin ETFs provide better protections for individual investors." One of the key cited reasons is the lack of ample regulation and supervision over cryptocurrency exchanges where futures are traded on the CME which is regulated by the CFTC.

However, what I've learned from participating in this new but growing market is that one development leads to another given enough time and demand.

WHAT TO WATCH FOR NOW?

THE IMPACT ON BITCOIN TRANSACTION VOLUME

Will BITO and BTF (as well as the other Futures-based ETFs that will follow) approval have a noticeable impact on Bitcoin transaction volume? Many analysts believe that this will allow more institutional and retail exposure to Bitcoin and may increase the cycle of bitcoin investors, resulting in larger transaction volumes.

THE IMPACT ON BITCOIN PRICE

What impact will it have on Bitcoin price, and will it be a one-time impact or something that's long lasting? Price obviously went up to an all-time high, much of it was touted as "in anticipation for BITO's launch," but was it truly due to the Bitcoin ETFs beginning to trade, or due to inflation fears as JPMorgan and some other analysts think?

THE IMPACT ON BITCOIN HOLDING DISTRIBUTION

We've already seen a shift in holding distribution over the past year. The on-chain market analysis group Glassnode claims that the number of Bitcoin whales with more than BTC 10,000 has fallen to 82, a figure that hasn't dipped to such lows since mid-December 2012. Will the introduction of Bitcoin ETFs drive more institutional investors into the market and change the makeup and distribution of Bitcoin across investors and investor type?

THE IMPACT ON BITCOIN PRICE BEHAVIOR

Will the introduction of Bitcoin ETFs impact Bitcoin correlation and behavior as a financial asset? Bitcoin Whales tend to hold on the average 75 percent of their Bitcoin for the long run, reducing the effective supply and impacting price dynamics. Will larger investments in Bitcoin ETFs by institutional investors, as well as the reliance on Bitcoin Futures and the ETFs', need to "recycle" them impact Bitcoin price volatility and correlation?

AND OF COURSE, THE 21 MILLION BITCOIN QUESTION: WHAT ABOUT SPOT BITCOIN ETFS? ARE THEY NEXT?

Whether you are considering investing in one of the new ETFs, directly in Bitcoin, or not at all, we are all collectively in the midst of a fascinating and potentially history changing moment unfolding in front of our eyes. The digital transformation driving the current trends in finance is here to stay, so make sure to take advantage of the early benefits.

The road to approval of a Bitcoin ETF has been long, dating back to 2013.

INVESTING IN BLOCKCHAIN-BASED ASSETS

Article #5   *12.22.2021, The Street*

Top Wealth Managers Reveal the Trends and the Truth about Digital Asset Investing

As more and more investors demand options for investing in digital assets like crypto, wealth managers are being forced to evolve with the market.

It's clear that mainstream investor interest in digital asset investing, which includes cryptocurrencies, Non-Fungible Tokens (NFTs,) and digital securities has skyrocketed in the last year. A recent CNBC Invest In You survey found that 10% of those surveyed said they're invested in cryptocurrency, ranking the digital coins fourth after real estate, stocks, mutual funds, and bonds. Plus, some 65% of those cryptocurrency investors jumped into the asset class in the last year.

This trend is not confined to the US. In fact, a survey of institutional investors and wealth managers from the US, UK, France, Germany, and the UAE, who collectively don't currently have exposure to cryptocurrencies and digital assets, reveals that 62% expect to invest in these for the first time within the next year.

The reasons for the growing appetite for digital asset investment include everything from the assets' long-term capital growth prospects to a general feeling of confidence in the asset class as more corporations and large institutional investors are participating in the market. Others believe it could be a good hedge against inflation. Yet, while the reasons are many, the fact is that investors (from Gen Z to Boomers) have a serious case of FOMO and are beginning to ask their financial advisors and wealth managers some tough questions.

This growing demand coming directly from clients has forced wealth managers to face an evolving digital economy head on. The financial sector is in a historical moment of digital disruption and transformation. We're never going back to the old way of doing business and only moving forward. With this in mind, how are family offices and wealth managers responding to their clients? What counsel are they providing with regards to digital assets? Where do they see their specific piece of the financial puzzle going from here?

In an effort to find answers to these critical questions, I decided to reach out to a few seasoned and savvy wealth management pros to get their take on the market, what they're seeing with their own book of business, and how they're responding to the demand for digital asset investment.

I spoke to some of the industry's most seasoned and successful financial advisors, including Anthony J. Kratofil, CFP®, founder of Vital Wealth Management, as well as a C-suite executive at one of the largest wealth management firms globally. While each of these individuals see varying pain points and opportunities, their experiences are similar allowing us to draw some significant conclusions.

WEALTH MANAGEMENT FIRMS ARE TRYING TO RESPOND TO CLIENT DEMAND

As more and more investors demand options from their advisors, firms are having to respond from the top down. For example, Morgan Stanley's wealth division opened up three bitcoin funds to US clients in March, followed by JPMorgan in August, with half a dozen fund choices for their US clients. Goldman Sachs will also link global wealth clients with crypto funds and Citi Private Bank acknowledged that an increasing number of clients are posing questions about crypto but are still working out what it might offer.

THE CURRENT STATE OF AFFAIRS: THE CLIENTS AND THEIR INVESTMENTS

Just as large intuitions are working on finding investment solutions on a macro level, the wealth advisors I talked to all agree that regardless of age, net-worth, risk tolerance or otherwise, investors are beginning to ask questions about digital assets, including cryptocurrency. However, according to these advisors, there seems to be different interests and approaches based on three types of investor groups:

- **Institutionalized approach:** This may include endowments, or larger investment firms that are already blockchain-focused and understand the impact of blockchain technology and the firms driving that technology on the modernization of the financial industry. While these investors want to participate, they prefer the fund of funds approach, which includes allocating investments across multiple funds that specialize in blockchain to mitigate the risk.

- **Family office approach:** For wealth managers with family offices there are typically two types of clients: the ones that lack understanding, but have a significant amount of FOMO, and the ones that have more understanding and are going out on their own without an advisor. Many family office managers don't have the access, ability, or the tools to include digital assets as part of a client's portfolio. Therefore, their clients don't have any other choice but to invest in crypto or other digital assets on their own terms. There is, however, a growing number of wealth managers that are doing the work, getting as knowledgeable as they can, and are seeking tools and funds to invest in for their clients.

- **Digital-savvy investors:** These individuals are more attuned to market dynamics and are comfortable making direct investments with or without their wealth manager's assistance. This seems to be the smaller group of the three.

STAYING EDUCATED AND INFORMED IS KEY

Through my conversations it became clear that many of the major firms are not implementing any kind of formal training for their advisors, which leaves the educational process up to each individual. It's no longer a "nice-to-know," but rather a "need-to-know" situation for advisors when it comes to understanding the digital asset investment landscape. This is a function of staying relevant and being knowledgeable enough to bring value to clients.

The experts I spoke with had a clear message for others in their industry: If you're interested in growing your practice in the next 10 years to 20 years and you're not educating yourself, you're going to be at a significant competitive disadvantage and struggle to grow.

WHERE THE OPPORTUNITIES FOR WEALTH CREATION EXIST IN THE DIGITAL FINANCE ECOSYSTEM

The digital finance ecosystem offers a variety of investment opportunities and tools each with their own pros and cons. At this moment, it's each advisor's responsibility to be educated enough to offer sound advice and recommendations about which investment options work best based for each clients' individual needs.

Below are a few key ways wealth managers can put their clients' money to work for them in the digital asset ecosystem.

GAINING EXPOSURE TO THE CRYPTO MARKETS:
- **Pure-play crypto:** The most straightforward approach to create crypto exposure, but one with arguably more risk, is to invest directly in cryptocurrencies. While Bitcoin's surge earlier this year to more than $60K in value may be

quite enticing to even the most experienced investor, take heed. Bitcoin, and others, can fall in value as quickly as it rises, as the last couple of months demonstrated. This option is for investors who can handle the volatility involved.

- **Crypto ETFs:** A more traditional way to invest in cryptocurrencies is to use an exchange-traded fund (ETF). ETF's are easier to own as they are a standard security and can be bought through any brokerage/investment account and even through your IRAs. US based examples include: ProShares Bitcoin Strategy ETF and Valkyrie Bitcoin Strategy ETF. There are also several non-US pure crypto ETFs. It is important to note that as of now, all SEC approved crypto ETFs are crypto futures ETFs, and not spot ETFs so they don't track 100% of the cryptocurrency movements. However, a crypto ETF has the same volatility and risk as the cryptocurrency it represents, so there's still no easy ride here.

- **Crypto trusts:** Bitcoin and Ethereum trusts are available and are traditional publicly traded securities that are accessible through one's investment, brokerage, or IRA accounts. Some examples include Grayscale Bitcoin Trust and Grayscale Ethereum Trust. Again, like the crypto ETFs, trusts carry the same potential volatility and risk as the cryptocurrency itself.

- **Crypto private funds:** There are private funds investing directly in cryptocurrencies. Some offer a basket of cryptocurrencies like Bitwise 10 Crypto Index Fund. Private funds are less accessible than the publicly traded ETFs and Trusts.

- **Hedge funds:** A crypto hedge fund is like a mutual fund, where a person can invest in a large group of underlying securities. Unlike an ETF, hedge funds are an active asset class and are managed by a team of experts. They typically focus on higher frequency trading for short term gains rather than long-term holding of assets.

GAINING EXPOSURE TO THE BLOCKCHAIN ECOSYSTEM:

- **Blockchain-focused stocks:** You can also invest in publicly traded blockchain related stocks. There are a few pure crypto or blockchain stocks such as Coinbase, Canaan, Hut 8, and Riot. To gain broader exposure the closest thing will be to invest in publicly traded stocks that have some digital finance exposure, like PayPal, Visa, Square, Microstrategy, Robinhood, NVIDIA, AMD, or IBM.

- **Blockchain focused ETFs:** These are ETFs that focus on publicly traded stocks of companies related to the blockchain ecosystem. These ETFs, which include names like Amplify Transformational Data Sharing ETF (BLOK), Siren Nasdaq Nexgen Economy ETF (BLCN), and First Trust Indxx Innovation Transaction & Process ETF (LEGR) are aiming to provide more diversified and broad exposure to the growth of the blockchain ecosystem.

VENTURE CAPITAL—EXTRACTING THE FULL VALUE OF THE MOMENT

Investing in private investment funds that are leading the way in identifying and funding the best and brightest players in blockchain is a strategic and deliberate way to invest in the blockchain ecosystem. Venture investing is not for everyone, but there are some excellent venture capital funds to invest in, including A16Z, SPiCE VC, and BCAP. These funds invest directly in the blockchain ecosystem, each with its own focus, and provide an investor with greater diversification.

In its recently published "Blockchain Venture Capital Report," Cointelegraph Research revealed that blockchain private equity has outperformed traditional private equity across one-, three- and five-year horizons.

These outsized returns are driving the potential for increased equity investments in blockchain startups both for blockchain and mainstream VC funds. The reason? VC investing offers an opportunity to participate in high-growth companies at the ground level. Venture Capital Funds are a long-term investment but allow investors to fully realize the tremendous growth of the digital finance ecosystem before it reaches maturity. This is especially true for industries that are growing and evolving rapidly, like the blockchain ecosystem, as the majority of value creation happens when companies are still private before going public.

Understanding investment opportunities and staying attuned to regulatory developments in this space will become a necessary part of their everyday job.

WHAT THE FUTURE HOLDS FOR DIGITAL ASSET INVESTING FOR WEALTH MANAGERS

Anthony Kratofil of Vital Wealth Management had this to say about where he sees this trend in wealth management moving: "I'm excited for the future of digital finance. I think it will allow the market to bypass many of the current system's intermediaries to keep costs down and provide better outcomes for investors and savers. As for blockchain, where we are in this period reminds me of the early days of the Internet."

"While many only saw it for what it was, others understood its disruptive power, invested early and did very well," Kratofil went on to say. "Wealth managers of all sizes have the opportunity and the obligation to responsibly seize the moment and the momentum for their clients, all while always keeping their clients' unique needs and interests at the center of everything."

As the digital finance market continues to grow, wealth managers will no longer have a choice to just avoid the conversation with clients. Understanding investment opportunities and staying attuned to regulatory developments in this space will become a necessary part of their everyday job. However, with sound strategies, smart advisors and their clients will reap the lucrative benefits this space offers now and in the future.

INVESTING IN BLOCKCHAIN-BASED ASSETS

Article #6   *01.20.2022 , The Street*

If Your Portfolio Has No Metaverse Exposure, It Should and Here is Why

The time is now to capitalize on the opportunities for investment and wealth creation as the colossal undertaking to create, build, and deploy the Metaverse takes shape.

I don't usually begin any of my articles, or any conversation for that fact, with an opinion about investment opportunities. This is different. This is the Metaverse. Therefore, I'll boldly proclaim that if your investment portfolio doesn't have any Metaverse exposure, you should do something about it right now. In full disclosure, it should come as no surprise that I do have Metaverse exposure in my portfolio.

As I mentioned in my "Dawn of the Metaverse" article, the first of the series, we are at a moment in history where the Metaverse is much like the Internet was in the late 80's and early 90's, social networks of the mid-90's, and the Cloud in the early 2000s. Much like the massive disruptive technology revolutions that came before, the Metaverse will change the way we interact, transact, and behave.

In this particular article, I'm taking a closer look at the opportunities for investment and wealth creation as the colossal undertaking to create, build, and deploy the Metaverse takes shape. Because of its pervasiveness and eventually universality, the Metaverse will impact every industry and almost every aspect of our lives. With a movement like that, the investment opportunities are immense, but you have to understand the space better before diving in.

WHAT WILL THE FUTURE OF THE METAVERSE LOOK LIKE?

EARLY BEGINNINGS OF THE METAVERSE— HOW GAMING HAS THE GOODS

By now, many can already visualize the early days of the Metaverse and understand that beyond the hype, some of the early adoption and implementation will come from gaming and entertainment. When it comes to gaming, the Metaverse is now. Companies like Roblox (RBLX), Minecraft owner Microsoft (MSFT), and privately held Fortnite creator Epic Games are already creating Metaverse-like experiences. Traditional game makers including Activision Blizzard (ATVI), Electronic Arts (EA), and Take-Two Interactive Software (TTWO) are also on their way to building their future Metaverse.

Early pioneers in this space, gaming companies have the design and tech know-how already baked into their operations to easily create mini-Metaverse experiences that have become important building blocks for the next wave of Metaverse innovations. This is exactly why these companies will see tremendous growth in the short and long-term. Corporations from every sector, unable to design and create Metaverse worlds in-house, will inevitably look to experienced organizations like gaming companies to help them in their pursuit.

DEEP AND WIDE INTO MANY ASPECTS OF OUR LIVES

Make no mistake, over the next decade we will experience the Metaverse disrupting many aspects of our daily lives from virtual office space and training to smart homes and concert experiences. Work, commerce, education, travel, finance, healthcare, retail, and everything in between will launch their own unique take on the Metaverse creating a global paradigm shift that will be lasting. Some iterations will work and some will fail. This type of technological Darwinism will take hold and, in the end, a set of standard frameworks, various popular devices and wearables, and a commerce engine using blockchain-based digital assets (i.e., NFTs and crypto) will be built and will win out.

But what exactly does it mean to build the Metaverse? The Metaverse isn't a single platform. Rather, it's a complex digital environment that relies on seven distinct layers (suggested by Jon Radoff, author of Building the Metaverse blog), as well as a variety of companies that will have the opportunity to play a significant role in the creation and evolution of the ecosystem. These layers include:

1. **Infrastructure:** Connectivity technologies like 5G, WiFi, cloud, and hi-tech materials like GPUs. Notable companies in this space: AT&T, Verizon, Broadcom, Qualcomm, AMD, Nvidia, Amazon, Alphabet, Microsoft, and Intel.

2. **Human interface:** VR headsets, AR glasses, haptics and other technologies users will leverage to join the Metaverse. Notable companies in this space: Oculus, Apple, Meta, Microsoft, Unity, and Magic Leap

3. **Decentralization:** Blockchain technology, DeFi, NFTs, IoT, AI, edge computing and other tools and assets of democratization.

4. **Spatial computing:** 3D visualization and modeling frameworks.

5. **Creator economy:** An assortment of design tools, digital assets and e-commerce establishments.

6. **Discovery:** The content engine driving engagement, including ads, social media, ratings, reviews, etc.

7. **Experience:** VR equivalents of digital apps for gaming, events, work, shopping, etc. Names like Axie Infinity, Decentraland, and Epic Games.

BUILDING THE METAVERSE WILL TAKE TIME

The Metaverse, like Rome, will not be created in a day. It will take over a decade or more of evolution for the Metaverse concept to become a permanent feature of many aspects of our daily lives. There are a variety of reasons for that. Some technologies still need to develop and improve in order to make the Metaverse experience fully immersive and captivating, while being practical and accessible (price and simplicity) for everyday use.

Think about it, every single device from refrigerators to mobile devices to TVs will be a part of the Metaverse. And that's just hardware. New applications and software will have to be developed, while existing ones will have to adapt. The wearables we know of now, like watches, glasses, and even earbuds, will all play a role, but don't underestimate the likelihood and impact of some "black swans" that will come along making what we have now obsolete.

THE METAVERSE WILL BE HUGE

For crypto investors, many Metaverse projects such as Axie infinity (AXS) have been running at full steam. To Wall Street, the Metaverse revenue opportunity, which could touch a wide range of industries including technology, entertainment, sports, education, and retail, is just getting started.

Following a laser focus on multiple corporations within the Metaverse ecosystem last year, Wall Street analysts have now started focusing on the Metaverse's market impact potential. While the analysts' predictions vary in size, they all agree that the Metaverse is a multi-trillion-dollar opportunity over the next decade.

Jefferies predicts the Metaverse will be the biggest disruption to how we live in history. In a December 6, 2021 note, Jefferies analysts wrote that the Metaverse could be the "biggest disruption humans have ever experienced" and lead to the "digitization of everything." While Jefferies' analysts predict that the Metaverse will encompass all aspects of human activities eventually, they believe that the adoption will start with games, entertainment, and social media followed by more than a decade of evolution.

Morgan Stanley analysts believe that the addressable US consumer expenditure to monetize within the Metaverse is at $8.3 trillion. This is looking only at the Metaverse market related to advertising and e-commerce.

Bernstein analysts estimate the size of Metaverse-related markets to be $2 trillion and growing. Evercore ISI analysts think that the Metaverse can account for trillions of dollars of value creation within the next decade. Ark Invest CEO Cathie Wood says the Metaverse will be a multi-trillion-dollar opportunity and impact every aspect of the economy in ways that "we cannot even imagine right now."

WHY SHOULD YOU INVEST IN THE METAVERSE?

Can you imagine going through the last three decades without your investment portfolio benefiting from the growth brought by the Internet revolution? Probably not.

Investors need to be thinking about the Metaverse as akin to the Internet in its early days. In addition to its immeasurable impact on our lives, the impact of the Metaverse and related technologies on investment opportunities will be monumental.

Make no mistake, over the next decade we will experience the Metaverse disrupting many aspects of our daily lives.

But contrary to the Internet revolution, the technology development and deployment, as well as the global mass adoption of the Metaverse will happen at a much faster pace.

As I mentioned in a previous article, we are at the precipice of what could be the largest transformational period in global history. Investors that take advantage of the early opportunities of building the Metaverse will only benefit when the reality of this new ecosystem comes to fruition. In that vein, the articles that follows will look at both short and long-term opportunities, in a variety of different industries, that offer readers a deeper understanding of the space and highlight the substantial upside to participating in the Metaverse wave, along with some of its inevitable challenges. The choice to act on that knowledge is squarely up to you.

INVESTING IN BLOCKCHAIN-BASED ASSETS

Article #7   *03.19.2022, The Street*

Getting in on the Metaverse: Investment Tips for Today with Upside for Tomorrow

The Metaverse is here and growing quickly, which is why investors should consider Metaverse exposure as part of their diversified investment portfolio now

While it may seem like the Metaverse is some far-off virtual world stuck in Mark Zuckerberg's head, it is certainly not. It's real, it's happening, and it goes well beyond Meta. The Metaverse will impact every aspect of our lives slowly and then all at once.

Understanding that the Metaverse is that transformational, while also realizing that it's in its infancy, you should consider including strategic Metaverse exposure as part of your diversified investment portfolio now.

For investors seeking to stake a claim and participate in the growth of the Metaverse ecosystem, there are three potential strategies:

It's real, it's happening, and it goes well beyond Meta.

**STRATEGY #1:
DIVERSIFICATION**

Investing directly in a new, complex, and very fast-moving ecosystem is challenging and a bit risky. It requires thorough due diligence and understanding of the various moving parts. The best way to reduce risk is to diversify and rely on a team of experts to select investments.

Here are a couple of ways you can do that:

- **ETFs:** One option is to invest through exchange-traded funds (ETFs). An ETF is a type of pooled investment security that operates much like a mutual fund but is a publicly traded security. ETFs can be an effective addition to any portfolio.

  With regards to the Metaverse ecosystem, there are a few options, but that will surely grow as the ecosystem expands and matures. These ETFs typically invest in around 50 different companies that participate in various aspects of the Metaverse or are expected to be impacted by the Metaverse ecosystem growth.

  Some of these ETFs include Roundhill Ball Metaverse ETF (METV), Fount Metaverse ETF (MTVR), Amplify Transformational Data Sharing ETF (BLOK), and the most recent, Subversive Metaverse ETF (PUNK).

- **Funds:** Venture Capital and Private Equity funds specializing in the Metaverse are playing a significant role in the overall funding of this growing space, but those funds are fairly limited, as is access to investment opportunities. Investing in such funds means high risk (but potential high return), a long period of illiquidity (typically over 10 years), and requires significant commitment of capital.

STRATEGY #2:
DIRECT INVESTMENT IN COMPANIES
WITH METAVERSE EXPOSURE

As with any traditional vertical-specific investment strategy, investing directly in a company can be riskier requiring a deeper understanding of the organization and its role within a particular industry. However, for those with the right aptitude and stomach for it, it may mean a better return than investing through an ETF.

How do you select relevant companies within the Metaverse ecosystem? To start, you need to understand what the Metaverse is and it's composition. You then need to know what industries are currently adopting it and to what extent. Based on that knowledge, you can assess which companies will either need or want to participate in the future. These tips by no means will make you an expert, but they will give you a better view of the investment landscape.

The Metaverse is an environment that is an amalgamation of multiple technologies and domains. It's a complex digital environment that relies on seven distinct layers, populated with companies that contribute to, or impact, each specific layer. There are many "pure play" players that are still private companies, but over time more of them will likely go public. Also, more incumbents currently not dabbling in the Metaverse development and adoption, will start doing so in the near future. This means the list of relevant public companies to choose from will constantly grow over the next few years. Some companies, like Meta Platforms (FB), Apple (AAPL), Amazon (AMZN), Tencent (TCEHY), and IBM (IBM) impact multiple layers.

To keep things simple, each layer is listed with some examples of publicly traded companies leading in these specific areas:

- **Infrastructure:** Connectivity technologies like 5G, WiFi, cloud and hi-tech materials like GPUs. Notable companies in this space: AT&T, Verizon, Broadcom, Qualcomm, AMD, Nvidia, Akamai, Lumen Technologies, Amazon, Alphabet, Microsoft, and Intel.

- **Human interface:** VR headsets, AR glasses, haptics and other technologies users will leverage to join the Metaverse. Notable companies in this space: Oculus, Apple, Meta Platforms, and Microsoft.

- **Decentralization:** Blockchain technology, DeFi, NFTs, IoT, AI, edge computing and other tools and assets of democratization. Notable companies in this space: Coinbase, Galaxy Digital, Block, PayPal, Tencent, and Alibaba.

- **Spatial computing:** 3D visualization and modeling frameworks. Notable companies in this space: Hexagon AB and PTC.

- **Creator economy**: An assortment of design tools, digital assets, and e-commerce establishments. Notable companies in this space: Matterport and Adobe.

- **Discovery:** The content engine driving engagement, including ads, social media, ratings, reviews, etc. Notable companies in this space: Naver Corp, Alphabet, Meta Platforms, and Snap Inc.

- **Experiences:** VR equivalents of digital apps for gaming, events, work, shopping, etc. Notable companies in this space: Roblox, Krafton, Electronic Arts, Shopify, and Amazon.

STRATEGY #3:
METAVERSE COINS (CRYPTOCURRENCIES)

As a high-risk and potentially high-reward strategy, investing in the digital finance layer of the Metaverse, which includes cryptocurrencies, requires more understanding of the future "Metaverse economy" and the prominent role of digital currencies like Bitcoin.

Many of the companies associated with the Metaverse are profitable, time-tested, and publicly traded (i.e., Microsoft and Meta). However, most Metaverse cryptocurrencies and related companies and projects have only been around for a couple of years. It's not yet clear if they'll survive and thrive as the Metaverse grows, but it's worth taking a closer look.

Three large players, Axie Infinity, The Sandbox, and Decentraland, have market values of $3.28 billion, $4.5 billion, and $3.02 billion respectively. If these projects can consistently gobble up a significant portion of the capital being invested in virtual worlds, these market values could be an absolute steal. These three companies have play-to-earn-styled games built atop the Ethereum Blockchain allowing users to purchase digital plots of land that can be upgraded to attract other users and stored as Non-Fungible Tokens (NFTs). The in-game NFTs provide immutable proof of ownership of a digital asset stored on the blockchain. The actual ownership of in-game creations stays with the developer in traditional PC and console gaming systems. Sandbox and Decentraland allow users to own and monetize their own creations via NFTs.

Pursuing the cryptocurrency investment path means betting on the Metaverse's growth in a decentralized fashion. Surprisingly, this is still not fully established. With powerful players throwing tens of billions of dollars at the Metaverse (i.e., Microsoft, Google, Apple, and Meta), a centralized future is a real potential outcome.

Regardless of your risk tolerance or preferred investment strategy, make sure your investment portfolio matures with some kind of exposure to the Metaverse. Making those moves early on in the building process is always the better bet.

Pursuing the cryptocurrency investment path means betting on the Metaverse's growth in a decentralized fashion.

INVESTING IN BLOCKCHAIN-BASED ASSETS

Article #8   *11.07.2022, The Street*

Goldman Sachs' New Digital Asset Classification System Fills a Gaping Hole in the Digital Finance Ecosystem

Together with Coin Metrics and MSCI, Goldman Sachs' answers the call to provide essential standardized data and analysis for digital assets helping investors make more informed digital investment decisions.

What should have been the most significant news of the year for the digital economy was glazed over by most media outlets. Goldman, however, launching a standardized classification system for digital assets, including cryptocurrencies, with Coin Metrics and MSCI is more important than you think.

The new collaboration led by Goldman answers the call by digital finance investors, entrepreneurs, and market participants of all types to have a consistent, unbiased system to rate, analyze, and classify digital currencies and security tokens. Acting almost like a "Bloomberg" for digital assets, Datonomy will help retail and institutional investors better navigate and understand the worth and behavior of the more than 20,000 coins and tokens.

Anne Marie Darling, the Head of Marquee Client Strategy and Distribution at Goldman Sachs, stated, "Datonomy is a consistent and standardized way to help market participants view and analyze the digital assets ecosystem giving them a better idea of what is going on in the different crypto spaces, such as DeFi and smart contact platforms."

THIS IS A BIG DEAL AND HERE'S WHY

As previously mentioned, there are more than 20,000 individual cryptocurrencies in existence today, over three times more than the approximately 6,000 publicly traded US stocks. However, those same stocks have an overwhelming amount of analysts and ratings agencies watching their every move. In contrast, until the announcement from Goldman, there was no significant standardized, data-focused system to classify, analyze, and report on the thousands of digital assets.

Now, instead of digital finance investors flying blind, there will be a consistent, neutral, and reliable guide, providing the data and insight crypto and security token investors desire.

MORE INSTITUTIONAL PARTICIPATION MEANS MORE PROGRESS AND LEGITIMACY

Goldman Sachs' Datonomy is a fairly straight forward step in standardizing, and at the same time helping to reign in, the digital finance ecosystem. Moves like this continue to chip away at the "wild west" references to the market little by little. More institutional participation like this gives others the confidence to enter this growing market creating a cascading momentum that benefits the ecosystem as a whole. While all investors, retail and institutional continue to wait for regulators to make moves and provide regulatory clarity, we'll take these wins as they come.

INVESTING IN BLOCKCHAIN-BASED ASSETS

Article #9   *08.14.2023, Newsweek*

Betting on a One Trick Pony in the Web3 Race is Risky Business

Winning Web3 Investment Strategies Must Combine Artificial Intelligence and Blockchain Technology

Artificial Intelligence (AI), specifically Generative AI, is definitely having its "moment" right now. While AI has been around for years, the introduction of consumer-facing ChatGPT changed minds and investment strategies overnight. In fact, the AI market is projected to reach a staggering $407 billion by 2027, experiencing substantial growth from its estimated $86.9 billion revenue in 2022.

And to think, right before AI burst onto the scene, a different, new technology was investors' darling, gaining momentum, and increased attention. Remember blockchain?

While blockchain technology is a force just as ground-breaking and pervasive as AI, its association with cryptocurrency volatility, along with a "failure of imagination" of its use-cases and possibilities, created a lull in attention. However, even with the crypto chaos, the blockchain market size is still rising exponentially globally as more and more institutional investors, multinational corporations, and governments consider blockchain's benefits. In fact, the blockchain market is on pace to grow from $17.57 billion in 2023 to $469.49 billion by 2030.

AI and blockchain are each changing the way we live, work, and play in the most profound ways. But, when these technologies converge, their true potential is unleashed, creating a new realm of possibilities. The combination of AI and blockchain empowers a generation of applications that harness the unprecedented productivity gains facilitated by AI, while leveraging the security and transparency offered by blockchain. This convergence opens doors to innovative solutions that bring about enhanced efficiency, trust, and accountability across various sectors.

With the blockchain AI Market projected to grow to $980.70 million in 2030, at a CAGR of 24.06%, companies that leverage both blockchain and AI to unlock new possibilities and seize on that value will experience exceptional wealth creation.

THE PITFALL OF A "ONE TRICK PONY" STRATEGY

Investors often fall into the trap of fixating on a single industry or company that captures their attention due to promising trends or extraordinary growth potential. While this approach might yield short-term gains, it carries significant inherent risks. Relying solely on one industry or company overlooks the dynamic nature of the market and the broader impact of technological convergence.

Major breakthroughs and transformative advancements seldom occur within the confines of a single industry or company. Technological progress often emerges at the intersection of multiple fields, where different innovations converge to create exponential growth and unprecedented possibilities.

For instance, blockchain's decentralized and immutable nature provides a secure and transparent infrastructure that can revolutionize antiquated processes. However, it is the integration of AI's capabilities, such as massive data processing, pattern recognition, and intelligent decision-making that unlocks the true power of blockchain.

The most successful investment strategies are those that consider how technologies will evolve together. True potential lies in companies that combine multiple technologies, diversifying their offerings, and creating synergies. Examples of such companies include NVIDIA, AMD, Apple, Microsoft, and Alphabet, which have embraced the convergence of blockchain and AI.

BLOCKCHAIN & AI PARTNERSHIP PROVE THEY'RE BETTER TOGETHER

From the Metaverse (yes, it's still a thing) to manufacturing, the Web3.0 dynamic duo of blockchain and AI is on the path to redefine entire industry sectors creating operational efficiencies and improving the human experience. The convergence of these technologies has the potential to reshape the way we interact, transact, and create content in the digital realm, leading to a paradigm shift in entertainment, commerce, and social interactions.

For example, the blockchain-based supply-chain market is expected to grow to over $14 billion in revenue by 2028, while the healthcare market transitioning to blockchain technology (a rapidly growing trend), is expected to reach more than $126 billion by 2030. The manufacturing industry is expected to see the largest financial impact due to AI. An Accenture report forecasts that the manufacturing sector will reap the greatest financial benefit from AI adoption, with a gain of $3.8 trillion.

- **Manufacturing:** Blockchain can provide a secure and transparent system for automating, tracking, and verifying the entire manufacturing process, from raw material sourcing to the final product. AI algorithms can analyze large volumes of data generated throughout the production line, identifying patterns, detecting anomalies, and optimizing manufacturing processes. This convergence can lead to improved safety protocols, predictive maintenance, streamlined supply chain management, and overall cost reductions for manufacturers.

- **Supply chain management and IoT:** Blockchain's distributed ledger capabilities create a transparent and traceable supply chain ecosystem, while AI can comb through vast amounts

Investors often fall into the trap of fixating on a single industry or company that captures their attention due to promising trends or extraordinary growth potential.

of data generated within the supply chain, optimizing inventory management, demand forecasting, and logistics. The integration of these technologies enables enhanced visibility, real-time tracking, and authentication of goods, reducing fraud, improving efficiency, and mitigating risks.

- **Healthcare:** Blockchain's secure and decentralized nature can facilitate the sharing and management of patient data, ensuring privacy, interoperability, and security. AI algorithms can improve diagnostic accuracy, develop personalized treatment plans, and enhance patient outcomes. Additionally, blockchain can address challenges related to pharmaceutical supply chain integrity and integrate with AI to revolutionize clinical trials, patient monitoring, drug development, and overall healthcare management.

- **Arts and entertainment:** Blockchain can help artists establish ownership rights and protect their intellectual property. Smart contracts enabled by blockchain can automate royalty payments and provide artists with greater control over their creations. Additionally, AI technologies can enhance the creative process by assisting in content generation, curation, and personalization.

The convergence of transformative technologies like blockchain and AI presents an opportunity to unlock unparalleled growth and innovation across multiple sectors but none of it is happening overnight. Innovators and entrepreneurs are discovering new ways to leverage these amazing technologies every day and are creating startups and high-growth companies that harness their combined potential.

Investors that are able to identify those companies and capitalize on our digital future will reap the benefits. An investment strategy that involves embracing the interconnectivity of technologies and considering how they will evolve together, will define success in the Web3 Era.

VENTURE CAPITAL INVESTING

VENTURE CAPITAL INVESTING

Article #1   *05.13.2022, The Street*

The Case for Venture Capital in an Uncertain Market

Uncorrelated to equities, commodities and crypto Markets, VC Funds are an evolving asset class that can help diversify portfolios during downturns and beyond.

Everything is down these days except for one thing: inflation. The feared "I-word," along with a laundry list of macro and micro headwinds, have pushed the S&P 500 to its lowest point in more than a year, crushed the Dow and caused the NASDAQ to officially enter bear-market territory. Even the celebrated FAANG stocks are off by at least 20%.

GOLD? DOWN. BONDS? NOT GOOD. CRYPTO? IT'S BAD.

We certainly can't ignore crypto's tragic fall from grace. To once again reiterate the point I've made several times about Bitcoin and crypto, their recent nosedive (losing over 50% of their value), just proves they are in no way an inflation hedge or a safe haven, and absolutely correlated to stock market behavior and volatility.

What's an investable asset class that's proven to be uncorrelated to the stock market? Venture capital funds. However, it would seem that in the midst of the current market slowdown and the possibility of a looming recession, it's not the best time to invest in VC funds, let alone launch an entirely new fund. But, if that's what you're thinking, then you've got VC investing all wrong.

Unlike the equity markets, venture capital has remained steady during this period of volatility after experiencing record-breaking growth over the past few years. In fact, global venture funding reached $143.9 billion in Q1 2022, the fourth largest quarter of funding on record even with a slight slowdown from the previous quarter.

Additionally, according to recent research, the share of VC funds in portfolios continues to increase as pensions, endowments, financial firms, insurance companies, and family offices are adding VC exposure and seeing it pay off.

From biotech to blockchain, VC activity remains strong and continues to offer investors, large and small, opportunities for long-term wealth creation beyond the usual stocks, bonds, and crypto.

VENTURE CAPITAL PROVIDES DIVERSIFICATION THAT'S UNCORRELATED TO THE MARKET

Diversification is key to avoiding some of the worst of a down market. However, as described above, it's hard to find assets and/or industries that aren't correlated in some way to market movements. No matter the asset or the industry, major market corrections are like a tsunami carrying everything with it in the same direction.

Unlike traditional stocks, bonds, and the newest asset class, crypto, venture capital funds are not correlated to the equity markets. In fact, long-term correlation between VC returns and the market (Nasdaq and S&P 500) is very weak.

In addition to their equity market independence, VC funds provide diversification by providing exposure to a variety of startups, at various stages in their growth journeys, and across a multitude of fast-growing industries. Whether it's a niche fund or a fund-of-funds, investors are able to put their money to work and potentially avoid the massive swings, daily dips, and emotional market sell-offs by participating in this long-term, diversified asset class.

Having said all of that, VC investing isn't for everyone. Depending on the fund and its investment strategy, VC investing can be risky. And, because of its long-term nature, it's fairly illiquid. However, those downsides are also evolving and the VC market as a whole is becoming more accessible and attractive to a wider swath of investors, not just the millionaires and behemoth institutional players.

.A NEW ERA OF VC INVESTING

SPiCE VC, the venture capital firm I founded and currently lead, recently launched a second fund, SPiCE II, after a successful close of our flagship fund, SPiCE I, the first fully tokenized VC fund to ever be available to investors. With a 350% increase in security token price in 2021, SPiCE I was named the top performing fund in the tokenization and blockchain market by *Security Token Market*, the largest security token financial data and media firm.

SPiCE I's real market significance is not just in its value creation for investors, but also in how it presented an entirely new way for investors at any level, to fully participate in the private VC market democratizing venture capital investing by tokenization. While most VC funds have a minimum investment size requirement, which is typically in the multi-millions and only available to a select few investors, SPiCE I has created greater access through issuing digital securities that are tradable on exchanges like Securitize Markets and INX. This strategy has allowed for much lower minimum investment requirements. The result is an instrument that allows much greater access to a lucrative financial asset usually reserved mostly for institutional investors.

While still a small portion of the total VC market, the tokenization trend continues to gain traction, with names like Blockchain Capital and Realio leveraging the power of blockchain technology to benefit investors.

SPiCE II is doubling down on this investment approach using a traditional VC model, to be followed soon with a tokenized version of the same fund, while continuing its focus on identifying innovative companies that stand to benefit the most from the mass proliferation of blockchain technologies across many industries.

ENTREPRENEURIAL INNOVATION DOESN'T PAUSE FOR DOWN MARKETS

Ideas, breakthroughs, and new approaches don't stop because the stock market is down. Entrepreneurs continue to create the next generation of companies that will build the systems and the solutions for our world well before they hit the NASDAQ. Instead of playing this market, which never ends well, it may make sense to consider taking advantage of this dynamic asset class that's fueling innovation and disruption. It may be simpler and more accessible than you thought.

VENTURE CAPITAL INVESTING

Article #2   *06.15.2022, The Street*

The VC FOMO Problem:
The Time-To-Deal Race is Leaving Many
Disoriented and Others Well-Positioned

The time for venture capital firms to execute due diligence around a startup has compressed from months to just a few weeks. This time crunch magnifies the strengths and weaknesses of the industry and forcing many firms to rethink their approach.

I started SPiCE VC in 2017 when the VC market was hot and getting hotter. In fact, venture capital has been on a tear over the last three to five years. Even with a slight decline this year, the first quarter of 2022 saw global venture funding totaling an estimated $195 billion. Back in 2015, there were roughly 142 unicorns in the world. According to CB Insights, there are now 1,146 unicorns.

However, this VC success has led to frenzy, which inevitably has led to FOMO. In actuality, the entire VC space has moved to a constant state of FOMO, with funds of all sizes trying to get their hands on the next unicorn. Because VCs are jumping on opportunities faster in fear of losing out to another firm, the timeline for reaching certitude around a startup's thesis and executing due diligence has become much more compressed. This shortening of VC "courting" period poses risks for VCs and their investors.

The market in which we invest includes blockchain, tokenization, and various aspects of the exploding digital finance ecosystem. The market is more nuanced, but challenges still exist. Due to the mega hype prevalent in the blockchain ecosystem, there are a good deal of startups touting technology that's looking for a problem rather than solving true existing problems. Additionally, unrealistic business cases, products that aim to solve very short-lived problems, and solutions that rely on technologies or ecosystem components that will disappear, all combine to create noise and distractions for novice investors. Identifying the real diamonds in this huge pile of shiny objects is not an easy task.

DUE DILIGENCE AND VC "COURTING"

The due diligence process for most venture capital firms involves extensive and in-depth research, including gathering market data, sifting through mountains of documents and financial data, while getting to know the founders and executive team as best they can. Traditionally, this process would take anywhere from six weeks to several months, with 18 months being the average time a startup goes from one round to the next.

VC's no longer have months to research a company and conduct thorough due diligence. In today's hyper-competitive and frenetic landscape, VC's looking to invest have much less time; if they're lucky, they may have a few weeks.

FOMO LEADS TO COMPRESSION

In order to combat this compression of time, VCs have been forced to adapt, pivot, and work smarter. Many are relying on data, while others are streamlining strategies focusing on efficiency without sacrificing quality. Others are looking at the due diligence process as a fluid, ongoing exercise, rather than a targeted one, i.e., VCs aren't waiting to be pitched, but rather tracking and gathering insights along the way. However, this is all easier said than done.

For generalist VC firms that don't have a niche vertical focus, the landscape to track is enormous and virtually impossible to monitor. This makes them less informed and more vulnerable.

FOCUS IS A VCS GREATEST ASSET

For VC firms like SPiCE VC, which is hyper-focused on high-growth companies in the blockchain and tokenization space, the surface area of which it must search and track is significantly smaller than what many other firms are facing. That focus makes niche funds nimbler, and provides them with the advantage of already fully understanding the market landscape, the technology, and the participating companies and players.

It's clear that when a firm is already deeply embedded in the industry it's looking to invest in, much of the tedious up-front work is done, making way for more time allowed to focus on the details that really matter: the company's leadership team and skills, product and technology, business model, product market fit, and go-to-market strategy, etc.

FOCUSING ON WHAT MATTERS

Knowledge matters, relationships matters, and data matters. The more a VC firm has of each of these components, the better. And, in the environment of FOMO and compression, they matter even more because, when in possession and used effectively, knowledge offers the gift of time.

VC's no longer have months to research a company and conduct thorough due diligence. In today's hyper-competitive and frenetic landscape, VC's looking to invest have much less time; if they're lucky, they may have a few weeks.

VENTURE CAPITAL INVESTING

Article #3 *01.18.2023, The Street*

Economic Downturns Mark a Return to Sanity (and Returns) for Venture Capital

Historically, VCs triumph over bubble bursts and recessions. Is this time any different or are VCs positioned well as the crypto winter thaws, the blockchain ecosystem continues its growth trajectory, and a new economic era takes hold?

The dot-com bubble was a speculative bubble created by a rapid rise and interest in internet companies. This five-year period leading up to the peak in March 2000 saw many companies focused primarily on gaining market share through brand building and networking.

The name of the game was getting big fast, as companies raced to acquire larger market share, sacrificing profitability for growth. The dot-com boom pushed the Nasdaq Composite Index to an all-time high of 5,048.62 on March 10, 2000.

Then, just like that, the bubble burst (as they all eventually do), and one company after another imploded, fueling an internet sector freefall that lasted for the following two and a half years. In the end, the Nasdaq lost 78% of its value.

Businesses and investors realized that large investments and rushing to IPO does not compensate for a lack of a sound business model. With the spectacular rise and colossal crash of many dot-com companies, only a few were left standing becoming some of the most well-known companies in the world. Companies like Amazon, eBay, and Shutterfly were lucky, as well as the investors and venture capital (VC) firms investing in them.

The dot-com bubble was a speculative bubble created by a rapid rise and interest in internet companies.

VC'S NEW DOWNTURN OPPORTUNITY

In 2023, if you substitute the dates and replace "Internet" with "crypto or blockchain," we're reliving the same old story. Over the past year, cryptocurrency prices have dropped by more than 75% and the colossal collapse of many crypto-focused companies like Terra-Luna, Celsius, BlockFi, and FTX. In parallel, many other crypto players are running into difficulties and are laying off employees, cutting budgets, and reducing revenue projections.

While the crypto crash has been a hot topic with leading headline, there's no denying significant economic headwinds exist throughout the economy, exaggerating the current trends in tech, Web3, crypto, and other high-growth, early-stage industries.

Whether it's a bubble or a recession, are today's economic woes similar to the crashes of old?

SIMILARITIES TO THE DOT-COM BURST

1. Both involve new and emerging technologies that have attracted significant attention and investment from VCs and other investors.

2. Both involve a high degree of speculation and risk, as these technologies are still in the early stages of development and adoption.

3. Both were characterized by a period of extreme hype and speculation, expectations detached from reality, which led to skyrocketing valuations for companies in the sector.

4. Both were fueled in part by a wave of new investors entering the market, many of whom were driven by the prospect of making quick and easy profits.

5. The two periods saw a similar magnitude of value drop—well over a 70% drop in Bitcoin price during this crypto winter vs. 77% drop in the NASDAQ composite index during the dot com era.

6. For VCs, both periods saw a shift in VC investment focus towards more mature, revenue-generating companies, rather than earlier-stage startups with unproven business models. There was also increased competition among VC firms to invest in the most promising companies, leading to higher valuations, and larger funding rounds.

However, there are some significant differences between today's market conditions and the dot-com era and even the Great Recession of 2008. Differences that create unique challenges, along with positive opportunities.

DIFFERENCES FROM THE DOT-COM ERA

1. The dot-com bubble was largely centered around traditional tech companies that were building new businesses and products, while the current blockchain and crypto boom is focused more on decentralized technologies and digital assets.

2. The dot-com bubble was largely driven by retail investors, while the current crypto boom has attracted a more diverse group of investors, including venture capital firms and other institutional investors.

3. The dot-com bubble burst was largely driven by the failure of individual companies, while the current situation for blockchain and cryptocurrency investments is more complex and involves a range of different factors, including regulatory developments, fraud and mismanagement, market trends, and technological advancements.

4. The impact of the dot-com bubble burst was more widespread, impacting not just the companies and investors involved, but also the overall economy. The crypto crash impacts a smaller segment of investors and organizations with exposure to crypto.

WHAT DOES THIS MEAN FOR VC INVESTING IN A NEW ECONOMIC ERA?

Some of the strongest vintages in private equity and venture capital were recession years; the dot-com crash of the 2001 period, for example, produced the best performing vintage in more than 20 years. However, beyond significant market corrections and the ability of smart VCs to get in on the ground floor of transformative startups, other factors have contributed to private equity's success in times of crisis include active involvement with portfolio companies, the ability to deploy capital more flexibly, and the ability to insulate investors from panic selling. Additionally, seasoned VC leaders understand the importance of staying the course, being confident in your strategy, and continuing to invest in promising companies, even during times of economic uncertainty.

Nevertheless, more critical than any factor, serious economic corrections breed more due diligence in the VC world. I recently wrote a piece about how the time it takes a VC fund to move from the discovery phase to the final investment phase has drastically shrunk in the last few years. There's been a feeding frenzy to find a unicorn in just about anything creating a culture of shortcuts and trigger-happy investing.

Specifically, the crypto crash and the resulting "crypto winter," along with a variety of other economic factors, has forced many funds to slow down and take a deeper look at companies, their leaders, and the inner workings of each startup they are courting.

Instead of the feeding frenzies of the pre-2021 VC investing, sanity will return and instead of deals getting done in days and weeks, it will be months or longer. Moreover, while much of the VC "hype" has been focused on crypto, there has been an entire universe built on blockchain technology experiencing incredible growth.

More critical than any factor, serious economic corrections breed more due diligence in the VC world.

Blockchain technology will endure and is already reshaping many large industries like capital markets, banking, insurance, healthcare, supply chain, and gaming. As such, VC funding has been shifting away from centralized crypto lenders and exchanges and taking a hard look at Web3 and blockchain-focused companies.

VCS WILL CONTINUE TO HELP FUND AND GROW OUR DIGITAL ECONOMY

Overall, similarly to the post-dot-com bubble burst, VC firms that stick to their strategy, become more selective and make intelligent decisions about where they're putting their money, investing in strong companies with sound teams and business models set to weather and navigate the current difficult times, are set to benefit from the continued growth of the ecosystem. Plus, let's not forget, entrepreneurs never pause for down markets, and neither will VC funding of their innovation.

VENTURE CAPITAL INVESTING

Article #4   *02.07.2023, The Street*

FTX Fallout:
Should VCs Be Held Accountable
for Missing Red Flags?

As impossible as it is to believe that venture capital funds did proper due diligence on mismanaged and allegedly fraudulent FTX, the inherent risk of early-stage investing makes regulatory change unlikely in the fallout.

Charges have been filed by the US Securities and Exchange Commission (SEC) against three top FTX executives, including Sam Bankman-Fried, but this is certainly not the end of the SEC's probe. Earlier this month Reuters reported that the SEC is also seeking information from financial firms (yet to be named) that made significant investments in FTX regarding their due diligence processes used prior to investing. While this particular area of the investigation is not necessarily an indication of any wrongdoing, the abundance of VC funds associated with, and deeply invested in FTX, raises some questions. Specifically, the SEC is focusing on details about what policies and procedures venture firms had in place when they chose to invest in FTX, and whether they were followed.

NO SHORTAGE OF VC'S JUMPING ON THE FTX BANDWAGON DESPITE RED FLAGS

The list of FTX investors who collectively invested over $2 billion, and subsequently had to write it all off, spans an impressive "who's who" of well-known investment firms, including: NEA, IVP, Third Point Ventures, Tiger Global, Insight Partners, Sequoia Capital, SoftBank, Lightspeed Venture Partners, Temasek Holdings, and BlackRock. It also includes one of Canada's largest pension funds with nearly $250 billion in assets under management (AUM), which will write down the entirety of its $95 million investment in FTX.

That's quite a lot of money flowing into an organization that had an accounting firm in the Metaverse, no board of directors, a questionable corporate domicile, and was highly leveraged from the very beginning, among a list of other "red flags." So, what gives? Each of the VC funds that invested in FTX said they conducted an appropriate amount of due diligence, including Temasek Holdings, that stated the firm spent eight months of due diligence without identifying a single red flag.

While I'm not in a position to Monday Night Quarterback the VC/FTX bandwagoning, it's undeniable that serious questions are being raised by the SEC and others. Were the funds acting responsibly on behalf of their own investors when they poured money into FTX as part of their fiduciary duties? How is it possible that not one of FTX's investors noticed anything amiss? And, what does the VC group think led to all of this?

While these questions about due diligence deserve answers, it's also about oversight. Did these investors exercise any oversight on how these funds were deployed at FTX?

When it comes to FTX, (and many others, including Terra-Luna, Celsius, BlockFi, Genesis, etc.) the stop gaps and oversight failed. We expect regulators to protect investors from fraud and mismanagement of their investment, while investors expect and rely on investment managers to do proper due diligence on investment and make risk-reward decisions as part of their fiduciary duty.

This delicate balance of oversight, trust, and accountability failed because, let's face it, FTX was the "cool" thing in which to invest.

VC GROUP THINK STRIKES AGAIN

This isn't the first-time venture capital and private equity money followed the cool, shiny object, throwing caution to the wind and betting the house. Remember the dot-com bubble? Apparently, investors in FTX forgot, because a cool kid that wore wrinkled shorts, never made his bed, and lived in a Bahamian penthouse wooed them. While Sam Bankman-Fried's rap sheet of fraud continues to grow, in my opinion, his single greatest fraudulent accomplishment was the massive heist of the global VC market. The popular "Crypto Kid" gave them a reason to swoon, and many of them fell in line one after another without questioning a thing.

WHAT DOES THE FTX FALLOUT MEAN FOR VC INVESTING MOVING FORWARD?

According to Politico, to potentially avoid another VC group think fail, the SEC is working on a rule that would preclude private funds from seeking indemnification for simple negligence, effectively making it easier for limited partners (LPs) in such funds to sue. This will, presumably drive higher accountability and will hopefully result in deeper due diligence and oversight on the part of fund managers. However, this issue has implications that go beyond just direct investors and often impact institutional investors, pension funds, etc.

SOUNDS GOOD, RIGHT? BUT IT'S NOT SO SIMPLE.

While I strongly believe that VC funds and their managers carry significant responsibility to their LPs and must do their best to make investment decisions based on solid due diligence and according to fund policies, my prediction is that the FTX-related VC probe is unlikely to amount to much from a regulatory perspective.

While these questions about due diligence deserve answers, it's also about oversight.

Even if some VC fund managers did little more than blindly follow Sequoia Capital in investing in FTX, it will be very hard to justify regulatory change from a singular event and a relatively small number of VC funds. In essence, LPs are rarely promised specific due diligence procedures, or requirements related to corporate governance, etc. LPs know this is a high-risk asset class, and that general partners often have little time to access the most popular deals. If they're dissatisfied with the fund's performance, they can and do vote with their feet during follow-on fundraising.

Also, LPs are already allowed to sue for gross negligence, which covers reckless or purposeful acts. However, expanding liability to simple negligence would effectively enable LPs to sue every time a deal goes bad, which would add a significant amount of unruly risk and cost to the VC business, risk and cost which will be passed on to investors and portfolio companies alike. Furthermore, most LPs will not take advantage of such rights, as earning a black-mark reputation for being overly litigious will preclude them from participating in future deals—no one wants to work with a tattletale.

VCS ARE RISKY, BUT SHOULDN'T BE RECKLESS

To quote Taylor Swift (no, I'm not a Swifty), VCs need to "keep their side of the street clean." As mentioned before, participating in the venture capital ecosystem is inherently risky. VCs make bets on early-stage companies, but those bets should be educated, informed, and researched. Furthermore, once the decision to invest in a startup is made, there should be an adult in the VC room making sure that whatever investment was made is being used wisely and for the right reasons.

There's no scenario in which a VC fund can guarantee a unicorn or even modest positive returns and that's okay. Investors not comfortable with those odds shouldn't be in the VC market. There will always be winners and losers, just like with the stock market. So, instead of opening the litigation flood gates, let's hold the fraudsters accountable and allow responsible venture capital funds to continue to invest in innovation.

Instead of opening the litigation flood gates, let's hold the fraudsters accountable and allow responsible venture capital funds to continue to invest in innovation.

REGULATION AROUND THE WORLD

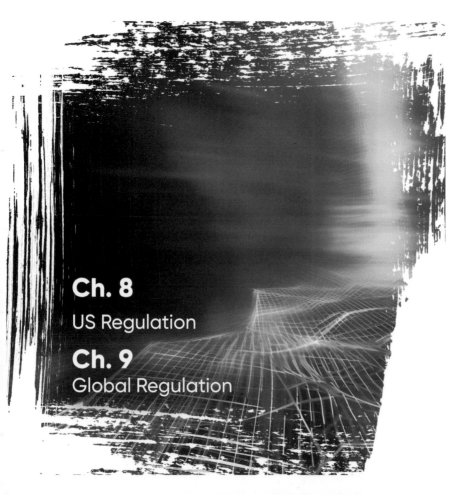

Ch. 8
US Regulation

Ch. 9
Global Regulation

INTRODUCTION

Mention regulation and watch eyes glaze over. It may not be the most exciting topic, but within the explosive context of blockchain, cryptocurrency, and digital assets, regulation is absolutely crucial. It's like the conductor in the orchestra of blockchain's symphony; without it, the whole thing falls out of sync.

Regulation plays a vital role for a multitude of reasons. Primarily, it acts as a growth enabler for substantial industries by providing a framework that encourages participation from institutional and blue-chip players. Especially in the wild west of cryptocurrency, having established rules can offer comfort and security to hesitant stakeholders.

Additionally, regulation is the compass that helps navigate the risk-laden waters of blockchain investments. Understanding the regulatory landscape in detail aids investors in assessing risks associated with particular business models and investment opportunities. It illuminates the path, highlighting the domains worth venturing into, and those likely to remain bogged down in regulatory quicksand.

One more fascinating aspect of regulation is its capacity to create and open new business and technology opportunities. Like a sculptor chipping away at a block of marble, regulations often reveal new forms and possibilities in the blockchain ecosystem.

However, the reality is that regulations are not universally applicable. They are jurisdiction-specific, often steeped in legislation, and can be heavily influenced by the prevailing political climate. Moreover, given the diverse applications of blockchain technology in various regulated industries—securities, payments, banking, lending, insurance, healthcare, and more—

there may be multiple regulatory bodies involved within the same jurisdiction, each with its own unique requirements.

It's a delicate balancing act. On one hand, regulation can fuel significant growth and development, as witnessed in the US securities industry or in Switzerland's progressive crypto regulation scenario. On the other, it can put a damper on growth, like in the US, where the lack of comprehensive crypto regulation has been a recurring issue.

One more fascinating aspect of regulation is its capacity to create and open new business and technology opportunities.

TO DELVE DEEPER INTO THIS COMPLEX DANCE OF TECHNOLOGY AND REGULATION, WE'LL NEED TO TAKE A CLOSER LOOK AT SEVERAL KEY THEMES:

In the US, we see a strange paradox. The nation is a pioneer in digital securities regulations but continues to lag behind when it comes to proactive legislation and regulations for cryptocurrency. The absence of legislative guidance often leaves regulators resorting to enforcement actions, which have had limited success. In contrast, the European Union, bolstered by the imminent rollout of the Markets in Crypto-assets (MiCA) and Switzerland's early bird approach to crypto regulation, is shaping up as a standard-setter, enabling more institutional investment and mainstream acceptance of crypto.

China, with its commanding lead in Central Bank Digital Currency (CBDC) with its digital yuan implementation, is noticeably absent from the crypto arena.

As we gaze into the crystal ball of blockchain regulation's future, the picture is decidedly mixed. In the US, despite mounting pressure on Congress, the prospects for sweeping legislative change appears bleak. The EU seems to be on a promising path with MiCA and CBDC, provided it remains steadfast in its current regulatory course. The UK and Switzerland continue to make strides, and Japan is emerging as a player to watch in the corporate and institutional tokenization space.

In this intricate tapestry of blockchain, crypto, and digital asset regulations, one thing is certain: while regulation may be complex, it's undeniably pivotal in shaping the industry's future around the world. It's not just a set of rules. It's the DNA of the digital finance revolution.

US REGULATION

US REGULATION

Article #1   *02.10.2021, Securities.io*

Three Key Biden Moves That May Signal New Era for Blockchain-Based Digital Finance

For the past few years, we've witnessed the digital finance arms race heat up across the globe. Whether it's central bank digital currency (CBDC), cryptocurrency, or digital securities, blockchain technology is driving the evolution of finance with global superpowers battling it out for supremacy.

More than 80% of the world's central banks are exploring their own versions of digital currencies, but China, the US, and the EU have the resources, technology, and infrastructure to determine the future of the digital economy. While many US enterprises embrace, and even lead, the digital finance revolution, the US government has been hesitant and arguably slow to act on cryptocurrency regulations and CBDC implementation. The result of this reluctance? In this turtle and hare scenario, China has hopped ahead gaining first-to-market advantages. However, just like in the fable, that doesn't mean the US is doomed.

Things might be about to change with the arrival of a new administration. Some interesting moves have recently been made by the Biden administration that signal some changes coming this year and beyond. Biden made two appointments that are key to moving the blockchain-based digital finance world forward:

JANET YELLEN

The Biden administration's new Treasury secretary is Janet Yellen, who has a good deal of interest in regulating cryptocurrency. In a written response to the Senate Finance Committee last month, Yellen said, "I think we need to look closely at how to encourage their use for legitimate activities while curtailing their use for malign and illegal activities. If confirmed, I intend to work closely with the Federal Reserve Board and the other federal banking and securities regulators on how to implement an effective regulatory framework for these and other fintech innovations."

From past history, it's clear that Janet Yellen doesn't shy away from regulation. But, while regulation has a negative connotation to some, the financial industry is screaming for common-sense regulation for this space in order for it to ever move forward. The grey murkiness of unregulated industries is seen as too risky for larger financial institutional players that see the world and their businesses through regulatory lenses. Janet Yellen just may be the woman to get the job done.

GARY GENSLER

Biden's pick for the chairman of the US Securities and Exchange Commission (SEC), Gary Gensler was the former chairman of the Commodity Futures Trading Commission (CFTC) and taught courses on cryptocurrency at MIT Sloan. He was also a director at Ripple and has testified before Congress about cryptocurrency many times. Gensler's appointment injects a broader perspective about frameworks for cryptocurrencies and blockchain.

At an MIT conference in 2018, Gensler posited that Ripple's XRP and Ethereum's ETH should be deemed digital securities. While ETH is no longer under the SEC's scanner, Ripple's XRP is. Back then, Gensler predicted that the courts would ultimately decide XRP's fate as a security. That event is already in motion, and his agency will have a big hand in deciding its outcome.

"The potential this technology has to be a catalyst for change is real," Gensler doubled down on the future potential of blockchain technology in a 2019 op-ed. "This last point—crypto and blockchain technology acting as a catalyst for change—may not fulfill the heightened expectations of maximalists but may be [Satoshi] Nakamoto's most enduring early contribution."

FINCEN HOLD

In addition to his picks to head the Treasury and the CFTC, the Biden administration put an immediate hold on a rule proposed by the Financial Crimes Enforcement Network (FinCEN). Under the bureau's proposed rule, banks and money service businesses need to submit reports, keep records, and verify the identity of customers that engage in transactions with private cryptocurrency wallets. This rule would require crypto exchanges to record name and address info for transactions aggregating over $3,000 per person per day that go to private wallets.

The record-keeping and counterparty detail is seeing a 45-day extension due to this complex the issue. This move, while not necessarily indicating a specific direction, signals interest on the part of the current administration to look at digital finance rules and regulations more closely to make informed decisions based on the future of the overall market.

THE WINDS OF CHANGE AND PROGRESS ARE BLOWING

This is an especially critical juncture for cryptocurrencies and blockchain. Institutional investors continue to warm up to the asset class. However, to date, no other mainstream retail investor has made such a bold move as BlackRock did this year. The world's largest asset manager filed prospectuses with the SEC for its new ETF, the first to include cryptocurrency (Bitcoin futures) as part of its offering.

Another nod to the firm's elevated interest in blockchain-based digital finance is a recent posting of a job vacancy for a New York-based VP of Blockchain. The person who fills the available position, as mentioned in the posting, will help with the valuation of crypto assets.

In order for cryptocurrency to become a mainstream asset, US financial institutions must take the necessary steps to make it available to the masses. Right now, it's difficult for just anyone to own cryptocurrency, but BlackRock's ETF development could make the crypto market accessible to everyday investors. Many of which have no idea how to trade cryptocurrency.

In addition to the promising BlackRock ETF initiative, two other significant developments in the marketplace have created some excitement. First, Tesla just bought $1.5 billion worth of Bitcoin and plans to accept it as a form of payment. Additionally, just as the combined cryptocurrency market passed $1 trillion in January, Coinbase, North America's largest cryptocurrency exchange by trading volume, filed for an initial public offering (IPO) with the SEC.

Congress and the SEC also want in on the action. The SEC recently filed a case against Ripple's XRP, the third-largest cryptocurrency by market capitalization, claiming that it is an unregistered security, offering a new clue about the possible direction of future SEC regulatory and enforcement activity. Separately, Congress is considering how it can implement new real-time payment services and boost financial inclusion this year, targeting various goals the crypto community has long discussed. This is certainly a critical conversation in which the industry wants to participate.

IN THE CARDS: DIGITAL FINANCE PREDICTIONS

The Biden administration has the opportunity and the inclination to create more clarity and, as a result, a favorable regulatory environment for digital assets and blockchain, a technology that's been around for more than a decade but is still viewed with deep suspicion by many lawmakers. Regulations will move faster during this administration, which will enable and encourage more market participation. Clear regulations are better for mass adoption and forward progress in the digital finance space, almost regardless of how strict they may be.

Institutional adoption of digital assets and blockchain/DLT will continue accelerating over the next few years. The current wave of adoption will further increase due to advances in the regulatory framework in the US and Europe, as well as the availability of more institutional-grade digital assets based financial instruments. Retail adoption of digital assets and blockchain will also increase, as financial instruments like ETFs make it much more accessible to retail investors.

There's no crystal ball and no one can predict what moves the Biden Administration will make next. However, what we do know is, momentum is building, interest is accelerating, and decisions and directions are just around the corner. Grab the popcorn.

In order for cryptocurrency to become a mainstream asset, US financial institutions must take the necessary steps to make it available to the masses.

US REGULATION

Article #2   *09.14.2021, Coindesk*

The Infrastructure Bill and its definition of "Broker" has caused a major crypto controversy

The definition of the word "Broker" in the Infrastructure Bill has sparked concern within the crypto and digital finance community.

On August 10, the contentious HR 3684 Infrastructure Bill cleared the Senate. Now, the document is in the hands of the House of Representatives, including the provisions expanding the definition of a cryptocurrency broker, designed to beef up crypto, and Decentralized Finance (DeFi) tax compliance.

But, the word "broker" has sparked the most concern within the crypto and digital finance community. That's because the Bill defines a "broker" as "any person who (for consideration) is responsible for regularly providing any service effectuating transfers of digital assets on behalf of another person." For digital finance leaders and investors, this definition is just way too broad, potentially driving the Internal Revenue Service (IRS) to target ecosystem participants like miners, developers, stakers, and others, who would be interpreted as brokers even if they don't have any customers or have access to information needed to comply. Many in the industry fear that this disconnect and misinterpretation could ultimately lead to blockchain and digital finance innovators and technologists to leave the US all together.

This doom-and-gloom scenario is not likely to materialize, though. Innovators do not just pack up and leave the US that easily.

While there was hope that the language in question would be amended—a relief to many—the House Democrats on Tuesday,

Aug. 23 blocked attempts to scale back digital currency tax rules. This was considered a significant setback for the industry, but not necessarily the end of the conversation. Advocates are looking at other legal avenues to provide clarity on the issue and definition. Regardless, according to treasury officials, the US Treasury is not likely to target non-brokers like miners even if the crypto tax provision language is not amended.

The Infrastructure Bill's language is certainly important and needs to be addressed. The greater challenge and opportunity is digital currency and digital finance regulation as a whole. Yes, major industry players are committing to the growth of the digital finance industry, but without sensible regulation that provides guidelines and guardrails, the industry will continue to exist on the sidelines.

Regulation is actually good for the industry and will provide clarity required for institutional investors to increase participation, so market participants can increase innovation and expansion right here in the US. If people want the market to be big, it has to be regulated.

US REGULATION

The Heat Is On:
The Crypto and DeFi
Regulation Debate Intensifies

*Does a recent uptick in regulatory activity signal
a new era for crypto and DeFi regulation?*

While the crypto and Decentralized Finance (DeFi) industries
continue their explosive expansion, regulators around the world,
and in particular the US, continue to struggle to catch up with
implementing regulatory approaches to this new, but lasting
domain. The gap between state and federal regulations make it
even more challenging to navigate for DeFi ecosystem players.

Regulators, with their intent to create some sensible guardrails for
the digital finance ecosystem, which will be met with significant
resistance from crypto-purists, still must fulfill their mandate of
protecting the public. Ultimately, their challenge will be to define
and implement rules to distinguish legitimate, innovative business
models from fraudulent activities all while not killing the industry.

IS IT OR IS IT NOT A SECURITY?

The Internal Revenue Service (IRS) classifies crypto as
property. The Commodity Futures Trading Commission
(CFTC) says crypto is a commodity. The Securities and
Exchange Commission (SEC) has indicated that it all
depends on circumstances. This is where much of the uphill
regulatory battle begins in the world of digital finance.

The confusion has caused some recent frustration and tension
between DeFi industry leaders and US regulators, including
industry darling, Coinbase, who was asked by the SEC to halt its

proposed crypto lending program titled "Lend." The SEC alleges that the company's yield is in fact a security, but Coinbase CEO insists on the contrary. Coinbase Lend would offer a 4% yield on holdings of USD Coin, known as USDC, a dollar-backed stablecoin that has reached more than $27 billion in circulation.

Similar debates continue with BlockFi's savings and loans product facing SEC scrutiny. Yet, while the back-and-forth is frustrating, it does signal a recent trend of elected officials and regulators taking notice of the rapid adoption of blockchain-based digital assets and digital currencies, as well as an inclination to provide some potential clarity to the market.

DEFI IN THE REGULATORS' CROSS HAIRS

It's clear digital finance is on the mind of regulators. In July, Treasury Secretary Janet Yellen pushed top US financial regulators to accelerate their consideration of new rules to police stablecoins, a type of cryptocurrency that's seen rapid recent growth and remains largely unsupervised. The spotlight on stablecoins triggered, among other things, the renewed debate on Tether (USDT), a stablecoin believed to be pegged to the US Dollar, and the degree to which it is really backed by USD.

Additionally, SEC Chairman Gary Gensler in his recent testimony before the Senate Committee on Banking, Housing and Urban Affairs, addressed among other topics the Crypto Asset Market. He said that, "Currently, we just don't have enough investor protection in crypto finance, issuance, trading, or lending—it's more like the Wild West." Gensler also said that while not every crypto token qualifies as a security, the fact that platforms have allowed the trading of so many tokens mean it is highly likely at least some securities are being offered on the platforms. And, to the extent that there are securities on these trading platforms, under SEC laws they have to register with the commission unless they qualify for an

The lack of clarity is driving instability in the market making it hard for ecosystem players to drive legitimate business innovation and growth.

exemption. Gensler added that regarding investor protection, the SEC is working with the CFTC, which has relevant and sometimes overlapping jurisdictions in the crypto markets.

Speaking of the CFTC, Biden's picks to the CFTC have rich crypto/digital backgrounds. Kristin Johnson specializes in complex financial products regulation and government officials, and Christy Goldsmith Romero also teaches cryptocurrency regulations at UVA. Biden also nominated acting CFTC Chairman Rostin Behnam to be the Senate-confirmed head of the regulatory agency further signaling a potential increase in regulatory focus on crypto and DeFi.

WHAT DOES THIS ALL MEAN FOR CRYPTO AND DEFI ECOSYSTEM?

While die-hard crypto enthusiasts want to see the original vision of decentralization live on in the crypto and DeFi ecosystem, others understand that "if you don't build it, they won't come." The lack of clarity is driving instability in the market making it hard for ecosystem players to drive legitimate business innovation and growth. Clear regulations are critical for stability and increased institutional participation in the industry.

A certain amount of regulation is also good for investors in DeFi products and services so they know they are being protected to the degree possible from fraud and scams. All this is key for the DeFi ecosystem to continue growing and achieve its potential to become the mainstream financial ecosystem.

TAL'S TAKE:
FIVE PREDICTIONS

1. **Regulators (SEC, CFTC, FINRA, the Fed and others) will struggle with defining responsibilities on regulating DeFi, thus sparking proxy wars:** What's a security and what's not? What's a commodity and what's not? And who actually is following the money?

   Take the Commodity Futures Trading Commission CFTC and SEC battle on domain authority. This struggle makes sense, as existing regulators' responsibilities were defined in the days of traditional finance. The DeFi ecosystem is challenging these traditional boundaries, which regulators will have to figure out, and eventually succeed, how to adjust to the new world of finance.

2. **Regulators will increasingly become more proactive:** We will see a much more proactive regulatory posture (i.e., Gensler and Biden's moves). I expect this proactive approach to adapt regulations for the crypto and DeFi ecosystem in parallel with increased enforcement of regulations, as demonstrated by the SEC's actions over the last few months.

3. **More Regulations:** Regulators and legislators will drive new regulations that are aimed at providing ample regulatory oversight for the DeFi ecosystem. Some of these new regulations may cause a meaningful shakeup in the industry. The major challenge regulators will face is being able to drive effective regulations without killing the transformational value behind decentralization as some regulatory approaches that worked well in a centralized financial ecosystem are not practical in a decentralized ecosystem.

4. **DeFi Infrastructure adapting to supporting new regulatory needs:** In parallel to the rapidly changing regulatory environment, DeFi infrastructure will need to evolve and adapt, adding new services and capabilities in order to enable DeFi while supporting the new regulations.

5. **Increased institutional adoption:** Increased regulatory focus will likely drive more institutional involvement both participation and investment in the DeFi. Together with some of the turbulence resulting from the increased regulatory focus, we will see significant continued growth of the DeFi ecosystem.

US REGULATION

Article #4   *10.07.2021, The Street*

How to Read the CFTC's Latest Legal Moves to Take on 14 Crypto Players

CFTC flexes its legal muscles, but what does it mean for the market and regulations moving forward?

Last week, the Commodity Futures Trading Commission (CFTC) issued a $1.25 million settlement order with Kraken, one of the crypto industry's largest market participants. The order charges that Kraken offered margined retail commodity transactions in cryptocurrency and failed to register as a Futures Commission Merchant (FCM). Kraken has been required to pay a $1.25 million penalty and to cease and desist from further violations of the Act. The CFTC stated that, "This action is part of the CFTC's broader effort to protect US customers."

A day later, the CFTC announced that it had charged 14 entities for offering cryptocurrency derivatives and margin trading without registering as a FCM, with two of them blatantly lying about being registered with the CFTC.

All of the complaints are somewhat similar in that the CFTC alleges that each of the cryptocurrency platforms "from at least May 2021 and through the present" have offered services to the public "including soliciting or accepting orders for binary options based off the value of a variety of assets, including commodities such as foreign currencies and cryptocurrencies, and accepting and holding customer money in connection with those purchases of binary options."

WHAT'S INTERESTING ABOUT THIS NEW STANCE?

Although the definition of CFTC's mandate as a regulator is fairly clear, the answer to the question of who regulates the crypto industry, or rather, what aspects are regulated by which regulator remains a debatable question.

Although the CFTC has issued regulatory guidance in the past, and engaged in some regulatory enforcement activities, it has traditionally taken more of a backseat role in crypto regulation. However, it seems the recent steps have established the CFTC as a key regulator of the crypto industry along with the Securities and Exchange Commission (SEC), the US Department of Justice (DOJ), and the US Department of the Treasury.

With all that said, the CFTC still has limited jurisdiction over spot markets in virtual currencies, participants buy and sell virtual currencies for prompt delivery, while it has broad jurisdiction over derivatives markets, i.e., cryptocurrency futures.

What makes this more aggressive and purposeful stance even more interesting is the CFTC has previously taken the position that Bitcoin, Ethereum, and Litecoin are considered commodities. In these recently filed complaints, the CFTC did not appear to limit the cryptocurrencies that would be considered commodities to just Bitcoin, Ethereum, and Litecoin. The CFTC broadly referred to commodities as foreign currencies and cryptocurrencies including Bitcoin. However, which of the hundreds of cryptocurrencies on the market will be considered commodities remains to be seen.

SHOULD WE EXPECT MORE SHOES TO DROP?

Where does this leave legitimate and successful digital finance organizations? According to a colleague and the CEO of a well-known crypto-focused digital bank and exchange, the regulatory uncertainty and lack of clear guardrails is forcing "a bank our size to spend way more than we should and more than other traditional banks just to keep up with evolving compliance demands from multiple regulators."

Given the current lack of clarity of jurisdiction over cryptocurrency trading and related financial instruments, as well as the latest round of regulatory actions, I expect that regulatory activity within the cryptocurrency space will increase from all US regulators, including the CFTC, SEC, Treasury, and the Office of the Comptroller of the Currency. While various guidance has been issued, it seems regulators are taking a "regulatory guidance by enforcement action" strategy. The result is that market players will need to thoughtfully consider all relevant regulatory regimes in order to determine what compliance activities they need to take to remain compliant.

Recent steps have established the CFTC as a key regulator of the crypto industry.

US REGULATION

Article #5   *11.09.2021, CNBC*

Stablecoins Need to Be "Stable" To Be Useful; The US Government is Making Sure of It

Stablecoins are a necessary digital asset with compelling uses, but need more regulatory oversight to build trust and legitimacy

Stablecoins are a widely-used digital asset pegged or directly connected to a traditional asset such as a currency like the US dollar or a commodity like gold. This unique type of cryptocurrency, with a $130 billion market value, is used by investors to buy and sell other digital assets, or as a secure place to hold wealth. That's because they are seen as much more "stable" than their crypto cousins.

Cryptocurrencies like Bitcoin or Ethereum do not carry a promise for future value. Their price is determined purely by market forces based on supply and demand. The price of a stablecoin, on the other hand, is pegged to a real asset of value, so it carries with it a promise of value identical to the asset it is pegged to. For example, USDC's value is always supposed to be $1.

Stablecoins are essentially a bridge between cryptocurrencies that do not appear as a traded pair. They are also used for cash transactions between crypto businesses and as a way to hold on to cryptocurrencies without the same risk of volatility. These versatile assets also play a significant role in many DeFi transactions.

In other words, stablecoins are to the crypto world as real money has become to the old-world style of bartering. They are the grease that smooths the machine's operations.

CAN A STABLECOIN'S PROMISE OF VALUE BE TRUSTED?

There are multiple types of stablecoins. For example, Tether (USDT) is run by Tether Limited, which is controlled by the Hong Kong exchange Bitfinex. USD Coin (USDC) is run by a consortium started by the payment company Circle, while the coin Binance USD (BUSD) is controlled by the exchange Binance.

But, with all of these various players in the stablecoin market, large and lucrative ones at that, who is making sure that the issuer of each stablecoin is doing what they need to do to support that promise of stability? Right now, no one does, so there is no way to know for sure what these companies are actually holding and whether it is enough to guarantee the stability of the coin.

For this reason, more and more regulators are taking notice and voicing concerns.

THE WATCHDOGS ARE STARTING TO WATCH

According to the President's Working Group on Financial Markets (PWG), which includes several top economic advisors to President Joe Biden, stablecoins could, "support faster, more efficient, and more inclusive payments options. Moreover, the transition to broader use of stablecoins as a means of payment could occur rapidly due to network effects or relationships between stablecoins and existing user bases or platforms."

This positive outlook on ongoing uses and future benefits is absolutely true, but only if stablecoins are regulated.

The Working Group is composed of Treasury Secretary Janet Yellen, Federal Reserve Chair Jerome Powell, Securities and Exchange Commission Chair Gary Gensler,

Stablecoins are to the crypto world as real money has become to the old-world style of bartering.

and ActingCommodity Futures Trading Commission Chair Rostin Behnam. Each of these individuals could designate a representative to participate in the group.

While this group understands the need for stablecoins in a growing crypto ecosystem, they also made it crystal clear these assets would need to be regulated. In fact, in a report released on Monday, Nov.1, the President's Working Group on Financial Markets urged lawmakers to subject stablecoin issuers to the same strict federal oversight as banks. They also added that Congress should require custodial wallet providers to be regulated by a federal agency and limit stablecoin issuers' interactions with non-financial companies such as tech or telecom providers.

And then they dropped the mic: If Congress fails to pass such laws, the regulatory agencies have the authority to take their own measures.

WHAT HAPPENS NOW?

Per the report from the President's Working Group on Financial Markets, it is preferred if Congress is the one to take action. Unfortunately, we all know the challenges with that course of action. Therefore, it's very likely US regulators will take the bull by the horns and begin making decisions about stablecoin oversight.

Which regulators will step up? Given the SEC Chairman Gary Gensler's track record and statements made regarding stablecoins and DeFi over the last few months, my bet is on the SEC. Gensler and the SEC's regulatory decision-making regarding the stablecoin will definitely impact the crypto market and the entire DeFi ecosystem, but how and how much greatly depends on the approach taken.

If we've learned anything about Gary Gensler over the past few months, it's that we know he has a deep understanding of the crypto ecosystem and we can assume he'll take a reasonable approach to regulatory oversight even if we can't predict how the market will react. My hope is that this regulatory action will provide the clarity the industry is craving.

US REGULATION

Article #6   *02.24.2022, The Street*

Talk is Cheap:
Congressional Hearings on Stablecoins
Feature Partisan Politics with
Little Regulatory Progress

As stablecoins grow in use, US lawmakers continue to grapple with how to legislate and regulate them

Stablecoins have exploded 500% to exceed a $127 billion market cap over the past year, according to the President's Working Group on Financial Markets. The report released on Nov. 1, 2021, in partnership with the Federal Deposit Insurance Corporation (FDIC) and the Office of the Comptroller of the Currency (OCC), urged Congress to enact legislation to ensure that stablecoins are subject to a regulatory framework.

The problem with stablecoins, as the PWG outlined, is that much like traditional banks, stablecoins face credit risk, liquidity risk, operational risk, and settlement risk. Why is so much risk associated with this type of digital asset? Let's provide a quick refresher:

WHAT IS A STABLECOIN?

The purpose of stablecoins is to provide price "stability" as people transact across coins or between fiat and digital currencies. As a type of cryptocurrency that relies on a more stable asset as a basis for its value, stablecoins are linked to a fiat currency, such as the US dollar, but they can also have value linked to precious metals or other cryptocurrencies.

From Tether (USDT), the largest stablecoin, to USD Coin (USDC), a stablecoin pegged to the US dollar, and many others circulating globally, stablecoins are essentially a bridge between cryptocurrencies that do not appear as a traded pair. However, there is no guarantee the issuers have on hand the assets to which the coin is pegged. Tether Holdings' story is the prime example. The company once claimed to have $69 billion in real currency to support that amount of its coin in circulation. Yet no one who went looking for the money was able to find any evidence of it. After being sued by the state of New York, the company revealed it had been loaning money from its reserves to prop up an affiliated cryptocurrency exchange that was hundreds of millions of dollars in the hole.

HOUSE OF CARDS

Congressional hearings aim to find solutions for stablecoins per the urging of the PWG to establish some regulatory clarity around stablecoins. Congress completed several hearings on the future of these digital assets. The hearings, which took place on Feb. 8 and Feb. 15, demonstrated not only the increasing interest in Congress in passing legislation to establish a regulatory framework for digital assets, but also the lack of agreement on the right approach.

The lack of agreement is not surprising given the current political environment that exists in the US. However, the House and the Senate at least gave it a solid try, emphasis on try.

Under Secretary of the Treasury for Domestic Finance, Nellie Liang, appeared before the House Financial Services Committee and the Senate Banking, Housing, and Urban Affairs Committee. During the House Financial Services Committee hearing, committee members expressed support for the report's recommendation for new legislation to regulate stablecoins. However, there were a number of members, both Democrats and Republicans, concerned about the Report's recommendation to only allow stablecoins to be issued through insured depository institutions (IDIs), saying that IDIs would needlessly burden stablecoin issuers, particularly those that provide coins backed by stable reserves, such as cash. The regulation of stablecoins, like regulating DeFi, needs to consider a different role and ecosystem than the traditional financial world for which IDI regulations have evolved. Although concerns and risks may be similar, the way to implement stablecoin regulations in order to mitigate these risks may manifest itself differently.

With that said, Under Secretary Liang highlighted the flexibility within the existing IDI regulatory framework that would actually reduce regulatory burdens of a stablecoin backed by reliable reserves such as cash or cash equivalents versus others backed by more volatile assets. She added that the IDI framework could address the payment and prudential risks associated with stablecoins.

During the Senate Banking Committee's hearing with Under Secretary Liang, Democratic senators were more concerned about the risks of stablecoins and digital assets more generally, particularly the risks of runs on stablecoins and the use of stablecoins in illicit transactions. Elizabeth Warren (D-MA) urged Under Secretary Liang to direct the Financial Stability Oversight Council (FSOC) to regulate stablecoins in advance of congressional action on the issue, since, according to Senator Warren, the FSOC has the authority to regulate emerging risks to the financial system before they become systemic. Under Secretary Liang noted that the FSOC was still analyzing stablecoins' potential threat to the financial system. Republican senators on the Banking Committee, much like Republicans on the House Financial Services Committee, were concerned about the PWG recommendations to regulate stablecoin issuers as IDIs.

A NOTHINGBURGER OR SOMETHINGBURGER?

Hearings, like the ones that took place, often kick the can down the road, which is exactly what's going on in this situation. While congress flexes their muscles and spews their partisan jabs, the world, along with the entire US financial sector waits for critical regulatory guidance on stablecoins. And, while the US continues to kick the stablecoin can further down the road, other countries, including China, are establishing themselves as leaders in the digital economy taking the lead on CBDCs, on digital assets in general, and more.

Until the US is fully able to develop and deploy its own CBDC, stablecoins are what people will continue to use more and more, growing the market exponentially. In this current scenario, regulation on stablecoins is needed and needed now. However, we can't lose sight of the benefits of stablecoins, if and when they're legislated and regulated sensibly, with the understanding of the key role they play within the digital economy and Decentralized Finance (DeFi), as well as their important role in continuing US leadership in international financial markets. In other words, the world is waiting for US leadership and foresight, which is exactly the opposite of what we've seen during the recent hearings.

If unregulated stablecoins are, in fact, one big house of cards, don't we want to stop an unfortunate collapse before it becomes a catastrophic one?

US REGULATION

Article #7   *11.16.2022, Newsweek*

Clear Regulation Is The Only Way To Civilize The Digital Asset Wild West

We know regulation always trails innovation, but this extraordinary innovation requires an equally extraordinary response from regulators.

The Wild West of the 19th century US was a period and a place of no laws, no courts, and little to no government authority. The only sheriff in town was, well, the sheriff, but even that role was often contested and unclear. There was only so much the sheriff could do when there were little to no rules to enforce and no established accountability protocol to enact. I guess they called it "wild" for a reason.

Nearly two centuries later, the narrative surrounding the present state of cryptocurrency and the digital asset market is heavy with "wild west" references. While it's meant to be hyperbole, it's hard to ignore the similarities: No clear sheriff in town, no clear rules or laws, and perpetrators ready to take advantage of the lawlessness, an apprehensive but determined portion of the investment population is ready to participate, but still in need of guardrails and security.

So, who's the sheriff in the wild west of the digital economy? As with sheriffs of old, it's a bit unclear. The same is true in the world of digital assets. Depending on how the asset is used or behaves, either the Security and Exchange Commission (SEC), Commodity Futures Trading Commission (CFTC), or the Treasury has jurisdiction. With that being said, the CFTC, which has regulatory authority over derivatives transactions and commodities markets, has been taking a much more proactive role in "policing" various aspects of the digital asset ecosystem.

POLICING WITHOUT REGULATION WILL LEAD TO DIGITAL ECONOMY GHOST TOWNS

Much like the old sheriffs of the Wild West who tried to find some semblance of law and order without the legal tools to do so, the CFTC is faced with similar dilemmas. Without regulatory clarity that provides sufficient and consistent guardrails, the CFTC is constantly in "enforcement mode." In fact, of the 82 enforcement actions brought by the CFTC this year alone, more than one-fifth were crypto-related.

With a reputation as the "good cop" of regulation and enforcement of the digital asset ecosystem, versus the Security and Exchange Commission's (SEC) "bad cop" association, the CFTC has had to step up its enforcement game in light of a series of questionable (at best) and fraudulent (at worst) actions made by a few market players negatively impacting the legitimacy of the entire ecosystem. Using what little tools they have, many of which are based on antiquated rules for traditional markets, the CFTC has identified and pursued these actors, including high-profile shakedowns of Coinbase, BitMex, Kraken, and Bitfinex to name a few.

Even when leveraging the enforcement tools available, the CFTC will be stuck in a doom loop of bounty hunting without a clear mandate or direction. The solution is not more enforcement. It's legislation and regulation.

THE DOOM LOOP ENDS WITH REGULATORY CLARITY

Summer K. Mersinger, a commissioner on the CFTC, recently noted that, "Congress must set some rules on regulation. Without more clarity in the laws, without some sort of statutory change, we're going to continue to see any kind of regulatory-related framework on the federal level in digital assets coming out of enforcement decisions made by court decisions. Unfortunately, that bypasses the public legislative process, the public input, and it's not an ideal way to govern."

While die-hard crypto enthusiasts want to see the original vision of decentralization live in the digital economy—a utopian scenario where the Wild West characters suddenly start policing themselves (spoiler alert: this never happened)—others understand that "if you don't build it, they won't come." The lack of clarity is driving instability in the market creating a cascade of skepticism. Without clear regulation and protections in place, "big money" institutional players won't fully participate in the market, and without them, the average consumer won't feel comfortable taking, what they believe is a risk, to participate in what could become a wealth of opportunities.

The fact of the matter is a certain amount of regulation is good for investors of digital assets so they know they're being protected to the degree possible from fraud and scams. More importantly, regulations are being called upon by the majority of crypto, blockchain, digital economy entrepreneurs, and business leaders.

Not everyone living in the Wild West was a criminal. But, how did they know if they were doing something wrong if there were no laws to reference and rules to live by? The same holds true with today's most innovative and pioneering companies shaping the digital economy. They, too, need to operate with clear regulations in order to continue to invest in, and innovate for, an inevitable digital transition of our entire financial system.

Enforcement is still part of the plan, penalizing the criminals that blatantly violate the laws. However, to close with another blatant Wild West reference, right now we've got the cart before the horse. The rules need to be in place first in order to have a civilized and thriving digital economy. Without them, the sheriff will always be shorthanded and outmatched.

Article #8   *11.20.2022, The Street*

Red Flags Are Harder to Miss with Regulation: An FTX Cautionary Tale and Industry Call-to-Action

Ignorance wasn't bliss in the case of FTX. As we dissect the tragedy of errors and the red flags that were missed, the answers become clearer: regulation and oversight could have prevented FTX's (and others) downfall.

The second largest crypto exchange in the world, British Virgin Islands-based FTX, halted all withdrawals and announced that it was filing for bankruptcy in the matter of one week. This news came as a shock to the cryptocurrency community, as FTX had been one of the most popular exchanges growing rapidly and expanding its user base from 100,000 to over 1.5 million people. It was seen as a crypto success story by most market participants and pundits, which led to the crowing of Sam Bankman-Fried (SBF) as the crypto exchange prince, only to be out-ranked by the self-proclaimed king, founder, and CEO of Binance, Changpeng Zhao (CZ).

SBF was regarded as a shy modest 30-year-old billionaire genius, looking to give away all his wealth. FTX was on the path to bringing the crypto world closer to Utopia, while SBF's Alameda Research was hailed as the savior of the industry acquiring multiple companies within the crypto ecosystem, and giving a second lease on life. This all sounded and looked great. But as we know now, it was one giant Ponzi Scheme no one saw coming or did they?

IGNORANCE WAS BLISS, UNTIL IT WASN'T

Now, I know hindsight is 20/20, but as we all take a step back and look at the rise of FTX and its business practices along the way, one can see that the writing was always on the wall. It was only a matter of time before FTX, and its over 134 companies across many jurisdictions, unraveled in epic fashion taking much of the crypto world with it. From allegations that SBF spent million on lobbying Washington for softer regulation, to encouraging his own employees to keep their life savings in the exchange, SBF's FTX was operating with reckless disregard the entire time. It was even lending its own investors' money to Alameda Research without any financial reporting of those movements. After reviewing FTX's financials, or lack thereof, the newly appointed FTX CEO, John Ray II said that he had never seen, "such a complete failure of corporate controls and such a complete absence of trustworthy financial information as occurred here."

The bombshell revelation that FTX was $8 billion in the red and couldn't pay its liabilities was the final nail in the coffin sending Bitcoin plunging by 4%, and causing other digital assets exchanges, including BlockFi, Gemini, and Crypto.com to suffer massive losses, being forced to halt withdrawals, and even file for bankruptcy.

Some of the biggest losers in the FTX debacle are also its biggest-name investors like Soft Bank, with their $1.3 billion stake, and Sequoia Capital, with their $260 million stake. Even its spokespeople like Tom Brady are feeling the burn as investors and creditors were out for blood. While these large institutions and celebrities can possibly handle the losses, FTX investors like the Ontario Teacher's Pension, which could lose up to $95 million, may not.

There's no doubt that there will be more shoes to drop before this saga is complete, but as the "experts" weigh in on the unraveling of FTX, it's clear that the cryptocurrency world has been rocked and many serious questions are raised about the stability of digital assets. FTX's rampant fraud and manipulation of unsuspecting investors has been a major black eye for the crypto industry and has left many investors shaken. But, with so much money at stake, many commentators are now asking probing questions about what went wrong at FTX and where were the regulators?

FTX was never regulated as an exchange by any government body because crypto exchanges are not currently regulated as exchanges.

WHAT REGULATION?

Since it was first established in 2018, FTX was running on a patchwork of insignificant and disparate licenses in various jurisdictions around the world. Instead of putting in the work needed to obtain legitimate licenses and registrations with the likes of the SEC and CFTC, FTX went on buying sprees to obtain just enough regulatory "green lights" to get by.

According to Aitan Goelman, an attorney with Zuckerman Spaeder, "It's a patchwork of global regulators and even domestically there are huge gaps." Many crypto firms like FTX are leaning on licenses that provide minimal consumer protection and don't cover their actual activity. FTX continued to operate with these small, insignificant license as it grew to a multi-billion-dollar behemoth.

FTX was never regulated as an exchange by any government body because crypto exchanges are not currently regulated as exchanges. This lack of regulation allowed FTX to act in a number of ways that would be illegal for other financial companies.

- FTX was not regulated as a bank or a lender, even though it was acting as one. This allowed FTX to avoid stringent capital requirements and other regulations that are designed to protect investors.

- FTX was not regulated as a financial company, even though it was acting like one. This lack of regulation meant that FTX was not subject to consumer protection laws or securities laws.

- FTX was not regulated as an exchange, although it was the second crypto exchange in the world, as crypto exchanges are not regulated as exchanges.

This fear is only going to be exacerbated as more cases of fraud come to light.

Would the situation be different if regulators were assigned to monitor FTX? One can only opine. However, it is interesting to note, the only part of the company complex where there was a regulator involved (CFTC) has not been pulled into the bankruptcy filings of FTX's US operations.

It is no secret that big time fraud and colossal implosion of huge operations can happen under regulators' eyes as well. One can easily remember Lehman Brothers and Enron as vivid examples. These events are much rarer and more spread apart than what we've seen in the crypto market just in the last year. In fact, Terra-Luna was the first major casualty, with Celsius and FTX following close behind. Each of these cases had a unique set of circumstances, but they all share one common theme: lack of oversight, transparency, and fiduciary responsibility. Investors are worried about the security and reliability of exchanges, which has led to a general mistrust of the entire sector. This fear is only going to be exacerbated as more cases of fraud come to light.

IS THIS THE REGULATORY MOMENT WE'VE BEEN WAITING FOR?

The events of the past few months have shown just how fragile the crypto industry is. Bitcoin and other digital assets may be revolutionary asset classes supported by innovative technologies, but they are still in their infancy. There are a lot of kinks to work out, and it will take time for the industry to mature. In the meantime, investors need to be careful and do their homework before investing in any project. The crypto ecosystem is full of scams and Ponzi schemes, so it's important to be vigilant if you want to avoid losing your money.

With that said, not every company or individual investor in the crypto space is criminal. But, how do they know if they're breaking the law if there are no clear laws to reference and rules to operate by? While the debate between those who believe tighter regulation is needed for the crypto industry, and those who advocate for decentralization, the FTX collapse has many more vocally advocating for clear crypto regulations. Regulators and legislators simply can't let the industry continue as usual. A certain amount of regulation is good for investors of digital assets, so they know they are being protected to the degree possible from fraud and scams. More importantly, regulations are also being called upon by the majority of crypto, blockchain, and digital economy entrepreneurs, and business leaders.

US REGULATION

Article #9   *02.28.2023, Federal Register*

Enforcement, Enforcement Everywhere but No Real Regulation in Sight

Dissecting the latest regulatory crackdown on crypto in the US and what it means for investors.

In the wake of the crypto industry meltdown of 2022, regulatory agencies, including the Securities and Exchange Commission (SEC), have been cracking down on crypto exchanges and lending firms. The SEC has issued significant fines and penalties against cryptocurrency lending firms in recent weeks, and several federal banking officials have released policy statements that would make it harder for crypto-related entities to engage with the traditional financial system.

While many of us speculated this would happen, especially in light of a gridlocked US Congress, the comprehensive and speedy nature of the crypto-related enforcement has been eye-opening. Understanding what has transpired can offer a glimpse of what's to come for digital finance participants, specifically in the crypto "wing" of the industry.

THE HOWEY TEST PUT TO THE TEST

The SEC has been targeting stablecoins, which are pegged to other assets like the dollar, in an effort to limit their volatility. SEC Chair Gary Gensler has focused on stablecoins, confident in the commission's ability to stretch the so-called Howey Test over the digital asset space. The Howey Test determines what qualifies as an "investment contract" subject to US securities laws. The SEC wants to send a message that no player, however big, is immune to regulation by targeting stablecoins.

Last month, the SEC levied a $45 million fine against crypto lender Nexo, while also charging one of its competitors, Genesis, with offering unregistered securities. The agency also announced a settlement with the Kraken crypto exchange that removed one of its popular investment products from the US market potentially impacting the wider industry. The SEC warned Paxos, a firm that issues stablecoins tied to the US dollar, about possible securities violations.

In addition to stablecoins, the SEC has recently taken aim at lending-related crypto products commonly known in the industry as staking, a way in which investors lock up their crypto tokens with a blockchain validator to be rewarded with new coins when their staked crypto tokens become part of the process for validating data on the blockchain.

The SEC's newly-aggressive enforcement regime is worrying and even angering many crypto participants, with some referring to it as "Operation Choke Point 2.0," a law enforcement campaign from the 2010s aimed at preventing banks from working with certain businesses. The Blockchain Association has filed amicus briefs on behalf of both Ripple and Wahi, defending tokens in question as "merely software."

The group argued it is, "devastating to the industry at large for the SEC to be able to proclaim, at will, and without meaningful review or challenge, that certain software packages are securities."

"It gives the SEC the ability to cause great damage to the industry, merely by making adverse allegations that may be proven untrue if contested in a court of law, but which the SEC knows will not be meaningfully contested."

YOU'LL BE TAXED FOR THAT

The SEC isn't the only sheriff in town. The Internal Revenue Service (IRS) is paying close attention to income derived from cryptocurrencies, treating them as capital assets, and requiring capital gains taxes to be paid when they are sold for a profit. Much like traditional securities, if you sell cryptocurrency for more than you paid for it, you're required to report the gain on your taxes.

This tax requirement may come as a surprise to some cryptocurrency investors who may not have been aware of the IRS's treatment of crypto as a capital asset. Nonetheless, the IRS has been and will continue to crack down on crypto tax evasion with increased enforcement efforts in 2023.

FRAUD CRACKDOWN

The regulatory crackdown also extends to fraud, which isn't surprising to anyone considering the recent fallout of crypto giant FTX. The SEC filed a lawsuit against Terraform Labs, the company behind digital coins Luna and TerraUSD, which collapsed last spring, triggering a broader decline in cryptocurrency prices. Former NBA star Paul Pierce agreed to pay $1.4 million to settle charges that he marketed a cryptocurrency without adequate disclosures.

Finally, three top financial regulators recently issued a letter warning banking organizations to exercise caution when dealing with cryptocurrencies. The Federal Reserve denied Custodia Bank's application to join its payment system, adding to concerns about the industry's future.

The SEC wants to send a message that no player, however big, is immune to regulation by targeting stablecoins.

ARE THE "WILD WEST" DAYS OF CRYPTO AND DEFI OVER?

The crypto industry faces an uncertain future as regulatory agencies continue to tighten their grip on the industry. While some argue the crackdown is a knee-jerk reaction to the industry's meltdown, others believe that regulatory agencies have been waiting for the perfect moment to enact the crackdowns they've planned all along.

Whatever the case may be, it is clear that the regulatory landscape for cryptocurrencies is evolving rapidly. Digital economy participants should not only be aware of the risks and challenges ahead, but should also be ready for new opportunities that will come now that a new "sheriff is in town" catching the bad guys.

US REGULATION

Article #10   *06.28.2023, The Street*

SEC vs. Stablecoins:
The Debate Over Their Status as
Securities or Money Heats Up

After its crackdown on crypto, the SEC seems to have their sights set on regulating stablecoins.

Stabelcoins and Decentralized Finance (DeFi) have caught the attention of the Securities and Exchange Commission (SEC), as suggested by recent public and private dialogue by the Commission and its leadership. In fact, according to a report by investment bank Berenberg, it is "much more likely that the SEC will focus on these areas following its recent enforcement actions against players in the cryptocurrency industry." Stablecoins were even a topic of debate a few months ago when the US House Committee on Financial Services discussed the Subcommittee on Digital Assets, Financial Technology, and Inclusion draft legislation related to stablecoins.

Federal Reserve Chair Jerome Powell and SEC Chair Gary Gensler have differing opinions on the viability of stablecoins as a form of payment and their classification as securities. Powell asserted his stance during a Capitol Hill hearing that stablecoins should be considered a form of money, emphasizing the importance of the central bank's credibility. He argued that the US central bank should have a "robust federal role" in overseeing stablecoins due to their potential to advance digital payment options, particularly since they are connected to the nation's sovereign currency.

In contrast, the SEC has consistently maintained that any cryptocurrency beyond Bitcoin, Litecoin, Bitcoin Cash, and Ethereum should be classified as securities. This stance has led to legal disputes involving major platforms such as Binance, Coinbase, and Ripple. SEC Chair Gary Gensler has expressed the need to grant the Commodity Futures Trading Commission (CFTC) greater authority over non-security tokens.

Specifically, Gensler stated, "In 2022, I think the CFTC could have greater authority. They currently do not have direct regulatory authorities over the underlying non-security tokens." He cited the example of TerraUSD, an algorithm-based cryptocurrency that deviated from its peg to the USD, as evidence of the risks associated with unregulated stablecoins.

WHY DO WE CARE ABOUT STABLECOINS AND HOW THEY'RE REGULATED?

The potential regulation of stablecoins is significant for several reasons. Stablecoins play a crucial role in facilitating DeFi and cryptocurrency trading. Their regulation will have a considerable impact on these domains, particularly affecting players in the ecosystem, including crypto exchanges and DeFi protocols. Berenberg pointed out that if US regulators target stablecoins like USDC, it could significantly impact the revenue of platforms like Coinbase.

In the first quarter of 2023, Coinbase generated $199 million in net revenue, with approximately 27% coming from interest income earned on USDC reserves. Additionally, the note from Berenberg suggested that Bitcoin, affirmed by the SEC as a commodity rather than an unregistered security, is likely to benefit from the regulatory crackdown.

There is a belief that the SEC's interest in regulating stablecoins stems from a desire to impact DeFi protocols indirectly. The ultimate classification of stablecoins as money, commodities, securities, or a combination thereof remains uncertain and will require legislative action down the road.

Ultimately the regulation will create a more inviting and hospitable environment for institutional business and will foster the growth that we all know is possible for the ecosystem.

REGULATING STABLECOINS IS INEVITABLE

Regardless of which regulatory body should oversee them, it is increasingly clear that regulation is inevitable for stablecoins. The writing is on the wall, and exchanges and DeFi protocols should be prepared for this eventuality. There should be no surprises here as the looming regulatory action will undoubtedly have a significant impact on DeFi protocols and decentralized exchanges.

However, as with much of the recent rulings and enforcement by the SEC and others, ultimately the regulation will create a more inviting and hospitable environment for institutional business and will foster the growth that we all know is possible for the ecosystem, mostly for participants who are willing and able to adapt to the regulatory landscape.

GLOBAL REGULATION

GLOBAL REGULATION

Article #1   *04.26.2023, The Street*

EU Approves MiCA – Unleashing New Era in Digital Asset Regulation

Europe creates new comprehensive regulatory regime to tame crypto while US uses patchwork of existing laws to enforce what it can

Last Thursday, April 20, the European Union Parliament voted 517 to 38 in favor of a new crypto licensing regime, called Markets in Crypto-Assets (MiCA). This is a major milestone, as the EU is the first major jurisdiction in the world to introduce a comprehensive crypto law. In the words of Stefan Berger, the lawmaker who led negotiations on the MiCA legislation, "the rules put the EU at the forefront of the token economy. The European crypto-asset industry has regulatory clarity that does not exist in countries like the US."

EUROPE PULLS AHEAD WITH MICA

MiCA is designed to bring more oversight to the cryptocurrency market, which has been operating in a largely unregulated manner. The new law will require crypto exchanges and digital wallet companies to get licensed in order to operate in the EU. Licensed companies will be able to offer regulated services and "passport" them across the EU. MiCA also requires stablecoin issuers to hold sufficient reserves.

The MiCA regulation has been in the making since it was first proposed in 2020. The rules will take effect 12 to 18 months after the legislation is published in the bloc's Official Journal, which is likely to happen in June. MiCA has been controversial with some industry players arguing that it will stifle innovation and investment in the sector.

According to a report from Reuters, the EU's approval of MiCA is part of a larger effort to regulate the digital economy. "Regulating the digital economy is a priority for the EU and today's adoption of MiCA represents a significant step towards creating a framework that will foster innovation while also ensuring that consumers and investors are protected," said Derville Rowland, the director general of financial conduct at the Central Bank of Ireland.

In addition to MiCA, the European Parliament also voted 529 to 29 in favor of another law known as the Transfer of Funds regulation. The law requires all crypto operators to identify their customers in order to fight money laundering. This is known as the "travel rule," which is already used in traditional finance, and will now cover transfers of crypto assets. Information on the source of the asset and its beneficiary will need to "travel" with the transaction and be stored on both sides of the transfer.

The Transfer of Funds regulation will also apply to transactions above €1000 from self-hosted wallets, a crypto-asset wallet address of a private user, when they interact with hosted wallets managed by crypto-assets service providers. The rules will not apply to person-to-person transfers conducted without a provider or among providers acting on their own behalf.

The body of legislation includes measures against market manipulation and against money laundering, terrorist financing, and other criminal activities. To counter money-laundering risks, the European Securities and Markets Authority (ESMA) will set up a public register for non-compliant crypto assets service providers that operate in the European Union without authorization.

GLOBAL CRYPTO COMMUNITY VOICES DISCONTENT WITH MICA

One of the biggest challenges of these laws is that they create major obstacles in the DeFi world, as current implementations of DeFi protocols and services do not support the identities of the source and destination being part of the transaction end-to-end. DeFi infrastructure and service providers, as well as operators, will have to adjust to EU regulation or avoid the EU market altogether.

While some in the crypto community are concerned about the impact of these new laws on innovation, others believe that clear and comprehensive crypto regulation is long overdue and is critical for the growth of the crypto assets ecosystem. According to a report from CoinDesk, "eliminating anonymity and requiring more accountability from operators on topics like crypto marketing, offering rules and requiring stablecoin issuers to keep ample reserves, will allow the industry to rebuild some of the trust that got eroded with scandals like Terra-Luna, FTX, and Bitfinex."

COMPARING THE EU'S MICA TO THE US SEC'S APPROACH

It's clear the EU is taking a more proactive and comprehensive approach to digital asset regulation. The SEC has been working on a number of initiatives to regulate digital assets, including the recent announcement of a working group focused on DeFi. However, the US still lacks a comprehensive federal regulatory framework for digital assets. Instead, the SEC has been relying on existing laws, such as the Securities Act of 1933 and the Investment Company Act of 1940, to regulate digital assets. This has resulted in a patchwork of state and federal regulations that have made it difficult for companies to navigate the legal landscape.

In the words of Maxine Waters, the chairwoman of the US House Financial Services Committee, "It is clear that the United States is falling behind other countries, particularly China, in the development of a comprehensive regulatory framework for digital assets." Waters has urged the SEC to take a more proactive approach to digital asset regulation and to work with Congress to develop comprehensive legislation that provides regulatory clarity and consumer protection.

MY TAKE ON MICA AND BEYOND

Despite the short-term pain, and to the dismay of crypto purists, I believe the EU's MiCA regulation represents a major milestone in the regulation of the cryptocurrency market. While some in the industry may be concerned about the impact on innovation and investment, the clear and comprehensive regulation is long overdue and is critical for the growth of the crypto assets ecosystem. The US and other major jurisdictions should take note of the EU's approach and work to create their own comprehensive regulatory frameworks for digital assets.

GLOBAL REGULATION

Article #2   *04.19.2022, The Street*

Japan's Collectivist Approach to Digital Securities is a Model for Rest of Us

Japan is proving that building and regulating the new digital economy may take more collaboration and compromise than we'd like to admit

While we haven't heard a lot lately about the digital securities ecosystem in Japan, the country is home to a thriving and inclusive market that isn't necessarily getting the credit it deserves. Japan's digital security market is interesting to watch for several reasons:

- Japan's Capital Markets is the 3rd largest worldwide after the US and the EU, and the largest in Asia, based on a recent SIFMA "Capital Markets Fact Book."

- Japan was one of the first countries to normalize cryptocurrencies making it ripe for increased participation and mass adoption of digital assets.

- Japan's equities market is structured differently than the US market. The US private offering securities market is very large, reaching an all-time high market value of $9.8 trillion. In contrast, Japan's private offering securities market is almost nonexistent. Most of the securities in the Japanese market are listed securities, unlike the US where digital securities started evolving with the private offering securities, the Japanese market has taken a different path. Evolution has occurred with and through some of the largest players in the market: Nomura Securities, MUFG, SBI, and SMTB.

JAPAN'S CULTURAL NORMS ARE A MAJOR FACTOR IN DIGITAL ECONOMY REGULATION

Unlike the US, which requires a top-down approach to regulation where companies generally wait for word from Washington on regulatory matters and frameworks, Japan is quite different. The country's tradition of collectivism drive's even its corporate culture, where compromise for the good of all is a means to a mutually beneficial end for all. You can see this in real time with Japan's approach to regulation in the digital economy.

In May 2020, the regulatory framework was officially defined by Japan for its ongoing financial technology and innovation efforts. Originally, a consortium of over 30 of the largest players in the market, broker dealers, investment banks, issuers, and large institutional investors, was formed to collectively develop industry standards and protocols for use of security tokens across the industry. Additionally, JSTOA (Japan Security Token Offering Association), the self-regulating body which is operated by its members, has offered guidelines for firms engaged in blockchain and crypto-related activities.

Basically, Japan's largest corporate entities in the blockchain and tokenization space are working together to determine the best regulatory framework, presenting those ideas to Japan's regulatory body for approval, and moving forward in a collective manner in implementation and execution of those frameworks. While this approach may not work in the US, it's driving Japan's digital economy forward with confidence and certainty.

You can see Japan's "corporate collectivism" in action as the country tries to persuade the global community to quickly and effectively regulate digital currencies as their use to skirt sanctions in Russia grows. In fact, a senior official from the Bank of Japan (JOP) communicated to the G7 nations that, "a sense of urgency is paramount if the G7 nations are to effectively coordinate regulation of cryptocurrencies and digital assets, as the current regulations do not fully consider their growing adoption and proliferation throughout the world."

It's in that vein of strategic coordination and collaboration that Japan may be an unlikely leader in the global effort to find effective and lasting crypto and digital asset regulations that work on a global scale and not just for an elite few.

NOTABLE DIGITAL SECURITY PROJECTS FAST-TRACKING IN JAPAN

In addition to establishing itself as a global leader in regulating the digital economy, Japan is also making major breakthroughs in other aspects of the blockchain and tokenization ecosystem.

In fact, Nomura Research Institute (NRI), published a report in late 2021 about the growing Security Token Offerings (STO) market potential in Japan, where the author of the report and Senior Researcher Kadai Sato stated in summary, "an increasingly wide variety of financial products are being issued on blockchains through security token offerings (STOs). The corporate bond market is expected to see widespread issuance of bonds for retail investors and bonds and bondholder perks through STOs. In the real estate securitization space, recent legislation has opened a path to eliminate legal impediments to STOs. The state is set for real estate security tokens' rollout."

There are a number of tokenized real estate developments in Japan, with the motivation for using security tokens to facilitate easier ownership registration and transfer. For example, Securitize Japan recently announced a partnership with Phillip Securities Japan to tokenize real estate. The company also launched a Japanese real estate investment platform using digital securities in collaboration with LIFULL to promote real estate crowdfunding using blockchain.

Another breakthrough in the tokenization of Japan's real estate market is the news Tokai Tokyo received a license from the Japanese regulator, the Financial Services Agency (FSA), allowing them to deal in digital securities. Tokai Tokyo will now partner with ADDX, the global private market investment platform, on security token issuances by Japanese real estate companies and banks. Additionally, Japanese investors will be able to trade the digital securities on the ADDX secondary exchange through Tokai Tokyo.

It's not just Japan's real estate market that's making exciting moves in the tokenization market. One of the largest retailers in the country is jumping in per the recent joint announcement by Nomura, Marui Group, the Japan-based multinational retail company, and Securitize to issue digital securities backed by a one-year corporate bond. Marui is working collaboratively with Nomura, as its financial advisory, while using Securitize's digital security issuance platform to enable issuers to identify investors, offer non-monetary interest payments, and sell corporate bonds to specific investor groups. The deal aims to raise a total of about 1.4 billion yen, 100 million of which will be issued as digital securities and is available for Epos Card members under the Marui Group.

AS JAPAN GOES, SO GOES THE MARKET

Japan isn't interested in doing anything just for attention's sake. It's humble, intentional, and collectivist cultural practices are guiding its business and tech leaders to make sound decisions that benefit its economy, its private sector, and its people. In the midst of the uncertainty that exists globally, especially with regards to digital asset regulation, we've never needed an "adult in the room" like we do now. Could Japan be that adult?

Article #3   *10.18.2021, The Street*

The OCC Officially Recognizes the Critical and Permanent Role of Blockchain in Banking

It's the first time the OCC refers to Distributed Ledger Technology (DLT) it in its Operating Plan and it's a really big deal

The Office of the Comptroller of the Currency (OCC), the bureau within the United States Department of the Treasury that regulates and supervises all national banks, thrift institutions, federally licensed branches, and agencies of foreign banks in the United States, refers to crypto in its recently published Bank Supervision Operating Plan. This is very significant because, after three years of extensive exploration of the crypto ecosystem, it is the first time the OCC refers to the term in its Operating Plan.

No less significant is the OCC's reference to Distributed Ledger Technology (DLT) and its adoption by banks. In its interpretive letter 1174, from January 2021, the OCC endorsed the integration of DLT with existing banking operations including the deployment of stablecoins and extension of banks' payments related activities. According to the OCC's latest plan, the regulator will "identify banks that are implementing significant changes in their operations using new technological innovations...[and] evaluate the appropriateness of the governance processes when banks undertake significant changes."

This is noteworthy for a couple of reasons. First, it is a recognition that many banks, along with a slew of other financial institutions, are adopting DLT as a technology enabling better processes. Simply put, financial institutions are moving past the exploratory phase of DLT and are now actually implementing the technology into their operations.

Secondly, the OCC is declaring its intent to explore and define appropriate governance processes for banks to deploy when such changes are implemented. In other words, the OCC is defining its intent to regulate how such changes should take place.

While much of the media hype focuses on crypto and other DLT-based technology and tools, the velocity at which the infrastructure and "under-the-hood" adoption of DLT by mainstream financial institutions gets missed in the news cycles. So, why are banks adopting DLT and how quickly is that adoption advancing?

DLT (A.K.A. BLOCKCHAIN) WILL MAKE BANKING BETTER

DLT can significantly simplify and speed up processes, improve customer experience, reduce risk, and increase inclusion. Here are some examples:

- **Financial inclusion:** There are about 1.7 billion adults that are reported to be unbanked globally. Advanced technologies built on DLT can offer more affordable and scalable solutions to increase financial inclusion. DLT has the ability to truly democratize the banking industry globally.

- **Payment settlement and clearance:** Blockchain can enable banks to settle transactions directly and keep track of them better than traditional methods such as SWIFT. A standard bank transfer takes a few days to settle due to the complexity of the current financial system. International money transfer is slow and expensive. A basic bank transfer must pass through a complex chain of intermediaries, such as custodial services, before reaching its destination. Bank accounts must also be reconciled across the global financial system, which consists of a huge network of funds, asset managers, dealers, and other businesses. A blockchain based system can facilitate immediate and low-cost transaction settlement.

- **Lending:** Some banks have formed syndicates to use DLT for syndicated lending. Lending can therefore take place with fewer intermediaries, while business processes can be simplified. Execution can be automated with smart contracts and risk and costs are dramatically reduced.

- **Identity services and enhanced security:** The immutability of a distributed ledger provides a new level of security. It is challenging to establish a single customer view across different jurisdictions and business lines. With mutualized data management, DLT allows permitted parties to share data securely and in real time, which could address challenges of Know Your Customer (KYC) and Anti Money Laundering (AML).

The themes are clear. DLT injected into the banking and financial ecosystem is an equalizer, a simplifier, and a fortifier. Given the transformational potential of DLT, why don't we witness faster adoption?

DLT adoption in the banking industry is already a reality. A research report from Bank of America published in February shows that 21% of the banks they cover have already incorporated blockchain technology into their businesses in some form. JPMorgan, Citi, Wells Fargo, US Bancorp, PNC, Fifth Third Bank, and Signature Bank are among the many banks that are already using DLT blockchain, while many more intend to implement the technology.

However, before adoption meets critical mass,
some challenges still need to be addressed:

- **Integration:** Banks and other financial institutions
  need to discover how to integrate the new technology
  with existing systems and business processes, as well
  as acquire the proper expertise to operate them.

- **Standards:** To realize its full potential, DLT requires
  widespread collaboration and agreement of common standards.
  Although banks have formed DLT syndicates for specific
  purposes, the real benefit will derive from the "network
  effect" of widespread adoption. All of this takes some time.

- **Legal:** Further clarity and guidance is needed from
  regulators on issues like ownership and jurisdiction
  of DLT data and transactions, as well as governance,
  reporting, transparency, etc. Regulators are beginning to
  provide more guidance related to DLT adoption, including
  the OCC, a trend that is expected to accelerate.

As these challenges are being addressed, the pace of adoption
and the number of traditional banks and investment banks
adopting DLT will increase dramatically. They understand that
DLT/blockchain is not just a techie fad for the crypto crowd.
They know that in order to stay ahead of their competition,
the world's leading financial institutions must embrace the
evolution of their industry, which now requires the use of DLT.

GEOPOLITICS AND THE NEW DIGITAL ECONOMY

Ch. 10
The Blockchain Arms Race

INTRODUCTION

In an age where headlines seem more like sci-fi excerpts and economies transition with a pace akin to Moore's Law, the world is undergoing transformations both subtle and seismic. I'd argue that among these dynamics, the confluence of geopolitics and the burgeoning digital economy stands out most prominently.

The historical echoes are palpable. Not since the monumental Bretton Woods agreement of 1944, which crowned the USD as the world's reserve currency and birthed institutions like the IMF and World Bank, have we teetered so close to a tectonic shift in the global financial order. The aftermath of World War II became the bedrock for that previous transformation. Today, as the Russia-Ukraine crisis continues to unfold, it reminds us that events of this magnitude aren't confined within geographical borders but ripple outward, influencing spheres beyond immediate contention. Much like how the cataclysm of the mid-20th century paved the way for systemic change, we are witnessing the precursors to another potential overhaul, one that's digitally charged and accelerating at an unprecedented rate.

As America increasingly pulls away from its traditionally assertive role on the global stage—be it in conflict resolutions or other world affairs—the European Union has asserted itself more. Elsewhere, China's economic footprint deepens across Asia, Africa, parts of Europe, and the Middle East, even as tensions simmer with the US. The ramifications of the Russia-Ukraine conflict echo, pulling the world into an economic quagmire, and Russia's subsequent alignment with China, India, and Iran, partly a strategy to sidestep crippling sanctions, reshapes trade dynamics.

Yet, what is truly fascinating isn't just the geopolitical dance itself, but its intricate choreography with the digital realm. The reverberations of China's closures, and later its reopening amidst the pandemic, and the global financial disarray

As America increasingly pulls away from its traditionally assertive role on the global stage— be it in conflict resolutions or other world affairs—the European Union has asserted itself more.

post-2022, are hard to overlook. The burgeoning digital economy isn't just a passive observer in this landscape; it's both a catalyst and beneficiary. The role of blockchain and digital innovations are inextricable with the emerging new world order. The Fourth Industrial Revolution, fresh trading alliances and shifts in world order, are all tethered to the digital realm. If money indeed makes the world go 'round, then the digital economy is the new centrifugal force.

If one were to gaze into the proverbial crystal ball, certain trends seem evident. China will likely continue to spearhead Central Bank Digital Currency (CBDC) advancements, while the EU, ever the regulatory trendsetter, will pave the way in crypto regulation and mainstreaming. The US, I predict, might remain somewhat inert on the digital currency frontier, at least for the foreseeable future. But, as with all prophecies, only time will confirm or confound these musings. Whatever the future holds, the symbiotic dance of geopolitics and the digital economy will undoubtedly keep us riveted.

THE BLOCKCHAIN ARMS RACE

THE BLOCKCHAIN ARMS RACE

Article #1   *01.21.2021, The Street*

A New Global Arms Race in Digital Finance is Heating Up

Today, we're on the precipice of what could be the largest transformational period in global history. With the first Industrial Revolution, new technologies like assembly lines, factories, and transportation fundamentally changed society. This time, instead of cogwheels doing the work, blockchain-based digitalization will continue to drive transactions. Specifically, this latest phase of progress has its sights set on a massive industry ripe for disruption: finance.

Digital finance and the monetary system are leveraging decentralized blockchain technology to modernize financial markets. Dominant players in these systems include the world's biggest financial institutions and global central banks.

THE RISE OF DIGITAL CURRENCIES AND CBDCS

As tokenization is an inevitable trend, Central Bank Digital Currencies (CBDC) are surging in adoption, since they are simply one kind of a more generalized digital asset, albeit one that is bound to risk-free central bank money. The global rivalry in digital currencies is heating up as central banks from an increasingly wider swath of countries, including China, Thailand, the EU, UK, US, and Australia, explore potential use-cases for tokenized money.

CBDC is the first place where we see top-down adoption of Distributed Ledger Technology (DLT) from central banks and governments. The adoption of CBDCs will drive significant DLT ecosystem innovation and development that will impact financial organizations. The widespread adoption of DLT will extend beyond finance to other industry verticals like security, supply chains, healthcare, retail, and ecommerce.

CBDCs will certainly make payments, settlement of deals, and trading simpler, especially when it comes to global trade. It will also potentially change the role current institutions are playing regarding money and payments. CBDC implementation will possibly make cross border payments simpler and much cheaper. One result will be the enablement of micropayments, allowing small businesses to be more competitive, and eliminate the need for aggregators in order to make them economically viable, resulting in a different distribution of value.

Winners and losers are made from historic periods of societal shifts and advancements. The US was obviously a dominant force during the first revolution. As the world embarks on a new transformational journey, who is driving it? The answer to this question is very complex and currently unclear, but there is an intense financial technology "arms race" brewing between the world's superpowers for dominance in digital finance infrastructure and technology, spurring short-term competitive innovation with critical long-term implications.

"I believe that if America does not lead innovation in the digital currency and payments area, others will," said David Marcus, head of Diem, the cryptocurrency project founded out of Facebook, in a statement to the US Senate Committee on Banking, Housing, and Urban Affairs.

Huw van Steenis of UBS said there will be a "three-horse race" around the future of money with private tokens and CBDCs developing in parallel with efforts to improve the current system. The implications of winning or losing the digital finance "arms race" are massive and far-reaching.

During the US and USSR space race, NASA harnessed tremendous intellectual and technical capital to enable the moon landing and further space exploration, leading to a variety of spinoff inventions, from global positioning systems (GPS) to advances in flight technology to Velcro and even freeze-dried food. In the same way, blockchain-based digital finance technology is a means to the end of greater technological sophistication.

THE THREE LEADERS IN THE DIGITAL CURRENCY ARMS RACE

More than 80% of the world's central banks are exploring their own versions of digital currencies, but it's China, the US, and the EU that have the resources, technology, and infrastructure to determine the future of the digital economy. A major event within the financial world started in early 2020: the World Economic Forum in Davos, where the WEF released a toolkit for policymakers regarding the creation of CBDCs.

CHINA

China is currently testing its digital yuan with a feature allowing people to send money to each other by simply touching their smartphones together. This particular effort is just one of many digital currency trials China is conducting across the country. These coordinated activities, in combination with their leadership in the crypto ecosystem, accounting for nearly 90% of trading volumes and hosting two-thirds of bitcoin mining operations, is giving China somewhat of an advantage.

Leveraging first-mover advantage, China has ambitious plans to leverage US innovation and its own digital currency to someday dominate other world currencies. As a purely aspirational endeavor, the jury is still out on whether China can actually achieve this goal.

Regardless, China is creating a significant advantage in this global race on CBDCs by investing in the technology and experimenting at a very fast pace. Even in the most isolated and underdeveloped areas, most people already use electronic forms of payment, like WeChat Pay, almost exclusively.

China has made the digital yuan a public priority, and it has an ambitious goal of competing with the US dollar by creating a digital Asian alternative. China will be able to track and control the movement of money in and out of the country, which is much easier to do with a digital yuan. Given its political structure, China is able to move faster than the US or Europe in implementing such changes.

EUROPE

Europe is in a strong position to create a CBDC, but unlike attempts by smaller, individual countries like Sweden, the size and scale of an EU digital currency would be sustainable long-term and could compete at scale. The European Central Bank isdiscussing launching a consideration phase for a digital euro this year and launching a digital euro is at least a five-year plan.

UNITED STATES

The US continues to lead in the innovation, regulation, and implementation of blockchain-based digital securities, banking, payments, insurance, etc., but may not be as far along as others when it comes to CBDCs. Over the last decade, American innovators have built compelling innovations in blockchain, digital currency, and cryptocurrency aimed at revolutionizing finance and creating new US tech superstars. And, as these technologies advance, they're innovating industries beyond just finance, including retail, cybersecurity, supply chain management, and many more.

Tech leaders in the space like Securitize are paving the way for widespread adoption and access to liquidity by building the mechanisms for the industry to take hold. The benefits of CBDCs will propel the US implementation of a digital dollar. The release of CBDC is not just a technical change, but it's also the revamp of a financial system centuries old. US policymakers should continue to foster US leadership in technological financial innovation and ensure that the American people enjoy its benefits first.

"The United States usually wins when we unleash the power of our innovative, dynamic private sector, with the government setting the rules rather than building the products," said Brian Brooks, former acting Comptroller of the Currency at the US Treasury Department. "But either way, given the intense focus of other countries in this area, let me say that because of the important role of the US dollar, we need the United States to step forward in this field."

THE FUTURE OF FINANCE

What happens with CBDCs will have far-reaching implications on the future of digital finance, including cryptocurrency and digital securities. Much like the space race didn't just put a man on the moon, but also catapulted the invention of important ancillary technologies, CBDC and DLT adoption will influence the forward-moving progress of every industry. There will be an exponential amount of innovations resulting from this digital finance arms race we don't yet know. The possibilities are endless and we're just at the starting line.

Whoever leads this race and determines the outcome of its infrastructure and operation will most certainly gain a significant advantage and may have the possibility to spearhead many of the other innovations that come from this technology. The conversation of this tech competition between countries was even brought to the US Senate. China is far ahead in implementing real digital finance and currency programs as we speak, giving them a first-mover advantage.

The US and its regulatory bodies are still the gold standard and will ultimately set the pace and the rules. US-based innovators continue to roll out viable solutions. But which powerhouse will roll out the standard solutions first to control the space and our digital economic destiny?

THE BLOCKCHAIN ARMS RACE

Article #2   *09.30.202, The Street*

El Savador's Bitcoin Bet: An Interesting Experiment or Visionary Leap Forward?

Bitcoin is now a legal tender in El Salvador.
Will it be a future template for success
or a mistake others will learn from?

Earlier this month, Bitcoin became a legal tender in El Salvador, despite warnings from the International Monetary Fund (IMF) against making it a national currency. The first few days were certainly rocky, with protests in the capital, glitches with a government-backed Bitcoin app, and a 15% dip in the cryptocurrency's value. However, according to a Twitter post by El Salvador's president, Nayib Bukele, as many as 2.1 million users, a sizable portion of El Salvador's population, are using the Chivo wallet, the country's official wallet dedicated to Bitcoin-related transactions. If this is factual, it would mean that, to date, the country has realized more than $63 million in Bitcoin transactions in less than a month.

Some of the immediate questions come to mind: Why is El Salvador doing this? Can Bitcoin actually be used by Salvadorans? What countries are likely to follow suit? And, what are the potential implications on the Bitcoin market and on the crypto ecosystem in general?

WHY ARE THEY DOING IT?

With this move, the government plans to boost El Salvador's economy, which for years has experienced low levels of economic growth. Most of the country's population does not have a bank account and almost a quarter of the GDP comes from remittances sent from the large ex-pat community working abroad, benefitting around 360,000 households.

One of the main reasons touted for declaring Bitcoin as a legal tender in El Salvador is exactly this—remittances-based portion of El Salvador's GDP—and the hope to save a large amount of fees paid for those remittances today.

CAN BITCOIN REALLY BE USED BY SALVADORANS?

It is true that Bitcoin is established already as a store of value and a tradable asset, but can it be used for small transactions relating to daily life in El Salvador? Probably not in its native form. Bitcoin is not built for micro transactions, and transaction processing pace and fees will make it impractical.

The Lightning Network and its likes may make it more feasible, at least in theory, to use Bitcoin as a method of payment. The Lightning Network adds another layer to the Bitcoin blockchain which allows users to settle transactions off the blockchain. This means that users of the network aren't constrained by the blocksize limit. Therefore, the transaction fees are much lower and are settled almost instantly.

In fact, The Lightning Network used in El Salvador and a video shared on Twitter showing a swift Bitcoin payment of a coffee through the scanning of a QR code in the coastal area of El Tunco in El Salvador.

However, The Lightening Network is not without issues. It is unclear if such solution can be successfully implemented across El Salvador and whether or not the Salvadoran social experiment will yield the desired outcomes.

WHO IS NEXT?

The move by El Salvador was applauded by politicians in a number of Latin American countries, including Panama, Argentina, and Brazil. It seemed that Paraguay was vying to be next in line. This July, Paraguayan Congressman, Carlitos Rejala, was driving similar Bitcoin adoption in that country. Coming shortly after lawmakers in El Salvador had established bitcoin as legal tender, many in the space assumed this legislation would attempt to grant Bitcoin similar status in Paraguay.

However, that is not the case. While El Salvador's final bill was just a few pages of text representing easily the most favorable and accommodating Bitcoin legalese ever passed, the early draft of Paraguay's legislation is a different story. It defines Bitcoin as property rather than legal tender, which will require Bitcoin miners to obtain government licenses. Its aim is to drive the mining industry towards becoming 100% renewable energy-based, detailing sanctions and penalties for those who would violate its proposed rules, while including measures to protect cryptocurrency investors.

All-in-all, it seems that Paraguay's approach is less about day-to-day transactions and more about growing the local Bitcoin mining industry.

CAN OTHER DEVELOPING COUNTRIES FOLLOW EL SALVADOR AND POSSIBLY PARAGUAY?

Eight sovereign nations, Ecuador, El Salvador, Zimbabwe, Timor-Leste, Palau, Panama, the Marshall Islands, and Micronesia, use the US Dollar as their official currency. The British Virgin Islands and the British Turks and Caicos Islands also use the USD as an official currency of exchange. Many other countries use currencies with fixed exchange rates to the USD.

While dollarization was implemented to reduce currency risk and increase international investment and trade, these nations are effectively outsourcing their monetary policy to the US Federal Reserve. By doing so they offer the ability to influence their own economies by adjusting the money supply or exchange rate.

Could any of these countries consider implementing Bitcoin as a replacement to the USD dependency? Because of Bitcoin's price volatility, as well as issues related to the practicality of daily use by consumers for small transactions, it has been largely discounted by countries until recently. The case for seeking alternative monetary solutions other than the USD for developing countries is still a compelling one. However, the jury is still out on whether or not Bitcoin is the answer. The outcome will depend on how the story unfolds in El Salvador.

WHAT TO EXPECT?

If El Salvador invests the necessary efforts in developing an environment for Salvadorans to use Bitcoin as a legal tender, including the implementation of a set of tools (a.k.a. The Lightning Network) that provide practical, every day, simple to use payment methods, the country could potentially drive other development in the crypto world. This would create a myriad of opportunities to enhance the crypto user experience that still leaves much to be desired.

Regardless of the outcomes, El Salvador will be a learning experience for other countries with USD-dependent currency, offering many key learnings as to whether crypto can provide an alternative to the USD and, if so, what would be required to make it practical.

The move by El Salvador is likely to encourage more US investors to buy Bitcoin as investment, although it may be some time, if at all, before they can use it to buy a coffee themselves.

THE BLOCKCHAIN ARMS RACE

Article #3   *02.17.2022, The Street*

For the Beijing Olympics, Medal Leaders Reflect World CBDC Leaders

An update to the global CBDC race and how the international debut of the digital yuan at the Winter Games is pure Olympic Gold

As I'm writing this article, the medal count at the 2022 Beijing Olympics looks very much like the state of play, or should I say "state of race" in the world of Central Bank Digital Currencies (CBDCs), with the EU and China leading and the US trying to keep pace. The only deviation is Japan and other Asian countries, that have pulled ahead of the US in CBDC development and deployment but aren't doing so well when it comes to Olympic medals.

Regardless of medal count, the apparent winner in the "Global Arms Race of CBDCs" is China. They have successfully leveraged the world stage of sports to showcase the progress they've made with the digital yuan. China is using the Winter Olympics to not only test its CBDC, making it one of only three payment options for foreign athletes and visitors (along with cash and Visa cards), but to also solidify its leadership position in the digital finance ecosystem. In fact, according to the Chinese Central Bank, more than $315,000 in digital yuan have been used every day at the Winter Olympics.

However, don't discount the progress others have made. The EU, Japan, South Korea, and others continue to create positive momentum in a transparent and judicious manner. Unfortunately, the same cannot be said about the US effort to establish its own digital dollar. In fact, very little progress has been made. What does that mean for the US and its opponents in the race for CBDC gold?

CHINA

For more than a year, the digital yuan has been aggressively rolled out and tested with more than 260 million using it already, completing more than $13 billion in transactions according to the Beijing Financial Supervision Authority. Even more impressive is that China has gone beyond the metroplexes of Beijing and Shanghai experimenting with the CBDCs even in the most isolated and underdeveloped areas where most people are already using e-payment platforms like WeChat.

The result? A year after writing my initial "Global CBDC Arms Race" article, China is pulling further ahead, an advantage of most likely four or five years compared to other advanced economies.

EUROPEAN UNION

The European Union has made significant progress with its "five year plan" for a digital euro, but the planning, testing, and execution has been at a much slower and more calculated pace compared to China. Earlier this month, the European Commission, the executive branch of the European Union (EU), proposed a digital euro bill in 2023 that will support the European Central Bank's (ECB) test and deploy its own CBDC. The Commission's plans to move forward with a bill is the most definitive sign so far that a digital euro could become a reality in the coming years.

Adding to the region's headway, one of its financial hubs, Switzerland, is taking a lead. The Swiss National Bank, the Bank for International Settlements' Innovation Hub Swiss Centre, and the country's stock exchange, SIX, completed a joint experiment, dubbed Project Helvitia, to integrate a wholesale central bank digital currency (CBDC) for interbank transactions.

This successful effort involved five of the largest and most prominent banks globally including Citi, UBS, Goldman Sachs, Hypothekarbank Lenzburg, and Credit Suisse. This is a defining moment for CBDC infrastructure development showcasing that digital (DLT) finance and traditional banking can work seamlessly together.

ASIA: JAPAN, SOUTH KOREA

Much like the EU, Japan is moving towards a digital yen in a premeditated and cautious manner. While efforts are clearly underway to research, develop, and eventually test a Japanese CBDC, they're also aware that the underlying infrastructure needs to work for their people (i.e., data privacy), as well as interoperate with other CBDCs and digital assets (i.e., a digital dollar or digital euro), in order to be effective and useful.

With that said, individual Japanese firms, like Soramitsu, are making some moves. Most recently, the firm is researching the possibility of a CBDC working in four Pacific island states. The Oceana Project is part of a wider partnership effort with 10 Oceanic governments, that will evaluate the viability, usability, and security of CBDCs in the wholesale and retail environments.

But while Japan remains somewhat restrained, the Bank of Korea recently announced it had completed its first phase of CBDC trials in December of 2021. Wasting no time, the initial phase tested basic use-cases to confirm that the CBDC "performed normally." Well, it did. Therefore, the Korean Central Bank will be moving on to its next phase, which will implement functions like payments, personal data security, and other enhanced technologies.

RUSSIA

Even Russia is all in on CBDCs. The Bank of Russia revealed that it has already started a pilot for the digital ruble, with three banks involved in the trial now and nine more joining soon. Similar to China, Russia has banned cryptocurrency, making way for a full-steam-ahead approach to a CBDC. The results of the digital ruble pilot will be announced later this year, with a plan for deployment accompanying it. However, based on their willingness to bypass rules and norms in the Olympic games (i.e., Russia's doping problem), it will be difficult for the international community to believe what Russia says is actually reality.

UNITED STATES

There's no denying that the US continues to lead in the innovation, regulation, and implementation of blockchain-based digital securities, banking, payments, insurance, etc. Yet, with all of this innovation, talent, and pure momentum at play, the US is far behind when it comes to CBDCs.

Let's be honest. The digital yuan's success at the Olympics, the EU's phased approach, and even the Oceania Project are all futile efforts in part because none of them have what they actually need to make their CBDC rollouts successful: the backing of the US dollar. The dollar is still the most redeemable currency for facilitation of global commerce and continues to have the trust and confidence of the world. Therefore, it's in the country's best interest to preserve the dollar's status as the world's reserve currency by transitioning it to a global standard-setting CBDC.

But, while the US has the gold standard in currency (literally), the powers that be are not using it to their advantage to take a more prominent leadership role in the CBCD race. According to a recent Fed report on the pros and cons of a digital dollar, no one is in any particular rush to act. Specifically, the Fed said, "it's not doing anything without clear support from Congress and the White House, ideally in the form of a specific authorizing law." With the way the US government is currently working or not, major decisions on

The EU, Japan, South Korea, and others continue to create positive momentum in a transparent and judicious manner. Unfortunately, the same cannot be said about the US effort to establish its own digital dollar.

a "highly significant innovation in American money" and its financial system are not likely to happen any time soon.

The release of CBDC is not just a technical change, but it's also the revamp of a financial system that is centuries old. It's always cumbersome to create that kind of foundational change, but US policymakers should continue to foster leadership in technological financial innovation and ensure that the American people enjoy its benefits first. We can't afford a silver or bronze in this competition.

THE ONGOING RACE FOR CBDC GOLD

The "three horse race" I mentioned in my previous article about CBDCs is no longer accurate. It's now a multi-horse race, with one very important horse walking the track.

As other countries, including many not mentioned, continue to roll out pilots and trials of their own CBDCs, the US and its modest pursuit of the digital dollar is falling further behind. If this trend continues, it may be too late to regain what's been lost.

American entrepreneurs and technologists have built compelling innovations in blockchain, digital currency, and cryptocurrency aimed at revolutionizing finance and creating new US tech superstars. It's up to us to leverage this significant groundwork and our prominence in the development of the underlying infrastructure of the digital economy to once again be the standard for the rest of the world.

THE BLOCKCHAIN ARMS RACE

Article #4   *03.02.2022, The Street*

What the War in Ukraine is Teaching Us About Crypto

As the war in Ukraine rages on, crypto's role in the conflict is becoming more significant for the good and the bad.

As the largest land war on European soil since World War II continues to progress, crypto's role in the conflict is becoming more significant. With many already noting that crypto may be the new "conflict currency," the digital asset is being used for good, as well as for bad. Yet, crypto is defying traditional safe-haven assets like gold, making moves that more closely mirror the equity markets than the commodity markets. In fact, cryptocurrency tumbled alongside global equity markets initially on news of the invasion but have rebounded since. Bitcoin (BTC) fell to below \$35,000 when Russian forces entered Ukraine but has since risen about 25%.

WHAT DOES ALL OF THIS TELL US ABOUT CRYPTO AND ITS ROLE IN BOTH THE MODERN ECONOMY AND IN MODERN WARFARE?

THE GOOD:

The unprovoked Russian invasion of Ukraine has shocked the entire world and has offset the global order that has existed for decades. Citizens from all over the world have been moved to help the people of Ukraine in any way they can. Additionally, Ukrainians themselves have seen their economic well-being crumble as businesses close and workers flee or fight.

Many Ukrainians have turned to crypto to avoid the obvious problems with carrying large amounts of cash and/ or trying to access bank accounts locally or abroad.

Specifically, Ukrainian refugees are using crypto so they can convert it into fiat currency in a new country. While still volatile, this new digital asset may help thousands of Ukrainians survive financially for the duration of the conflict.

Crypto is also being used as another force for good in the form of donations. Crypto users all around the world have donated more than $35 million since the start of the invasion, according to Elliptic, a blockchain analytics firm, with at least $14 million already disbursed to Ukrainian citizens and the military. The first fund leading the crypto-support charge is The Crypto Fund of Ukraine, created with the help of Kuna, the Kyiv-based crypto exchange. Announced in a tweet from Ukraine's official Twitter account, the Crypto Fund of Ukraine is helping fund food, gas, medical supplies, and other necessities for civilian populations. The second fund is a wallet, coordinated by the Ministry of Digital Transformation, which is helping fund the military.

Additionally, $6.5 million in proceeds from a Ukrainian flag NFT was auctioned off by the Ethereum-based group Ukraine DAO making it the 10th most expensive NFT ever sold.

THE BAD:

The brazen attack by Russia has galvanized world leaders of NATO countries and beyond to take swift and decisive economic action against the Russian government, its oligarchy, and its citizens. So, at the same time the lives of millions of Ukrainians are in turmoil, so is the Russian economy, worrying many that crypto could be seen as a safe haven asset and a potential sanction evasion tool.

The sanctions imposed by the United States, European Union, United Kingdom, and other countries are some of the harshest ever targeting Russia's central bank to freeze the country's war chest. While there has been some activity to bypass sanctions, or mitigate their impact by using crypto, by and large, it just isn't as widespread as some were predicting. That's because crypto transactions can be traced. Crypto wallets are stored on the public blockchain, which makes sanctioned wallets easily identifiable. Additionally, most crypto exchanges have Know-Your-Customer (KYC) and Anti-Money Laundering (AML) protocols in place. And let's not forget, at some point any sanctioned Russian wallets will have to transfer its crypto to a fiat currency sounding off alarms everywhere.

Most recently, the US has put pressure on crypto exchanges to monitor movements and even initiate their own "soft sanctions" by any wallets in question, a request that has been met with pushback by the crypto community and leaders of those exchanges. However, the EU took further steps by announcing it will be, "taking measures, in particular on cryptocurrencies or crypto assets, which should not be used to circumvent the financial sanctions." France's finance minister, Bruno Le Maire, and Germany's finance minister, Christian Lindner, agreed that EU leaders should, "take steps to prevent listed individuals and institutions from switching to unregulated crypto assets."

The question remains, how can any bans on crypto movements by even the wealthiest Russians be enforced? Crypto is decentralized and based on anonymity, so even with some measures in place to thwart illicit activity, there will be Russians that generate income using crypto during the conflict. How much? Only time and crypto price movements will tell, but it will not be enough to save the Russian economy.

THE TRUTH:

By focusing on cryptocurrencies during this chaotic time, the digital finance community and the markets are learning more and more about the behavior of these digital assets. While things continue to evolve at a rapid pace, it's clear what cryptocurrencies are and what they are not:

CRYPTOCURRENCIES ARE:

- A force for good creating a new opportunity for people and entities to come together quickly and seamlessly to help fund and support a cause.

- An investable financial asset, but not necessarily a "safe-haven" asset because of its volatility.

- A digital currency that may be a "lesser evil" than a tumbling sovereign currency, which can make it desirable during times of uncertainty.

CRYPTOCURRENCIES ARE NOT:

- A commodity like gold. Crypto's behavior and its swings in value mirror the stock market more than anything else.

- A systemic tool for Russians to sidestep global sanctions on a mass scale.

- Going to replace fiat currencies, including the Ruble, but may play a bigger role in the economies of struggling and emerging nations around the globe.

The question remains, how can any bans on crypto movements by even the wealthiest Russians be enforced?

As a community of digital finance participants, let's collectively work to make cryptocurrencies and other digital assets a force for good for Ukraine and for the world moving forward. Behind the stories about crypto's role in the war in Ukraine as a "conflict currency," let's remember there are real people with lives and livelihoods at stake. While hoping for a quick resolution in Ukraine, my hope is also that crypto's prominence in this particular conflict will create progress that impacts infrastructure, technology, and regulatory framework development well beyond this point in history. Let's use this moment to make things better.

THE BLOCKCHAIN ARMS RACE

Article #5   *03.25.2022, The Street*

Is the War in Ukraine Accelerating Global Digital Economy Adoption?

Just as the pandemic rapidly accelerated digital transformation, so is the geopolitical crisis in Ukraine, fast-tracking global use of digital assets.

It seems that we're living through one historic and global crisis after another. Our universal "pause from history" seems to be over, with both natural and man-made forces creating epic challenges that are determining a new world order as we speak. While no one can predict the future, we can look to the past and be sure that challenging times accelerate innovation and disruption at mass scale.

Take the Coronavirus pandemic. In just one year, after the start of the pandemic, almost every aspect of our professional and personal lives was impacted by rapid digital transformation. A full 85 percent of CEOs indicated that their organizations had significantly accelerated digital transformation during the COVID-19 crisis. But, it's not just companies. From remote working via video conferencing, to grocery delivery, our ability to adapt and to adopt a digital-first way of life increased with little proof that we'll ever go back to the "old way of doing things."

The same is true for the geopolitical crisis that we're facing now, which started with the Russian invasion of Ukraine. We're already seeing clues that this global catastrophe is accelerating the implementation and adoption of digital assets within a greater digital economy. Whether its new use-cases for crypto or increased fervor around Central Bank Digital Currency (CBDCs), countries large and small and from regions around the world are leveraging digital assets during uncertain times.

In fact, in a recent letter to shareholders, Larry Fink, CEO of Black Rock, indicated that the Russia/Ukraine conflict will fast-track the adoption of digital currencies and payment tools to, "help bring down costs of cross-border payments, for example when expatriate workers send earnings back to their families." Fink also went on to say that the current geopolitical conflict, "will push countries to reassess currency dependencies and look to means of payments that can bring down the costs of cross-border transactions." Fink also acknowledged that his firm is experiencing growing interest from clients around digital currencies, something that has only increased since the Ukraine crisis began.

With the increased interest in large-scale adoption of digital assets, comes new insight about how these assets behave and the psychology around why people are flocking to them. Crypto is defying traditional safe-haven assets like gold making moves that more closely mirror the equity markets than the commodity markets.

Beyond Ukraine, the sustained volatility of fiat currencies of countries like El Salvador, Paraguay, Nigeria, and many others, make digital assets like crypto and stablecoins more attractive.

Aforementioned geopolitical factors combined with substantial progress in overall digital economy infrastructure development, technology innovation, and user experience, has created the perfect storm for accelerated adoption and use around the world.

CRYPTO IN UKRAINE

Recently, Ukraine signed a law that will create a legal framework for digital assets. Among other things, that law is expected to help businesses manage crypto donations more effectively. Ukraine's expedited regulatory actions and its efficient use of crypto funds is not happening in a vacuum. In fact, this pioneering activity is being noticed throughout the world amplifying the many use-cases of digital finance tools and increasing the public's comfort level in leveraging them in a variety of ways.

RUSSIA ACCEPTS CRYPTO FOR OIL

At the same time Ukraine is demonstrating the use of digital currencies to help their people and the defense of their nation, Russia just took a major step to leverage these assets as well, some would argue a nefarious one. In a recent and sizable turn of events, a report from Russian news agency, RBC, revealed that Russia will now accept Bitcoin as payment for their oil. Pavel Zavalny, Chairman of the State Duma Committee on Energy, stated that Russia will let "ally" countries trade Russian energy resources with their local currencies or in cryptocurrency.

Whether it's a shock to some that Russia would take this bold step to evade sanctions, or an inevitability by others who knew this move from Putin was coming, the point in all of it is that digital currencies are being thrust onto the international stage in new ways. Whether Russia's use of crypto is good or bad is irrelevant. Their willingness to put Bitcoin to use in global trade has opened the door for others in the international community to use digital assets as payment mechanisms on a broad scale. This is a new chapter in the digital economy, accelerated by conflict and chaos.

CHINA'S DIGITAL YUAN QUESTION

China became the world's first major economy to pilot a digital currency in April 2020, aiming for widespread domestic use of the e-CNY, or digital yuan this year and beyond. It currently has more than a hundred million individual users and billions of yuan in transactions, according to the IMF. Plus, with China's banning of all cryptocurrency transactions, it's clear that the country is totally focused on the digital yuan's success and dominance.

There's no doubt that China wants to expand the digital yuan's global influence, but how far are they willing to go? Could the geopolitical unrest in Russia offer China an opportunity to compete with the US dollar? Could the stiff sanctions on Russia imposed by the United States, European Union, United Kingdom, and others give China an opening to establish digital finance supremacy? These questions will have answers sooner than we think.

CBDCS AS EFFICIENT MONEY

"The history of money is entering a new chapter," said Kristalina Georgieva, IMF Managing Director. "Countries are seeking to preserve key aspects of their traditional monetary and financial systems, while experimenting with new digital forms of money."

This is especially true in countries that are either experiencing recent unrest, or have been dealing with decades of corruption, stagnation, and poor economic conditions.

- Nigeria became the first country in Africa to launch a CBDC last October. The eNaira is stored in a digital wallet and can be used for contactless in-store payments, as well as for transferring money.

- The seven countries that make up the Eastern Caribbean Union, Antigua and Barbuda, Dominica, Grenada, Montserrat, St. Kitts and Nevis, Saint Lucia, St. Vincent, and the Grenadines, have created a form of digital currency to speed transactions and serve people without bank accounts.

The move towards CBDCs continues to gain momentum, especially now as Central Banks look to bolster their economy in uncertain times. All told, around 100 countries are exploring CBDCs at one level or another. Some researching, some testing, and a few, like China, already distributing CBDC to

Ukraine is demonstrating the use of digital currencies to help their people and the defense of their nation,

the public. However, we will see these programs pick up speed to unprecedented levels over the next few months and years.

The Ukraine crisis has only sharpened the vision and hastened the rollout of digital asset programs in many countries around the world. The war is turning out to be the catalyst for action in the new digital economy.

THE EVOLUTION OF THE DIGITAL ECONOMY

Ch. 11
A Look Back at
Forward-Looking Predictions

INTRODUCTION

In the fast-paced, ever-evolving world of digital innovation, the past three years have felt like a whirlwind. Capturing the zeitgeist of these moments isn't just about being a bystander; it's about living and breathing the changes as they unfurl. The articles from this period encapsulate that sentiment, documenting real-time reactions to the nascent stages of technologies, ecosystems, and a digital renaissance that was blossoming across industries.

But here's the thing. These writings aren't just valuable for their predictions, they're a vibrant tapestry of the aspirations, vision, and relentless spirit of innovation that characterized these emergent days.

And yes, I'll admit, I had a few moments of clairvoyance: the somewhat overstated emergence of the Metaverse; the transcendence of NFTs from fleeting trend to significant digital artifact; the ripening of decentralized systems; the surge of Ethereum's rivals; and the incremental yet crucial strides in the regulatory sphere of crypto and Digital Finance. My prophesying at the end of 2022 about "Darwinism in the Digital Age," especially as it relates to crypto, has only become more prescient, with both survivalist trends in the space and the SEC's discerning stance on major players like Bitcoin and Ethereum.

Peering into the digital horizon, a few things seem certain: we've witnessed at least two significant cycles in the crypto realm, and Bitcoin's current ascendancy hints at more to come. Expect more oscillations, more bulls, more bears. The volatility of crypto is as predictable as its unpredictability. Moreover, mass adoption seems inevitable. From finance to healthcare, from gaming to logistics, digital integration is the future.

Expect more oscillations, more bulls, more bears. The volatility of crypto is as predictable as its unpredictability.

Yet, what truly excites me is the evolving cast of this digital drama. The stage will be shared by agile newcomers who carve their niche, and stalwart traditionalists who, with foresight and adaptability, harness the digital wave to redefine their legacies. Through it all, one thing's for certain: this digital epoch, with all its tumult and triumphs, is a story worth telling.

A LOOK BACK AT FORWARD-LOOKING PREDICTIONS

Article #1   *01.12.2022, The Street*

DeFi's 2022 End of Year Summary – One Year Early

Is it a prediction or a review? It's a little of both as we predict what a 2022 "Year in Review" may look like in the world of blockchain and DeFi.

It's become a standard practice for executives and thought leaders in every industry to publish "2021 in Review" or "A Look Back at 2021," articles, blogs, and newsletters. While it's always interesting to remember what has transpired in a year gone by, I believe that spending energy on what's ahead is more productive. In the words of Walt Disney, "never look back, darling. It distracts from the now."

In that vein, I thought I'd turn the "review" concept on its head and predict what these same thought leaders will be writing about as we all collectively take a look back at 2022 in the world of Decentralized Finance (DeFi). What technologies and companies will have had the greatest impact on the DeFi industry in 2022? What was a success and what was a bust? What did we learn from another year of innovation and advancements in the growing Blockchain and digital finance sector?

While I don't have a crystal ball to confirm if these predictions are correct, I'll take an educated guess that the following events and experiences will dominate our dialogue in 2022:

"YEAR OF METAVERSE" WAS MOSTLY HYPE

The year 2021 ended with major Metaverse hype, with Facebook rebranding as Meta, and multiple other corporations like Epic Games, Microsoft, Coinbase, and Tencent joining the Metaverse game. All of this activity set the stage for 2022 to be the "year of the Metaverse." While the hype and the funding continued to roll in, 2022 (as expected) did not see the Metaverse come to fruition. On the contrary, 2022 was one of the many years of building, developing, fine-tuning, failing, and succeeding. The Metaverse is a complex journey that will take on many forms for a variety of industries. It's better to look at 2022 as the beginning of that multi-year journey.

More importantly, what we saw this year is many new startups and ventures emerging, which sparked new infrastructure development and early applications, along with corporations investing in and beginning to experiment with the Metaverse in multiple industries.

NFTS MOVE BEYOND THE HYPE

MORE MARKETPLACES (SOME DEDICATED) JOIN THE NFT ECOSYSTEM

If anything was a strong indicator of what was to come in 2022 in the NFT market, it was OpenSea's valuation of more than $13.3 billion after a Series C funding round. The NFT aggregator and marketplace continued to be a dominant decentralized platform for users looking to mint, buy, sell, and trade NFTs. However, other marketplaces and NFT search engines gave OpenSea a run for its money.

Coinbase NFT's initial waitlist exceeded $1.1 million, which was more than OpenSea's total active user-base at the time. In addition to Coinbase NFT, exchanges like FTX NFTs, Rarible, Zora, and others exploded onto the scene creating more opportunities for NFT market participation.

MAJOR GROWTH IN NFT USE BY THE GAMING AND GAMBLING INDUSTRIES

The value of NFT transactions more than doubled this year as NFTs became the central source of monetary transactions in gaming and the burgeoning Metaverse. According to Deloitte, four to five million sports fans globally purchased or were gifted an NFT sports collectible in 2022. This growing interest in sports NFTs fueled NFT gambling. The sports betting landscape is huge and the NFT market certainly capitalized on this trend and designed gambling projects aimed specifically at sports enthusiasts.

Speaking of gaming, "play-to-earn" gaming grew in usage and popularity with new releases in 2022 that pushed the boundaries of what genres and mechanics can be adapted to this model. Beyond "play-to-earn," NFTs also played a new role in giving gamers ownership of digital assets purchased within a game and putting more power and autonomy in gamers hands.

ROBUST COMMERCIAL APPLICATIONS AND CORPORATE USERS OF NFTS BEYOND THE ART AND COLLECTIBLE MARKETPLACE

The funnel of innovative ways to leverage NFTs continued to widen creating rapid growth opportunities in 2022. From supply chain and logistics to healthcare, real estate and retail, NFTs had a significant impact on industries that for years have struggled to find effective ways to truly digitize their operations. 2022 marked the beginning of mass adoption of NFTs by corporations in a variety of industries to identify, track, secure, and share goods, much of which were seamlessly integrated and invisible to the consumer.

PROGRESS ON CRYPTO AND DIGITAL FINANCE REGULATIONS

Earlier in the year, lack of oversight and regulatory clarity continued to make it hard for ecosystem players to drive legitimate business innovation and growth. However, that changed gradually as regulators took steps to provide more clarity and guidance for the industry. Specifically, the SEC, CFTC, FINRA, the Fed, and others made major steps to define their own regulatory domains and subsequent responsibilities, while becoming increasingly more proactive in their regulatory posture. These steps, which began with decisions about the backing requirements for Stablecoins like Tether, resulted in more institutional involvement both participation and investment in DeFi.

Even with all of the positive movement in 2022, the regulators still faced the monumental challenge of balancing effective regulations for crypto and DeFi without killing the transformational value behind decentralization.

MATURING OF DIGITAL SECURITIES

Digital securities were used in more ways and by more people in 2022 from fundraising to traditional workflows. The industry saw an upswing in innovation, with an increased amount of mainstream assets securitized and issued as digital securities allowing for more access to global liquidity. Simultaneously, traditional exchanges reinvented themselves, much like the Swiss SIX did, as interest in digital asset trading from both retail and institutional investors grew. Finally, new and regulated digital exchanges launched with a focus on vertical integration among players within the ecosystem.

Before 2022, most digital securities were issued under Reg D. However, this year saw additional digital securities offered under other regulations like Reg A+, S-1/F-1, etc. This allowed for greater market participation among all investors, not just accredited, which also led to increased liquidity.

ETHEREUM COMPETITORS (SOLANA, AVALANCHE, LUNA) GREW DRAMATICALLY

As Ethereum (ETH) became too expensive for many projects, alternative blockchains experienced a mega growth period in 2022 following a similar trend in 2021. One of the reasons for the adoption of other blockchains is they were ready to onboard projects and users before the Ethereum layer-2 infrastructure could be available for users. Base layers like Solana, Avalanche, and Algorand launched massive incentive campaigns to build or port on top.

Bitcoin shattered its record highs of 2021. However, the cryptocurrency continued its roller coaster ride of volatility throughout the year. More importantly, it became clear in 2022 that Bitcoin is, in fact, partially correlated with stock market movements, contrary to what we thought prior to 2021 (viewing crypto/Bitcoin as an uncorrelated asset).

2022 IN SUMMARY

None of us really know what will happen this year in the universe of digital finance but taking our cues from 2021 and understanding where progress and focus is being channeled, we can be fairly confident that a 2022 "Year in Review" will look very similar. Obviously, we live in uncertain times where macro events can change the trajectory of innovation, behavior, and even funding. However, the digital finance evolution has progressed too much to go back. 2022 will be a year we move forward in exciting and historic ways.

It became clear in 2022 that Bitcoin is, in fact, partially correlated with stock market movements.

A LOOK BACK AT FORWARD-LOOKING PREDICTIONS

Article #2   *12.20.2022, The Street*

SPiCE VC's Tal Elyashiv Predicts What's Ahead for the Digital Economy in 2023

From Crypto to the Metaverse, the market will continue to evolve in interesting ways after a volatile but clarifying 2023

PREDICTION #1
NATURAL SELECTION OF THE CRYPTO ECOSYSTEM

Natural selection of the digital asset ecosystem will be a powerful force in 2023 and that's a positive development. The good companies will get stronger, and the bad ones will fade away or be restructured leaving a better positioned market for the future.

If 2021 was the "Year of the Cryptocurrency," then 2022 was the year it collapsed. Millions were made and lost by crypto investors, while crypto companies were built and folded.

With 2023 right around the corner, one thing is clear: the "Roaring Twenties" era of 2022 crypto parties and the market's overall irrational exuberance is over. 2023 is the year crypto will have to grow up and clean up its act.

We're already seeing the Darwinism sweep through the market with only the well-managed, well-intentioned companies surviving. While there will be more shoes to drop as we head into 2023, this process is needed and very healthy for the future growth of the digital assets ecosystem. The reshaping and rebuilding of the industry's reputation and the way it does business, will continue to be driven by institutional investors requiring more controls, risk management, transparency, and reality checks.

While we're on the subject of institutional investors, firms like Softbank, Sequoya, and Temasek, to just name a few, have some sobering up to do as well. This maturation and sobering up process will weed some of the fraud, incompetence, and lack of experience out of the industry and that's a good thing. The companies left standing will be stronger for it and the industry will be in a better position to begin thriving once again.

While the Darwinism in the US will mostly be led by the private sectors, in other jurisdictions like Europe (MiCA regulation) and Asia, there may also be further regulatory implementation that will provide better guidance on how to effectively reboot the industry.

PREDICTION #2
REGULATION EVERYWHERE BUT HERE (US)

Countries across the globe will make critical decisions on crypto regulation in 2023, while in the US, no meaningful regulatory movements will occur due to legislative dysfunction. However, if it doesn't happen in the US this year, the prospects of regulations moving forward on crypto in the US in 2024 is all but dead.

One thing we know for certain, in 2023 as it relates to crypto regulation in the US, infighting and lots of it. From the SEC and the CFTC, to the Democrats and the Republicans, and the DeFi versus TradFi crew, 2023 will be just as entertaining as WWE, so grab the popcorn. However, no one benefits from stalemates, from unresolved power struggles, and this coming year won't be any different in the digital economy. While one would like to hold out hope that a new Congress can accomplish meaningful crypto legislation, the likelihood of it happening is as high as SBF keeping his Bahamian penthouse.

But, while the US squabbles and debates, countries around the world are making progress and 2023 should see many of these regulatory regimes take shape.

The EU is taking a massive step early in 2023 to vote on and implement the Markets in Crypto-Assets Regulation (MiCAR/MiCA), which lays out a framework to regulate both the issuance of cryptocurrencies and assets, and transactions, i.e., trading, investment, and payments. Specifically, the MiCA bill contains several provisions regulators say are necessary to "reign in the Wild West of the crypto world."

Meanwhile, Asian regulators are each taking on crypto guardrails differently. Hong Kong's goal for 2023 is to increase retail access to crypto, which requires a specific regulatory strategy to support those objectives. In sharp contrast, nearby Singapore has signaled that it will tighten regulations after big losses this year for investors, while Korea, still dealing with the aftermath of the collapse of the Terra/Luna tokens, will focus solely on enforcement. On the other hand, India, somewhat uniquely in the region, is using tax policy to drive behavior.

PREDICTION #3:
THE METAVERSE AND NFTS COME BACK FROM THE DEAD (BUT NOT THE WAY YOU THINK)

The glitz and glamour of the Metaverse and NFTs may be tarnishing, but the practical, versatile, and inevitable uses for both will be much clearer in 2023.

The recent narrative about Metaverse's demise, partly based on Meta's dismal financial outlook, are premature, the same way the exuberance on its immediate relevance and market adoption was a year ago. No one should look at Meta and the overall building of the Metaverse infrastructure as a 2023 or 2024 project.

The truth is, the Metaverse is inevitable, but it will take years to fully come to fruition. With that said, 2023 will mark the beginning of how we perceive "Metaverse" experiences. New use-cases in enterprise, healthcare, education, and more will bring the practical utility of smaller doses of the Metaverse to our collective attention even in our daily lives. Advances in identity technology, along with AR/VR devices, think Apple's XR project, will come into focus as well in 2023.

The same is true about NFTs. The NFT market will also go through a rebirth of sorts in 2023 moving further away from being a value driver on its own in the digital art and collectibles domain and closer to being what the technology was meant to be, mostly digital proof of provenance and authenticity of an object, with its value deriving only from what it represents. 2023 will also see the NFT's versatility beginning to shine. The funnel of innovative ways to leverage NFTs will continue to widen in 2023. From supply chain and logistics to healthcare, real estate, and retail, NFTs will have a more pervasive and permanent role in digitizing operations.

PREDICTION #4:
2023 MAY BE THE "YEAR OF THE CBDC" AROUND THE WORLD BUT NO DIGITAL DOLLAR IN SIGHT

The CBDC arms race continues as central banks will create alliances with commercial banks and technology providers to strengthen their position to test, launch, and execute their unique CBDC strategies all in 2023.

With more than 80% of the world's central banks already considering launching a Central Bank Digital Security (CBDC), 2022 was mostly full of trials and testing. However, the movements by nations across the world to make CBDCs a reality is picking up speed and will become a major priority in 2023 especially as the race to set a global standard is in sight. Additionally, commercial banks are increasingly interested in the space and will begin or continue to partner with central banks and software vendors to ensure success and mass adoption.

While China's digital yuan is far beyond the rest, many countries are making headway with 2023 goals of rollout a possibility. The Bank of Japan is piloting a rollout with major banks in early 2023. Turkey announced it would launch its CBDC this year, while the ECB intends to start work to develop a rulebook in early 2023 on rolling out a digital euro. The money and payments world is clearly on a path of adopting blockchain more broadly in 2023, with SWIFT even recognizing the need to move in this direction.

PREDICTION #5:
INSTITUTIONAL INVESTMENTS IN THE DIGITAL ECONOMY WILL SKYROCKET

After the "Darwinism Phase" of the crypto boom and bust lifecycle unwinds and a bit more regulatory parameters are in place, at least globally, institutional investors will make BIG moves with their BIG money all in 2023.

We learned in 2022 that beyond crypto's organizational woes, it's closely tied to traditional market movements and the overall economy. For 2023, the domain's performance will again depend on the sentiment around the world economy. If concerns ease, we may see an uplift in crypto prices as well as investing in the digital asset market.

Regardless of the market trends, we will likely see more traditional, blue chip funds, i.e., KKR & Hamilton-Lane together with Securitize, tokenize making them more accessible to a broader sphere of investors. Additionally, more and more large cap market players will move into the tokenization space, i.e.,

JP Morgan, HSBC, Fidelity, Goldman Sachs, and we'll see a significant uptick in M&A activity as a result. However, a caveat to all of this, as mentioned prior, is whether or not legislators and regulators step up to provide some needed stability.

Also, as part of the "Darwinism phase," 2023 will see significant M&A activity of distressed companies in the crypto ecosystem being acquired at rock bottom prices by stronger/healthier players.

2023 will also be an excellent time to invest in venture capital funds focused on the blockchain ecosystem, not crypto funds. It's a shameless plug, but I would be remiss if I didn't highlight how SpiCE VC is now in the process of raising SpiCE II after achieving stellar performance with SpiCE I. History shows that VC funds with recession year vintage tend to show superior performance compared to other vintage years. Plus, it makes a lot of sense, since valuations in the blockchain ecosystem are going to be much more reasonable and down to earth over the next couple of years.

INDUSTRY LEADERS' THOUGHTS

CARLOS DOMINGO
CO-FOUNDER & CEO, SECURITIZE

I was drawn to blockchain because I saw it as a way to solve real world problems. For example, enabling individual investors to participate in venture capital funds. Since Tal and I launched SPiCE VC and made its first fund accessible to even retail investors, I am proud that we, and Securitize, have been one of the biggest forces in using tokenization to open up access to even more asset classes: equity in private businesses, private equity, private credit, secondaries, fixed income, and more. Looking forward, all financial products will be digitized and tokenization is just the means to do so. Tokenization is new to most people now, but within a few years, it will be a given, in much the same way that The Cloud was a few years ago. People got comfortable with it, and now most of our data is in The Cloud and we hardly think about it.

As a technologist, I find blockchain and all the creative use cases fascinating. But what I find most rewarding is seeing blockchain, and our efforts, doing productive things that will make it possible for people like you and me to access opportunities we never could have in the past, and to improve traditional financial products in ways we haven't even imagined yet.

GRAHAM RODFORD
CEO, ARCHAX

Archax started in 2018 with a belief that not just cryptocurrencies, but every single financial instrument would eventually be "on chain." We believed when that happened, institutions would seek out credible, regulated partners.

For our part, the key benefit of this emerging sector isn't about avoiding centralized parties and avoiding trust, but leveraging the sheer benefits this technology provides throughout the full value chain of an instrument's creation and lifetime management. Our core belief underneath the vision for Archax, is that anything to do with an ownership register properly benefits from being on DLT/blockchain.

When we started, very few understood the vision that we had and believed we were just talking about these new security token offerings (STOs). But companies such as SPiCE VC, of which the author was a founder, understood this is more than just a small number of emerging instruments but a fundamental rewrite of everything that exists today. Since the beginning, we have seen virtually every asset class become demonstrated "on chain," an increased focus by all of the tier-one institutions on "digital," and a significant increase in the value being deployed into these new instruments.

KONSTANTINOS SGANTZOS
RESEARCH ASSOCIATE ON AI AND BLOCKCHAIN, SHARJAH UNIVERSITY, UAE, RESEARCH INSTITUTE OF SCIENCE AND ENGINEERING [RISE]

Contrary to the popular belief, blockchain and its derivative technologies are not "contraptions that print money." Blockchain was designed in Bitcoin (Wright, 2008) as a Triple Entry Accounting (Grigg, 2004) record keeper on a Distributed Ledger Medium. The infrastructure was carefully planned so that the participants' identity could be obscured behind a pseudonymous Public Key. However, the immutability of records which is ensured by the multiplicity of copies between the nodes and their integrity which is guaranteed via a cryptographic proof, both ensure that in case of a financial dispute, the participants' identity will be able to be revealed and a paper trail will prove who is right and who is wrong.

Humans have often proved their inability to understand technical terms in depth; therefore "pseudonymity" was translated by many as "anonymity", and people thought "it was cool" to use this technology for illicit activities. After the FBI raid on Silk Road in October 2013 and the capture of its owner Ross Ulbricht, it was evident even to the most unfamiliar to this technology that this was never a proper way to pursue such ventures. Nevertheless, as human nature has embedded the personal interest at the expense of others as Plato describes it in the parable "Ring of Gyges" (Woods, 2010,) similar ventures continued via the ICO frenzy of 2016, NFT craze, the plethora of stable coins that most of them were never either stable, nor coins, the whole infrastructure lead to an infinite "crypto party" that lead to multiple disasters like the latest FTX collapse.

So, is blockchain dead? I think not. With the upcoming age of AI both technologies will thrive. They have the potential to collaborate through IPv6 protocol to establish a secure infrastructure for global growth. By utilizing IPv6, every Internet of Things (IoT) device can incorporate Public Keys and Private keys, enabling safe, secure, peer to peer, and hack-resistant communication via microtransactions (microTXs), representing a fraction of a fraction of a cent. By the tokenization of fully auditable digital currencies, like digital CHF (Centi, 2023), blockchain technology will function as an "application" operating on IPv6 infrastructure, thereby fostering the emergence of what can be termed as Web3: The Internet of Value. This technological advancement is expected to yield numerous benefits in the coming years.

One of them is leveraging stored microTXs as a verifiable source to detect patterns of activity to learn from and adapt to society's logistics and supply chain. The accuracy of data can help AI generate more precise forecasts related to sustainability, green economy, reusability, and minimization of CO_2 emissions. Accurate data is essential for driving positive change in these areas. Blockchain's ability to audit every record can facilitate this pursuit without compromising users' privacy. Another field that can benefit is to ensure that Artificial Intelligence (AI) remains auditable as well, by making datasets open and obtaining the consent of original creators before incorporating their work into AI models. With Web3, this is possible through either "per use" micro payments or a one-time down payment for those whose works have been included in the model.

In conclusion, the combination of these technologies can contribute to the fight against "fake news," misleading websites, and prevent malicious actors from perpetrating harmful actions upon others. By embracing AI advancements while maintaining security and privacy, we can collectively create a better and more honest future for all of us.

REFERENCES:

1. (Centi, 2023). Centi Franc, the CHF Stablecoin. Retrieved from: https://centi.ch/centi-franc/ (accessed August 10, 2023).

2. Grigg, I. 2005). Triple Entry Accounting. Systemics Inc. Retrieved from: https://iang.org/papers/triple_entry.html (accessed August 10, 2023).

3. (Woods, C. 2010). Glaukon's Challenge (Republic 2). Available online: https://ssrn.com/abstract=1661519 (accessed on 4 August 2022).

4. (Wright, C. S. 2008) Bitcoin: A Peer-to-Peer Electronic Cash System. Article. SSRN: https://ssrn.com/abstract=3440802 or http://dx.doi.org/10.2139/ssrn.3440802

KYLE SONLIN
CEO, SECURITY TOKEN MARKET (STM)

For over a decade, the blockchain industry has been in pursuit of a defining application—a "killer use case"—that would revolutionize our economy and financial system. While many championed cryptocurrencies and decentralized finance as the answer hoping they'd provide permissionless banking on a global scale, these assets often lacked tangible underlying value. This made them just as susceptible to debasement as the very fiat currencies they aimed to supplant. Despite the extreme fluctuations in crypto asset prices, we must acknowledge the industry's achievements. Together, we've crafted a sandbox financial environment from scratch, introducing a permissionless system for asset exchange, instantaneous settlement, programmatic auditing, recordkeeping, leverage, market making, and governance. These financial rails were rigorously tested using assets that, over time, gained value primarily due to their transactional ease and global convenience.

Consider the rollout of any new technology: it undergoes multiple testing phases and beta versions. In these stages, the focus is on identifying and rectifying flaws. For a technological infrastructure to gain the trust and adoption of a global network of banks and financial institutions that handle hundreds of trillions of dollars worth of real assets like equities, debt, and real estate, it's imperative to demonstrate comprehensive robustness. This requires staking, transacting, and exchanging tens of billions of dollars worth of test assets in a controlled environment. While cryptocurrencies do hold value, they represent only a fraction of global asset markets. However, they've served as an invaluable exploratory phase for blockchain technology, showcasing its potential benefits for financial markets. After enduring stress tests—marked by high volumes, price volatility, hacks, and financial innovations—the industry has proven its worth and potential to reshape traditional financial systems, making them more apt for the high-frequency, global economy of the 21st century.

I firmly believe that the future will see the tokenization of all investment assets, transforming them into digital tokens on blockchain systems. This shift is akin to automating our financial markets. It paves the way for programmatic enforcement of compliance, instantaneous reconciliation of trades, and immediate transaction settlements. In the past, banks relied on vast workforces to manage these processes. With the advent of smart contract architecture, we can achieve superior outcomes at just a fraction of the cost. As financial services evolve to be increasingly driven by the ever-present need to reduce capital costs, the full realization of these savings at scale will ignite a worldwide race towards infrastructural transformation. From bank deposits to securities, I envision a future where all assets are managed on distributed ledgers, with multiple blockchains seamlessly integrated into a unified financial framework.

SHAI DATIKA
CEO, INX

Blockchain came to the world following a breach of trust in the financial market infrastructure brought on by the 2008 Financial Crisis, and before a series of destabilizing macro events (i.e. the global pandemic and the Russian invasion of Ukraine, among other seismic events), which altered what we perceived as a stable global world order. After an initial hype phase, with crypto and NFT exuberance, the true value of the underlying Distributed Ledger Technology (DLT) and a more "boring" blockchain came into focus. It's clear that the technology will enable new digital assets that are designed for a digital age.

While the power of blockchain is facilitating the tokenization of traditional securities as we know them today, the future may hold something completely different. As capital markets evolve beyond the shareholder structure of the 20th century, we will see an era where our wallets don't just hold our finances, but also our data.

The blockchains in our everyday lives may take shape as a CBDC, or a big tech giant's stablecoin, but there is no doubt they will be the main conduit for digital transactions and human verifications in an AI first world.

CHRIS KELLY
FORMER GENERAL COUNSEL, META (FACEBOOK)

Beyond changing the current paradigm of payments where centralized networks are constantly looking for the next way to skim from what are at their core peer-to-peer transactions, blockchain-based trust proofs of available value and the desire to exchange that value offer wonderfully transformative and empowering options for citizens around the world. The transparency that can be provided by public ledgers and the ability to build in user-selected privacy options about particular transactions is an additional empowerment for so many who are currently effectively excluded from the world's financial systems.

Providing ease of access and liquidity around the very real but illiquid assets that so many people in the world hold so they can make economically rational decisions that allow them to maximize returns and build wealth over time is one of the greatest potential developments in the space. It is incredibly exciting how many entrepreneurs are exploring these areas and making blockchain-based proofs more extensible and available to citizens around the globe.

DR CATHERINE LEPHOTO
EXECUTIVE DIRECTOR, GLOBAL PARTNERSHIPS, VX TECHNOLOGIES

My passion for blockchain technology and its impact in Africa is centered around its potential to transform two systems: health and education. As with every new technology, it is normal to see a slow uptake at the beginning. In Africa, the case for blockchain adoption is currently following a similar, frustratingly slow adoption. The slowness is further influenced by the fact that most people believe that blockchain technology is synonymous with cryptocurrencies.

Nonetheless, I predict that as the blockchain ecosystem inevitably increases in Africa, we will soon see an exponential rise in the uptake of the technology for use-cases outside of crypto and DeFi. This will happen as decision-makers in enterprises and governments begin to appreciate and harness the leapfrog opportunity the technology presents to the continent.

Currently the countries that are at the forefront of adoption of blockchain technology in Africa include Nigeria, Egypt, Kenya, and South Africa. However, there is evidence of increased activity in the space from other sub-Saharan African nations: notably Rwanda, Zambia, Uganda, Zimbabwe, Ethiopia, Ghana, the Democratic Republic of the Congo.

My prediction for the health sector is that more and more patient records will be securely written to blockchain platforms resulting in better health care delivery and patient outcomes. The value of health records on blockchain will increasingly become important as AI-empowered healthcare delivery takes root, particularly in countries in the developed world that may be finding themselves having to provide care to patients from different populations as a result of immigration. It is crucial that verified data on blockchain is used as input data for training AI solutions for healthcare in order to avoid bias that could lead to misdiagnoses and poor health outcomes in immigrant populations.

Another area of healthcare where blockchain technology will have a massive positive impact is in curtailing the proliferation of counterfeit medicines throughout the continent. The global counterfeit medicines market is estimated to be worth between USD 200 and USD 432 billion[i] with about 42% of that coming from African countries. Blockchain solutions with unbounded scale for supply chain management will be harnessed to solve this problem, too.

In the education sector, I foresee many countries in Africa accelerating reform strategies for education curricula to better include the myriad use-cases of blockchain technology along with other 4IR programmes.

Students in Africa are increasingly seeking material online for learning about blockchain technology and increasingly seeking knowledge that they can use to start their own businesses. This is very encouraging; it means the continent will not be left too far behind and the possibilities for equitable collaboration and partnerships with tech entrepreneurs from the global north will be enhanced. I could also imagine daily use of blockchain technology in students' lives through increased use of decentralized Apps.

Ultimately, blockchain technology will become an integral aspect of students' education experience before, during, and after they leave academic institutions. In turn, this will likely transform the job market and how people seek employment once they receive their academic qualifications.

Digitalization is the great equalizer Africa has been waiting for; blockchain is the pathway to realizing this dream.

[i] Ofori-Parku SS Fighting the global counterfeit medicines challenge: A consumer-facing communication strategy in the US is an imperative. Journal of Global Health 23 April 2022

STEPHAN NILSSON

CEO & CO-FOUNDER AT UNISOT, A WEB3 SUPPLY CHAIN TRACEABILITY PLATFORM

How the Public Blockchain & AI is revolutionizing global Supply Chains and the world economy.

The fusion of blockchain, IPv6, and AI, which facilitates tokenization and monetization, is poised to reshape the global landscape, with the supply chain industry at the forefront. In parallel to how private networks like CompuServe and America Online transitioned into the Internet we all know and use today, the current landscape of "private blockchains" and "crypto blockchains" is gravitating towards a singular global public blockchain.

Supply chains extend beyond mere logistics, encompassing everything from raw materials, food, to digital information, and covering the entire spectrum from raw material extraction and processing to recycling and repurposing. Embracing a global public blockchain as the universal "source of truth" guarantees unmatched transparency, efficiency, and truth. This evolution ensures that every step in global supply chains is verifiable, fostering a culture of trust and ethical practices.

Merging the public blockchain with AI through Decentralized Federated Learning (DLF) enhances data privacy by keeping data decentralized. This approach is not only energy-conservative but also optimizes bandwidth usage and reduces data duplications, leading to efficient and streamlined operations.

As the global industries recognize the transformative power of blockchain coupled with decentralized AI, we're on the edge of an innovation and collaboration renaissance. This will empower businesses to address long standing challenges, optimize expenses, and strengthen consumer engagement and confidence. Anchored by the public blockchain, this digital transformation will set the stage for a healthier, more transparent, and efficient global economic framework.

YONI ASIA,
CEO, ETORO

My 'discovery' of bitcoin in 2010 was an aha moment for me and eToro, the trading and investing platform I co-founded with my brother Ronen in 2007. Here was a technology that could transform financial services.

Back in 2008, I'd written about a new economic framework that would make money more transparent and enable philanthropy to create more economic value. Blockchain technology has enabled that vision to become a reality. Launched in 2020, GoodDollar is a community-driven non-profit project which generates and distributes digital money as a means of creating access to wealth for those facing poverty and inequality. Anyone in the world can claim G$ as a daily universal basic income. More than half a million people from over 180 countries and territories have opened a GoodDollar digital wallet with 100,000+ currently doing so daily.

While it is still in its infancy, for me Web3 is bigger than finance—it's about value, with the potential to revolutionize the world. It's as simple as making a reality of it.

Change takes time, uncertainty exists, and progress will not be linear, I do know that digital assets are inevitable. I divide digital assets into three buckets:

1. Non-financial assets such as NFTs, Roblox etc.

2. Financial assets such as stocks and bonds.

3. Digital gold, by which I mean bitcoin.

For me, Bitcoin is an unstoppable technology. It's hard to change it and therefore hard to break it. The smartest people I know own crypto. They understand that it marks the intersection of finance, economics, and technology.

I'm excited to see this revolution play out.

DR. MOHAMED AL HEMAIRY,

BLOCKCHAIN/WEB3.0 EXPERT, HEAD OF IP & TECH. TRANSFER OFFICE,
SHARJAH UNIVERSITY, DUBAI

I believe that blockchain technology has the potential to
revolutionize many industries, from finance and healthcare,
to supply chain management and the Internet of Things. It
has the power to create a more transparent, efficient, and
secure world. However, there are still many challenges
that need to be addressed before blockchain can reach
its full potential. These challenges include regulatory
uncertainty, security risks, and the lack of user adoption.

Despite these challenges, I am optimistic about the
future of blockchain technology. I believe that it has
the potential to make a positive impact on the world
and create a more just and equitable society.

KETAN MAKWANA,

CHAIRMAN AND MANAGING PARTNER, SEVENTY7 VENTURES

In my opinion blockchain is the future of technology and
will only go forward to enhance the security and privacy
of data, along with increasing efficiencies by streamlining
business operations. Industries that will immediately
benefit from blockchain technology adoption are finance,
legal & compliance, advertising, supply chain, and
cybersecurity, among others. Future considerations include
logistics, health, and local government protocols.

We are seeing a dynamic change in the understanding of the
relationship between Crypto, tokenization, and blockchain.
This will only continue to crystallize and, as this happens,
more and more utilization of the technologies will come
to the surface. Blockchain and tokenization are the future
of our economies, societies, and how we live our lives.

MANUEL EBNER,
FORMER CEO, MERILL LYNCH, SWITZERLAND

My first contact with blockchain technology was when a friend, who grew up in Patagonia, invited me to a week-long motorcycle ride from the South of Patagonia to the North of Patagonia. Wences Casares had just launched a Bitcoin Wallet called Xapo. I immediately accepted the invitation to jump on board.

After opening a wallet and purchasing some Bitcoin, I was immediately struck by the elegance and simplicity of the idea that this could be a breakthrough allowing the exchange of value via the internet on a peer-to-peer level without the need for any intermediaries, just like we exchange information instantaneously and with ease. It could also serve as a store of value as the maximum number of Bitcoin was clearly defined and could not be exceeded.

In addition to the idea of Distributed Ledger Technology (DLT) opening up a new paradigm of solving and simplifying complex multistep processes, I also imagined its implications on financial services. DLT could finally be the force that would redesign financial applications like letters of credit/ trade finance, proof of ownership, exchange of OTC securities, fully digitized exchanges, and digital land registries that would simplify real estate transactions.

The possibilities are rich but the challenges of reforming a global industry, which has spent decades optimizing suboptimal processes, is real. In the U.S., retail customers still use personal checks to pay bills. In Europe, this seems archaic as we use digital payments. But the U.S. has optimized checks, for example, by allowing the automatic deposit of a check by taking a photograph of the check.

Similarly in equities trading, the decades old processes have been optimized to allow for high frequency and high-volume trading at minimal costs per share. But if a retail investor buys shares, it still takes several days before the transaction is completed, as it takes multiple steps and several intermediaries to settle, clear, and transfer the shares to the new owner. In the industry the talk is of T+3 going to T+2 where 3 and 2 refer to days, not milliseconds.

So, despite the industry being ripe for reform and ready for a radical redesign of processes to achieve a dramatic step change in processing costs, efficiency, and speed, the fact that the industry is highly regulated with antiquated processes, will make it a challenge to take hold. The industry will also try to stifle change to protect its own position in the value chain, as DLT technologies threaten to disintermediate banks and other financial institutions, their own existence is at risk.

I know very smart, determined teams and companies are working on these and many other valuable applications, but they are not yet mainstream. As time progresses, I am convinced we will be enchanted by new applications of DLT that our imagination cannot dream of today.

ANTOINE TARDIF,
CEO, SECURITIES.IO

In the fast-paced world of finance and investment, the name of the game is innovation. As traditional methods of investment become increasingly outdated, a new wave of digital securities backed by venture capital funds is quickly capturing the attention of the global investor community. Central to this revolution is SPiCE VC and its critical alliance with Securitize, a regulatory compliance platform for issuing and trading digital securities.

Digital securities, often referred to as security tokens, are cryptographic tokens that represent ownership in a real, underlying asset. These can range from equity in a company, to real estate, to art. What makes them truly remarkable is their ability to streamline complex financial processes, while also ensuring enhanced transparency and security for investors.

VC funds were among the first to be implemented, but it's reasonable to predict that crowdfunding, which currently faces liquidity challenges, could be the next significant advancement. Presently, when investing in early-stage startups, the only exit opportunities are through a company acquisition or an IPO. However, with tokenized crowdfunding platforms, investors would be able to liquidate positions at more convenient times, rather than waiting 5 to 10 years (or even longer) for a liquidity event.

At Securitie.io, we've been closely monitoring and reporting on this development. Few people have been as instrumental to this vision as Tal Elyashiv and the Securitize team, who have been among the primary catalysts propelling the digital securities space forward.

OFER ROTEM,
FOUNDER AND MANAGING PARTNER OF COLLIDER VENTURES

I've been in the blockchain space since 2012, back then it was just Bitcoin. I started learning about it, becoming more and more interested in it, buying bitcoin, quitting my job as a programmer, and then becoming an entrepreneur and venture capitalist in the space.

Since diving into the blockchain ecosystem years ago, a few beliefs remain steadfast:

1. There's huge value and potential in reaching a consensus between a large and diverse group of people without a central authority.

2. When it comes to money, the above point is even more important. Distributing power from centralized authorities to a decentralized consensus can bring a lot of certainty, stability, and security for all.

3. This field is and will continue being significant and growing.

A few things have changed:

1. The realization that changes so significant like the one we're witnessing now can take much more time than what I originally had hoped for back in 2012.

2. This type of transformation requires decades, and possibly some periods of tumult, as public trust in governments and the global economy work to get to a place of acceptance and consensus.

I think the best way to approach blockchain integration is by understanding the genuine needs and economic motivations of people. Only then can we design systems with blockchain where it truly adds value. Often, starting centralized and nimble may be best, transitioning to on-chain operations when growth makes centralized trust a potential hazard. It's the system's users who perceive this risk, not necessarily its operators. The challenge arises when a platform becomes so influential that the creator becomes the potential risk. Relinquishing such power demands a higher perspective and an expansive understanding of one's long-term benefits. By ceding control, one might discover that they stand to gain even more over time.

I can only wonder how things will unfold; I remain optimistic.

W BRADFORD STEPHENS,
FOUNDER & MANAGING PARTNER OF BLOCKCHAIN CAPITAL

It has now been a little over a decade since I began my musings on where blockchain technology is going to take our world. Many of my original theses from back then have far exceeded my predictions for the future, while others have been slow to emerge. But, my base overarching thesis that blockchains will become the defacto standard for moving value around the world has always and still remains a question of when and not if.

Over the past three decades, nearly every sector of our global economy has been transformed by a shift from analog to digital, with the one outlier of antiquity being finance. This final segment of our society lacked the technology advancements to enable the shift away from centralized opaque finance, until the invention of the blockchain. And now with these intermediary-free trust platforms for exchanging value, we have the plumbing to re-create our global financial system: A new system that is free from censorship, exclusion, toll-takers and sovereign manipulation.

As I look to the future, I have never been more convinced that the entire global financial system will eventually be run off of blockchains. We have entered the next era of finance, where we are building supra-sovereign financial systems, and supra-sovereign equivalents of the corporation.

Inevitably, sovereign nation states, who have wielded undue power through centralized finance, will fight back. But this technology does not need permission to exist and isn't going away. Its ubiquitous global adoption will occur, and those that fight it will be left behind.

I love waking up every morning, to continue advancing our world through new technologies that have the ability to better all of mankind. While at the same time, neutering those corporations and institutions that have wielded their centralized power for their own benefits, instead of the people.

EPILOGUE

Charting the Uncharted –
The Blockchain Prophecies in Retrospect

In examining the blockchain's trajectory, one cannot help but marvel at the nuances it uncovers. The chapters and "current events" provided in this book are not merely snapshots of time; they were handpicked for their long-lasting relevance in the grand narrative of blockchain technology. As with all prophecies, each story is both a reflection and a nod to the future.

Blockchain's current significance is undeniable. It's reshaping industries, influencing policy-making, and quietly becoming an integrated part of our everyday lives. Yet, its importance doesn't merely rest on today's implications, but looms larger in the chapters yet to be written in our collective story.

There's a peculiar thing about mainstream acceptance of technology. It's not measured just by the sheer number of adopters but by its quiet omnipresence. The Internet protocol, once the talk of every tech town, now hums silently in the background, powering almost every facet of our lives. Blockchain seems destined to follow a similar arc.

As predicted and prophesied throughout the book, blockchain, once a peripheral concept, has grappled with its own success and the challenges it poses. From fraudulent activities, spurred on by anonymity, speedy transactions, lax KYC (You're your Client) requirements, and regulatory voids, to the very nature of its international reach, the vulnerabilities are evident.

Blockchain's intersection with existing regulations is much like fitting a square peg into a round hole. Our current legal frameworks were not built with crypto in mind, thus necessitating the creation of new ones tailored to this distinct domain. This is a global effort, requiring cooperation and collaboration on an epic scale.

While the U.S. has been ineffective so far to pass any meaningful legislation, regulatory bodies elsewhere, like the EU's MiCA, have begun to address these issues. Regardless of who leads the charge, it's clear that the age of unregulated crypto will inevitably sunset.

By 2023, the blockchain landscape has flourished into a verdant expanse of over 1,000 networks, each catering to diverse sectors. While this boom is a testament to innovation, it' also a cauldron of inefficiencies. Consolidation is inevitable, and for investors, understanding the interplay between applications and their underlying blockchains is paramount.

Blockchain's fusion with AI and other emerging technologies heralds an exciting future. The blend of machine learning, augmented and virtual reality, and blockchain is giving birth to groundbreaking solutions. Yet, with this convergence comes its share of challenges, especially in a world that's fast gravitating towards Web3. Blockchain's role in addressing the issues of artifact and identity authenticity will be pivotal.

Reflecting on blockchain's journey from its embryonic stage, spearheaded by the visionaries and their avant-garde concepts, to its current state, where it's courted by governments, industries, and regulators alike, is nothing short of awe-inspiring. It echoes the progression of past revolutions, yet with a twist. The blockchain revolution is poised to be exponential, with the upcoming decade promising seismic shifts.

Within blockchain's evolving narrative, one thing stands clear: its story, much like the technology itself, is decentralized. It belongs to everyone: the early adopters, the regulators, the skeptics, and the future innovators. As we stand on the precipice of a new era, this epilogue is but a brief pause, a moment of reflection, before the next exhilarating chapter unfolds.

ENDNOTES

Prologue

Dune Analytics. (n.d.). NFT Marketplaces Overview—OpenSea, LooksRare, Genie, OpenSea Pro, Blur, X2Y2. https://dune.com/sealaunch/NFT?undefined=&Select+Timeframe_ef4aff=720+days

Fortune Business Insight. (2023, May). Blockchain Technology Market Size, Share, and COVID19 Impact Analysis. https://www.fortunebusinessinsights.com/industry-reports/blockchain-market-100072

Tokachev, A. (2021, November). DeFi Can be 100 Times Larger Than Today in Five Years. Coin Telegraph. https://cointelegraph.com/news/defi-can-be-100-times-larger-than-today-in-5-years

Chapter 1

Block Data. (2021, July). Top Banks Investing in Crypto and Blockchain Companies. LinkedIn. https://www.linkedin.com/posts/blockdata_blockchain-cryptocurrency-dlt-activity-6830788189872013312-fBZ4/

FWS Institute. (2021, April 30). European Investment Bank Issues Inaugural Digital Bond on a Public Blockchain. https://www.swfinstitute.org/news/86061/european-investment-bank-issues-inaugural-digital-bond-on-a-public-blockchain

Ledger Insights. (2020, March 30). Nomura Research Issues First Japanese Blockchain Bonds, Forms Research Consortium. https://www.ledgerinsights.com/nomura-research-issues-first-japanese-blockchain-bonds-forms-research-consortium/

Elyashiv, T. (2021, December 15). Interview with Securitize's Carlos Domingo on Digital Assets, Tokenization and the Exciting Journey Ahead. The Street. https://www.thestreet.com/defi/digital-finance-investing/interview-with-securitizes-carlos-domingo-on-digital-assets

Elyashiv, T. (2022, January 26). Q&A Session with INX's Shy Datika on Recent Wins and the Future of Digital Assets. The Street. https://www.thestreet.com/defi/digital-finance-investing/q-a-session-with-inxs-shy-datika

Elyashiv, T. (2023, October 9). Tokenized real estate assets – the purpose, the promise and the path ahead. The Street. https://www.thestreet.com/defi/digital-finance-investing/tokenized-real-estate-assets

Elyashiv, T. (2021, September 22). Why is No One Talking About the Digital Security Explosion? The Street. https://www.thestreet.com/defi/digital-finance-investing/digital-security-growth-explodes

Chapter 2

Coinspeaker. (2021, July 26). How Aimedis Wants to Reform the Healthcare System Using Blockchain. https://www.coinspeaker.com/aimedis-reform-healthcare-system-using-blockchain/

Elyashiv, T. (2021, November 30). Healthcare is the Newest Frontier for NFTs. The Street. https://www.thestreet.com/defi/digital-finance-investing/healthcare-is-the-newest-frontier-for-nfts

Elyashiv, T. (2021, December 7). Tal's NFT Take: Can NFTs Take the Headache Out of Real Estate Transactions? The Street. https://www.thestreet.com/defi/digital-finance-investing/can-nfts-take-the-headache-out-of-real-estate

Elyashiv, T. (2021, October 21). Tal's NFT Take: Discovery and Search is Key to NFT Growth. The Street. https://www.thestreet.com/defi/digital-finance-investing/discovery-and-search-is-key-to-nft-growth

Elyashiv, T. (2021, October 28). Tal's NFT Take: From Crafts to Concerts, NFT Possibilities Expand. The Street. https://www.thestreet.com/defi/digital-finance-investing/nft-possibilities-expand

Elyashiv, T. (2021, November 10). Tal's NFT Take: NFTs are a Supply Chain's New Best Friend. The Street. https://www.thestreet.com/defi/digital-finance-investing/nfts-are-a-supply-chains-new-best-friend

Elyashiv, T. (2022, June 17). The Anatomy of a Successful NFT: Value, Brand, Community. Newsweek. https://www.newsweek.com/anatomy-successful-nft-value-brand-community-1716548

Lin, M. (2021, August 2). How NFTs Can Track Patient Consent for Clinical Trials and Give You Greater Control Over Your Own Health Data. Forkast. https://forkast.news/how-nfts-can-track-patient-consent-clinical-trials/

Louise, N. (2021, June 9). Enjin Teams Up with Health Hero to Launch NFT-powered Wellness App. Tech Startups. https://techstartups.com/2021/06/09/enjin-teams-health-hero-launch-nft-powered-wellness-app/

Chapter 3

Elyashiv, T. (2021, September 9). Bitcoin is the currency of choice for global ransomware attacks. The Street. https://www.thestreet.com/defi/digital-finance-investing/bitcoin-is-the-currency-of-choice-for-global-ransomware-attacks

Elyashiv, T. (2022, December 1). Crypto Exchange Proof of Reserves – A Real Solution or Just a Band Aid? The Street. https://www.thestreet.com/defi/digital-finance-investing/crypto-exchange-proof-of-reserves

Elyashiv, T. (2022, September 3). Is Crypto Giving Blockchain and Decentralized Finance a Bad Name? Medium. https://medium.com/spicevc/is-crypto-giving-blockchain-and-decentralized-finance-a-bad-name-b372f5652baa

Elyashiv, T. (2021, October 13). What Bitcoin's Non-Reaction to the Pandora Papers Tells Us About Crypto Behavior. The Street. https://www.thestreet.com/defi/digital-finance-investing/bitcoins-non-reaction-to-the-pandora-papers

Elyashiv, T. (2021, November 16). Welcome to Miami: The New Crypto Capital of the U.S.? The Street. https://www.thestreet.com/defi/digital-finance-investing/welcome-to-miami-the-new-crypto-capital-of-the-u-s

Investing. (2022, November 25). Binance Publishes Official Merkle Tree-Based Proof of Reserves. https://www.investing.com/news/cryptocurrency-news/binance-publishes-official-merkle-treebased-proof-of-reserves-2952088

Knight, O. (2022, August 22). Wall Street Giant DTCC Launches Private Blockchain in Big Crypto-Milestone for TradFi. Coin Desk. https://www.coindesk.com/business/2022/08/22/wall-streets-dtcc-launches-private-blockchain-platform-to-settle-trades/?fbclid=IwAR2jvhQTN9k-Y1bxQlghEJ70jw3spijx1kxT-OmVHdNlYv4q6DtJlXuJETw&mibextid=893gbd

The Securities Industry and Financial Market Association. (2023, July 26). Research Quarterly: Equities. https://www.sifma.org/resources/research/research-quarterly-equities/

Chapter 4

Cairns, R. (2022, June 30). Crypto is Crashing but the Tech Behind it Could Save Luxury Brands Billions. CNN Business. https://www.cnn.com/2022/06/26/business/aura-blockchain-luxury-counterfeit-hnk-spc-intl/index.html

Daley, S. and Whitfield, B. (2023, February 24). Blockchain and AI: How They Integrate and 26 Examples. Built In. https://builtin.com/artificial-intelligence/blockchain-ai-examples

Elyashiv, T. (2023, May 2). Blockchain is Changing the Retail Industry from the Container Ship to the Closet. The Street. https://www.thestreet.com/defi/digital-finance-investing/blockchain-is-changing-the-retail-industry-from-the-container-ship-to-the-closet

Elyashiv, T. (2023, March 16). Cha-Ching on the Chain: Why DLT-Powered Payments Are Here to Stay. The Street. https://www.thestreet.com/defi/digital-finance-investing/cha-ching-on-the-chain-dlt-powered-payments

Elyashiv, T. (2023, April 10). From Life to Health: Blockchain is Transforming the Insurance Industry. The Street. https://www.thestreet.com/defi/digital-finance-investing/blockchain-is-transforming-the-insurance-industry

Elyashiv, T. (2023, May 5). Is It Really A Smart Factory Without Blockchain? Industry Today. https://industrytoday.com/is-it-really-a-smart-factory-without-blockchain/

Elyashiv, T. (2023, June 5). Potential Solutions to the Carbon Credit Problem. Newsweek. https://www.newsweek.com/potential-solutions-carbon-credit-problem-1804181

Elyashiv, T. (2023, July 2). Unleashing Blockchain's Potential to Solve The Entertainment Industry's Toughest Challenges. The Tokenizer. https://thetokenizer.io/2023/07/02/unleashing-blockchains-potential-to-solve-the-entertainment-industrys-toughest-challenges/#:~:text=As%20a%20result%2C%20when%20a

La Rock, Z. (2019, April 23). Blue Cross Has Formed a Blockchain Consortium. Insider. https://www.businessinsider.com/blue-cross-blue-shield-forms-blockchain-consortium-2019-4

Market and Markets. (2018, July). Blockchain in Insurance Market. https://www.marketsandmarkets.com/Market-Reports/blockchain-in-insurance-market-9714723.html

Miliard, M. (2022, January 14). Blockchain Built Avaneer Health Network Gets $50M Boost from Aetna, Cleveland Clinic, others. Healthcare It News. https://www.healthcareitnews.com/news/blockchain-built-avaneer-health-network-gets-50m-boost-aetna-cleveland-clinic-others

Chapter 5

Amplify EFTs. (2023, September 1). What is Blockchain Technology? https://amplifyetfs.com/blok/

Constin, J. (2014, July 21). Facebook's $2 Billion Acquisition of Oculus Closes, Now Official. TechCrunch.

https://techcrunch.com/2014/07/21/facebooks-acquisition-of-oculus-closes-now official/?guccounter=1&guce_referrer=aHR0cHM6Ly93d3cuZ29vZ2xlLmNvbS8=&guce_referrer_sig=AQAAANHgIBNxoxjp0J5ioiO7RCBsH8UBkiHjwqzvUXNZ_HvogGCV26scCkeLUqTJGVEASuXFEEC3fW40u38_pZXSgbVoBn96XuC0BH5N1hmtx--MbqSqLHB1hDMf-2NTVfNDUcMsKZ6v3EHxWXabfnvDw9U0A8sOIELR8Wb12pNcaO_i

Elyashiv, T. (2021, November 2). Making Sense of the Metaverse and the Role of Decentralized Finance (DeFi). The Street. https://www.thestreet.com/defi/digital-finance-investing/metaverse-and-the-role-of-defi

Elyashiv, T. (2022, February 8). METAWORK IS ON ITS WAY TO A COMPANY NEAR YOU. The Street. https://www.thestreet.com/defi/digital-finance-investing/metawork-is-on-its-way-to-a-company-near-you

Elyashiv, T. (2023, June 12). 7 Stats That Prove the Metaverse is Definitely Not Dead. The Street. https://www.thestreet.com/defi/digital-finance-investing/7-stats-that-prove-the-metaverse-is-definitely-not-dead

Elyashiv, T. (2022, January 6). The Dawn of the Metaverse: A New Series on The Street/DeFi. The Street. https://www.thestreet.com/defi/digital-finance-investing/the-dawn-of-the-metaverse-a-new-series-on-the-street-defi

Gates, B. (2021, December 7). Reasons for Optimism After a Difficult Year. Gates Notes. https://www.gatesnotes.com/Year-in-Review-2021?WT.mc_id=20211231120000_YIR2021_BG-LI_&WT.tsrc=BGLI

Ridley, M. (2017, November 12). Amara's Law. MattRidley. https://www.mattridley.co.uk/blog/amaras-law/

Chapter 6

Accenture. (2017, June 21). Accenture Report: Artificial Intelligence Has Potential to Increase Corporate Profitability in 16 Industries by an Average of 38 Percent by 2035 | Accenture. https://newsroom.accenture.com/news/accenture-report-artificial-intelligence-has-potential-to-increase-corporate-profitability-in-16-industries-by-an-average-of-38-percent-by-2035.html

Comparison of the Number of Listed Companies on the New York Stock Exchange (NYSE) and Nasdaq from 2018 to 1st quarter 2023, by Domicile. (n.d.). https://www.statista.com/statistics/1277216/nyse-nasdaq-comparison-number-listed-companies/#:~:text=While%20the%20 NYSE%20has%20generally,had%20a%20much%20higher%203%2C788.

Elyashiv, T. (2021, October 26). Bitcoin Futures ETFs Are Here – Paving the Way for Spot-Based Bitcoin ETFs. The Street. https://www.thestreet. com/defi/digital-finance-investing/bitcoin-futures-etfs-are-here

Elyashiv, T. (2021, September 9). DeFi 101: Decentralized Finance and How To Invest in its Rapid Growth. The Street. https://www.thestreet. com/defi/digital-finance-investing/defi-101-decentralized-finance-how-to-invest#:~:text=One%20of%20the%20ways%20to

Elyashiv, T. (2021, September 9). Digital Finance Investing Strategies That Work. The Street. https://www.thestreet.com/defi/digital-finance-investing/investing-in-digital-assets-and-currencies

Elyashiv, T. (2022, March 18). Getting in on the Metaverse: Investment Tips for Today with Upside for Tomorrow. The Street. https://www.thestreet. com/defi/digital-finance-investing/metaverse-investing-tips

Elyashiv, T. (2022, November 7). Goldman Sachs' New Digital Asset Classification System Fills a Gaping Hole in the Digital Finance Ecosystem. The Street. https://www.thestreet.com/defi/digital-finance-investing/goldman-sachs-new-digital-asset-classification-system

Elyashiv, T. (2022, January 20). If Your Portfolio Has No Metaverse Exposure, It Should and Here is Why. The Street. https://www.thestreet.com/defi/digital-finance-investing/your-portfolio-needs-metaverse-exposure

Elyashiv, T. (2022, April 8). THE BLOCKCHAIN ECOSYSTEM: Review of the Investable Publicly Traded Universe. The Street. https://www.thestreet.com/defi/digital-finance-investing/the-blockchain-ecosystem-review-of-the-investable-publicly-traded-universe

Elyashiv, T. (2021, December 22). Top Wealth Managers Reveal the Trends and the Truth about Digital Asset Investing. The Street. https://www.thestreet.com/defi/digital-finance-investing/wealth-managers-and-digital-asset-investing

Elyashiv, T. (2023l, August 14). Winning Web3 Investment Strategies Must Combine Artificial Intelligence and. Newsweek. https://www.newsweek.com/winning-web3-investment-strategies-must-combine-artificial-intelligence-blockchain-technology-1819218

Globe Newswire. (2022, February 11). Blockchain Market Size Worth $227.99Bn, Globally, by 2028 at 72.9% CAGR—Exclusive Report by The Insight Partners. https://www.globenewswire.com/news-release/2022/02/11/2383531/0/en/Blockchain-Market-Size-Worth-227-99Bn-Globally-by-2028-at-72-9-CAGR-Exclusive-Report-by-The-Insight-Partners.html

Goldman Sachs. (2022, November 3). Goldman Sachs, MSCI, and Coin Metrics Collaborate to Introduce DatonomyTM, a Taxonomy of Digital Assets. https://www.goldmansachs.com/media-relations/press-releases/2022/introducing-datonomy-11-03-2022.html

Jones, C. (2022, September 21). Are There Too Many Cryptocurrencies? Coin Telegraph. https://cointelegraph.com/news/are-there-too-many-cryptocurrencies

Kharif, O. (2021, July 26). Goldman Asset-Management Arm Files to Offer a Crypto-Related ETF. Bloomberg. https://www.bloomberg.com/news/articles/2021-07-27/goldman-asset-management-arm-files-to-offer-a-crypto-related-etf#xj4y7vzkg

Markets and Markets. (n.d.). Artificial Intelligence Market Size & Trends, Growth Analysis, Forecast [2030]. https://www.marketsandmarkets.com/Market-Reports/artificial-intelligence-market-74851580.html

McCall, V. (2020, November 13). What is Epic Games? Here's What You Need to Know About the Game Developer and Distributor Behind the Success of Fortnite. Insider. businessinsider.com/guides/tech/what-is-epic-games

Nagarajan, S. (2021, October 21). Bitcoin is Soaring Because Inflation Fears are Eating at Investors—Not Because of Crypto ETFs, JPMorgan says. Insider. https://markets.businessinsider.com/news/currencies/bitcoin-price-crypto-record-etf-inflation-jpmorgan-high-concern-hedge-2021-10?utm_source=facebook.com&utm_medium=social&utm_campaign=sf-bi-main&fbclid=IwAR1AF1V71ydgQtp7Fb_GCMSp5BHmMANpM34FPykhDkWaKXktGQk8YP9TKmo

Rapoza, K. (2021, March 21). What's The Big Deal About DeFi and How Do You Invest In It? Forbes. https://www.forbes.com/sites/kenrapoza/2021/03/21/whats-the-big-deal-about-defi-and-how-do-you-invest-in-it/?sh=6727c05ce89c

Research Dive. (2021, September). Blockchain in Supply Chain Market: Leading Technologies, Top Key Vendors & Insight Scope till 2028. https://www.researchdive.com/8493/blockchain-in-supply-chain-market

Robertson, H. (2021, December 7). Jefferies Predicts the Metaverse will be the Biggest Disruption to How We Live Ever Seen, as Wall Street gets excited about virtual worlds. Insider. https://markets.businessinsider.com/news/stocks/metaverse-investing-wall-street-jefferies-land-sales-sandbox-crypto-nfts-2021-12

Son, H. (2021, March 17). Morgan Stanley Becomes the first big U.S. bank to offer its wealthy clients access to bitcoin funds. CNBC. https://www.cnbc.com/2021/03/17/bitcoin-morgan-stanley-is-the-first-big-us-bank-to-offer-wealthy-clients-access-to-bitcoin-funds.html

Spherical Insights. (2022, August). Blockchain AI Market Size—Global Analysis, Forecast 2021-30. https://www.sphericalinsights.com/reports/blockchain-ai-market

Statista. (n.d.). Comparison of the Number of Listed Companies on the New York Stock Exchange (NYSE) and Nasdaq from 2018 to First Quarter 2023, by domicile.

Zerucha, T. (2021, October 5). Nickel Survey Shows Increased Risk Appetite for Digital Assets from Professional Investors. Crowd Fund Insider. https://www.crowdfundinsider.com/2021/10/181257-nickel-survey-shows-increased-risk-appetite-for-digital-assets-from-professional-investors/

Chapter 7

Ashraf, A. (2022, November 18). Pension Giant Ontario Teachers' Plans to Write Off All $95M Invested in Crypto Exchange FTX. Coin Desk. https://www.coindesk.com/business/2022/11/18/pension-giant-ontario-teachers-plans-to-write-off-all-95-million-invested-in-crypto-exchange-ftx/

Cambridge Associates. (2020, March 31). US Venture Capital: Index and Selected Benchmark Statistics. https://www.cambridgeassociates.com/wp-content/uploads/2020/07/WEB-2020-Q1-USVC-Benchmark-Book.pdf

CB Insights. (2022, April 7). State of Venture Q1'22 Report. https://www.cbinsights.com/research/report/venture-trends-q1-2022/#:~:text=Global%20venture%20funding%20reached%20%24143.9,quarter%20for%20funding%20on%20record.

Elyashiv, T. (2023, January 18). Economic Downturns Mark a Return to Sanity (and Returns) for Venture Capital. The Street. https://www.thestreet.com/defi/digital-finance-investing/economic-downturns-mark-a-return-for-venture-capital

Elyashiv, T. (2023, February 7). FTX Fallout: Should VCs Be Held Accountable for Missing Red Flags? The Street. https://www.thestreet.com/defi/digital-finance-investing/ftx-fallout-should-vcs-be-held-accountable-for-missing-red-flags

Elyashiv, T. (2022, May 13). The Case for Venture Capital in an Uncertain Market. The Street. https://www.thestreet.com/defi/digital-finance-investing/the-case-for-venture-capital-in-an-uncertain-market

Elyashiv, T. (2022, June 15). The VC FOMO Problem: The Time-To-Deal Race is Leaving Many Disoriented and Others Well-Positioned. The Street. https://www.thestreet.com/defi/digital-finance-investing/the-vc-fomo-problem#:~:text=Digital%20Finance%20Investing-

Global Data. (2022, April 27). Global Venture Capital Investment Down by 16% in Q1 2022 but Stays Resilient, finds Global Data. Global venture capital investment down by 16% in Q1 2022 but stays resilient, finds Global Data

Invesco. (n.d.). The Case for Venture Capital. https://apinstitutional.invesco.com/dam/jcr:1f35880c-bdf9-42ea-8afe-ab69b85bc7a4/The%20Case%20for%20Venture%20Capital.pdf

Long, T. (2010, March 10). March 10, 2000: Pop Goes the Nasdaq! Wired. https://www.wired.com/2010/03/0310nasdaq-bust/

Prentice, C. (2023, January 5). U.S. Securities Regulator Probes FTX Investors' Due Diligence Sources. Reuters. https://www.reuters.com/technology/us-securities-regulator-probes-ftx-investors-due-diligence-sources-2023-01-05/

Quittner, J. (n.d.). Why 2015 was the Year of the Unicorn. Inc. https://www.inc.com/jeremy-quittner/best-of-inc-2015-unicorns-then-and-now.html

Sutton, S. (2023, January 6). The Legal Threat Coming for Venture Capital. Politico. https://www.politico.com/newsletters/morning-money/2023/01/06/the-legal-threat-coming-for-venture-capital-00076697

Woodley, K. (2022, May 9). Stock Market Today: Stocks, Bonds, Crypto and More Take a Dive. Kiplinger. https://www.kiplinger.com/investing/stocks/604655/stock-market-today-050922-stocks-bonds-crypto-dive

Chapter 8

Anderson, D. (2023, January 27). Fed Denies Custodia Bank Application to Join the Federal Reserve System. Coin Telegraph. https://cointelegraph.com/news/fed-denies-custodia-bank-application-to-join-the-federal-reserve-system

Canny, W. (2023, June 21). Stablecoins, DeFi Likely to Be SEC's Next Targets in U.S. Crypto Crackdown: Berenberg. Coin Deck. https://www.europarl.europa.eu/news/en/press-room/20230414IPR80133/crypto-assets-green-light-to-new-rules-for-tracing-transfers-in-the-eu#:~:text=Uniform%20EU%20market%20rules%20for,crypto%2Dcurrencies%20(MiCA)

De, N. (2021, August 3). State of Crypto: Infrastructure Bill Shows Congress Sees Crypto as Here to Stay. CoinDesk. https://www.coindesk.com/policy/2021/08/03/state-of-crypto-infrastructure-bill-shows-congress-sees-crypto-as-here-to-stay/

Elyashiv, T. (2022, November 16). Clear Regulation Is the Only Way To Civilize the Digital Asset Wild West. Newsweek. https://www.newsweek.com/clear-regulation-only-way-civilize-digital-asset-wild-west-1759761

Elyashiv, T. (2021, October 7). How to Read CFTC's Latest Legal Moves to Take on 14 Crypto Players. The Street. https://www.thestreet.com/defi/digital-finance-investing/cftc-flexes-its-legal-muscles

Elyashiv, T. (2022, November 20). Red Flags Are Harder to Miss with Regulation: An FTX Cautionary Tale and Industry Call-to-Action. The Street. https://www.thestreet.com/defi/digital-finance-investing/an-ftx-cautionary-tale-and-industry-call-to-action

Elyashiv, T. (2023, June 28). SEC vs. Stablecoins: The debate over their status as securities or money heats up. The Street. https://www.thestreet.com/defi/digital-finance-investing/sec-vs-stablecoins-the-debate-heats-up

Elyashiv, T. (2022, February 24). Talk is Cheap: Congressional Hearings on Stablecoins Feature Partisan Politics with Little Regulatory Progress. The Street. https://www.thestreet.com/defi/digital-finance-investing/talk-is-cheap-congressional-hearings-on-stablecoins

Elyashiv, T. (2021, September 16). The Heat Is On: The Crypto and DeFi Regulation Debate Intensifies. The Street. https://www.thestreet.com/defi/digital-finance-investing/crypto-and-defi-regulation-debate

Elyashiv, T. (2021, March 1). Three Key Biden Moves That May Signal New Era for Blockchain-Based Digital Finance. Securities.io. https://www.securities.io/three-key-biden-moves-that-may-signal-new-era-for-blockchain-based-digital-finance/

Federal Register. (2023). Federal Register/Vol. 88, No. 39., https://www.govinfo.gov/content/pkg/FR-2023-02-28/pdf/FR-2023-02-28.pdf

Franck, T. (2021, November 1). Stablecoins are a compelling payment option, but they need to be regulated, Biden administration report says. CNBC. https://www.cnbc.com/2021/11/01/congress-should-regulate-stablecoins-biden-administration-report-says.html

Gensler, G. (2021, September 14). Testimony Before the United States Senate Committee on Banking, Housing, and Urban Affairs. SEC. https://www.sec.gov/news/testimony/gensler-2021-09-14

Goswami, R. (2022, November 17). Never seen 'Such a Complete Failure' of Corporate Controls, says New FTX CEO who also Oversaw Enron Bankruptcy. CNBC. https://www.cnbc.com/2022/11/17/ftx-ceo-shreds-bankman-fried-never-seen-such-a-failure-of-controls-.html

Goswami, R. (2023, February 13). Crypto Firm Paxos to Face SEC Charges, Ordered to Stop Minting Binance Stablecoin. CNBC. https://www.cnbc.com/2023/02/13/paxos-ordered-to-cease-minting-binance-stablecoin-by-new-york-regulator.html

Isaac, C.L., Mikhael, C., Riemer K.E. (2022, May 6). CFTC and SEC Perspectives on Cryptocurrency and Digital Assets—Volume 1: A Jurisdictional Overview. K&L Gates. https://www.klgates.com/CFTC-and-SEC-Perspectives-on-Cryptocurrency-and-Digital-Assets-Volume-I-A-Jurisdictional-Overview-5-6-2022

Katz, M. (2022, November 11). Ontario Teacher's Pension Could Lose $95 Million on FTX Investment. Chief Investment Officer. https://www.ai-cio.com/news/ontario-teachers-pension-could-lose-95-million-on-ftx-investment/

Ligon, C. (2021, September 29). CFTC Files Charges Against 14 Crypto Companies. Coin Desk. https://www.coindesk.com/business/2021/09/29/cftc-files-charges-against-14-crypto-companies/

Ligon, C. (2022, October 20). Over a Fifth of Cases in CFTC's 2022 Crackdown Were Crypto-Related. Coin Desk. https://www.coindesk.com/policy/2022/10/20/over-a-fifth-of-cases-in-cftcs-2022-crackdown-were-crypto-related/

Locke, T. (2021, August 24). Treasury will Not Target Non-Brokers Like Miners even if the Crypto Tax Provision isn't Amended. CNBC. https://www.cnbc.com/2021/08/24/treasury-will-not-target-non-brokers-even-without-crypto-tax-amendment.html

Olinga. L. (2023, February 10). Coinbase Receives Bad News. The Street. https://www.thestreet.com/cryptocurrency/coinbase-receives-bad-news

Prentice, C. (2021, September 28). Digital Asset Exchange Kraken to Pay $1.25 million Penalty to Settle U.S. CFTC Charges. Reuters. https://www.reuters.com/technology/digital-asset-exchange-kraken-pay-125-mln-penalty-settle-us-cftc-charges-2021-09-28/

Reuters Euro News. (2022, November 18). Exclusive: How FTX Bought its Way to Become the 'Most Regulated' Crypto Exchange. https://www.euronews.com/next/2022/11/18/fintech-crypto-ftx-regulators

Velasquez, F. (2022, October 6). CFTC's Regulation by Enforcement Needs to Change, Commissioner Says. Yahoo Finance. https://finance.yahoo.com/news/cftc-regulation-enforcement-needs-change-175825515.html

Chapter 9

Elyashiv, T. (2023, April 26). EU Approves MiCA – Unleashing New Era in Digital Asset Regulation. The Street. https://www.thestreet.com/defi/digital-finance-investing/eu-approves-mica-unleashing-new-era-in-digital-asset-regulation

Elyashiv, T. (2022, April 19). Japan's Collectivist Approach to Digital Securities is a Model for Rest of Us. The Street. https://www.thestreet.com/defi/digital-finance-investing/japans-collectivist-approach-to-digital-securities#:~:text=Japan

Elyashiv, T. (2021, October 18). The OCC Officially Recognizes the Critical and Permanent Role of Blockchain in Banking. The Street. https://www.thestreet.com/defi/digital-finance-investing/occ-officially-recognizes-role-of-blockchain-in-banking

Eur-Lex. (n.d.). European Union Law Journal (database). https://eur-lex.europa.eu/oj/direct-access.html

European Parliament. (2023, August 20). Proposal for a Regulation on Information Accompanying Transfers of Funds and Certain Crypto-Assets (recast). https://www.europarl.europa.eu/legislative-train/theme-an-economy-that-works-for-people/file-revision-of-the-regulation-on-transfers-of-funds

Hori, T., Iijima T., Okada, A. (2023, May 9). The Financial Technology Law Review: Japan. The Law Reviews. https://thelawreviews.co.uk/title/the-financial-technology-law-review/japan

Jones, H. (2023, April 19). EU Urges Others to Copy its Rules for Crypto-Assets. Reuters. https://www.reuters.com/technology/eu-urges-others-copy-its-rules-cryptoassets-2023-04-19/#:~:text=MiCA%20requires%20crypto%20firms%20to,money%20laundering%20and%20terrorism%20finance.&text=It%20is%20being%20rolled%20out,the%20sector%20time%20to%20adapt

Kikuchi, T. (2022, March 9). Marui to Issue Token Bonds Nomura is FA, Foundation is Securitize. Coin Desk Japan. https://www.coindeskjapan.com/142731/

McKinsey. (2023, March 21). McKinsey Global Private Markets Review: Private Markets Turn Down the Volume. https://www.mckinsey.com/industries/private-equity-and-principal-investors/our-insights/mckinseys-private-markets-annual-review

Nikkei. (2022, February 24). US-based Securitize Partners with Phillip Securities to Develop Digital Securities. https://www.nikkei.com/article/DGXZQOUB2211P0S2A220C2000000/

Sato, K. (2021, September 15). STO's Market Potential in Japan. NRI. https://www.nri.com/-/media/Corporate/en/Files/PDF/knowledge/publication/lakyara/2021/09/lakyaravol346.pdf?la=en&hash=EFF5FF44ECEB9CC6BB52ED0FBC83BAF6F08A2404

The Securities Industry and Financial Market Association. (2021, July). 2021 Capital Markets Fact Book. https://www.sifma.org/wp-content/uploads/2021/07/CM-Fact-Book-2021-SIFMA.pdf

Chapter 10

Bank of Korea. (2021, January 25). CBDC Simulation Research Project Phase One Results and Future Plans. https://www.bok.or.kr/viewer/skin/doc.html?fn=202201240938308670.pdf&rs=/webview/result/P0000559/202201

Bukele, N. (2021, September 25). This is a tweet? Don't Entirely Know How to Cite This! Twitter. https://twitter.com/documentingbtc/status/1435326975120482306

Chawaga, P. (2021, June 5). El Salvador to Declare Bitcoin as Legal Tender. Bitcoin Magazine. https://bitcoinmagazine.com/business/el-salvador-to-declare-bitcoin-as-legal-tender

Cheng, E. (2022, January 18). China's Digital Yuan Notches $8.3 billion in Transactions in Six Months, Taking a Tiny Share of Payments. CNBC. https://www.cnbc.com/2022/01/18/chinas-digital-yuan-notches-8point3-billion-transactions-in-half-a-year.html

Deloitte. (n.d.). Summer 2021 Highlights. https://www2.deloitte.com/content/dam/Deloitte/us/Documents/about-deloitte/us-fortune-deloitte-CEO-survey-summer-2021-highlights-new.pdf

Documenting Bitcoin. (2021, September 7). This is how you buy Starbucks coffee with #bitcoin in El Salvador. Twitter. https://twitter.com/documentingbtc/status/1435326975120482306

Elyashiv, T. (2021, September 27). Central Bank Digital Currencies (CBDC) Have Created a New Global Arms Race. The Street. https://www.goldmansachs.com/media-relations/press-releases/2022/introducing-datonomy-11-03-2022.html

Elyashiv, T. (2021, September 30). El Salvador's Bitcoin Bet: an Interesting Experiment or a Visionary Leap Forward? The Street. https://www.thestreet.com/defi/digital-finance-investing/el-salvadors-bitcoin-bet

Elyashiv, T. (2022, February 17). For the Beijing Olympics, Medal Leaders Reflect World CBDC Leaders. The Street. https://www.thestreet.com/defi/digital-finance-investing/olympic-medal-leaders-reflect-world-cbdc-leaders

Elyashiv, T. (2022, March 25). Is the War in Ukraine Accelerating Global Digital Economy Adoption? The Street. https://www. thestreet.com/defi/digital-finance-investing/is-the-war-in-ukraine-accelerating-global-digital-economy-adoption

Elyashiv, T. (2022, March 2). What the War in Ukraine is Teaching Us About Crypto. The Street. https://www.thestreet.com/defi/digital-finance-investing/what-the-war-in-ukraine-is-teaching-us-about-crypto

Everstake. (2022, March 14). Ukraine's Ministry of Digital Transformation, FTX, and Everstake Launch Crypto Fundraising Site Aid For Ukraine. PR Newswire. https://www.prnewswire.com/news-releases/ukraines-ministry-of-digital-transformation-ftx-and-everstake-launch-crypto-fundraising-site-aid-for-ukraine-301501959.html

Hamilton. J. (n.d.). How Bitcoin Brought the Lightning Network to El Salvador. Cloud Tweaks. https://cloudtweaks.com/2021/07/how-bitcoin-brought-lightning-network-el-salvador/

Jones, Marc. (2022, February 16). Over $315,000 in Digital Yuan Used Every Day at Olympics, PBOC Official says. Reuters. https://www.reuters.com/technology/around-300-mln-digital-yuan-used-every-day-olympics-pboc-official-says-2022-02-15/

Keh, A. (2022, February 11). Why Are Russians in Beijing if Russia Is Banned for Doping? New York Times. https://www.nytimes.com/article/russian-doping-olympics-ban.html

Ostraff, C. (2022, February 25). Bitcoin Price Falls Below $35,000 After Russia Advances into Ukraine. Wall Street Journal. https://www.wsj.com/livecoverage/russia-ukraine-latest-news/card/bitcoin-price-falls-below-35-000-after-russia-advances-into-ukraine-qrfrH4buURVnPwKAFVwP

Post, K. (2020, November 30). European Central Bankers Predict that the Digital Euro is at Least Five Years Away. Coin Telegraph. https://cointelegraph.com/news/european-central-bankers-predict-that-the-digital-euro-is-at-least-five-years-away

Reuters. (2022, March 24). BlackRock's Fink Says Russia-Ukraine Crisis Could Accelerate Digital Currencies. https://www.reuters.com/technology/blackrocks-fink-says-russia-ukraine-crisis-could-accelerate-digital-currencies-2022-03-24/

Tan. E. (2022, March 2). Ukrainian Flag NFT Raises $6.75M for Country's War Efforts. Coin Desk. https://www.coindesk.com/tech/2022/03/02/ukrainian-flag-nft-raises-675m-for-countrys-war-efforts/

Weil, D. (2022, January 21). Digital Dollar Not Imminent: The Fed's Pros and Cons. The Street. https://www.thestreet.com/cryptocurrency/digital-dollar-fed-pros-cons

Williams, C. (2022, March 16). Ukraine Signs Virtual Assets Bill to Legalize Bitcoin. Crypto Briefing. https://cryptobriefing.com/ukraine-signs-virtual-assets-bill-legalize-bitcoin/

Yakubowski, M. (2020, December 27). Did CBDCs Affect the Crypto Space in 2020, and What's Next in 2021? Experts Answer. Coin Telegraph. https://cointelegraph.com/news/did-cbdcs-affect-the-crypto-space-in-2020-and-what-s-next-in-2021-experts-answer

Chapter 11

Elyashiv, T. (2022, January 12). DeFi's 2022 End of Year Summary – One Year Early. The Street. https://www.thestreet.com/defi/digital-finance-investing/defis-2022-end-of-year-summary

Elyashiv, T. (2022, December 20). SPiCE VC's Tal Elyashiv Predicts What's Ahead for the Digital Economy in 2023. The Street. https://www.thestreet.com/defi/digital-finance-investing/spice-vcs-tal-elyashiv-predicts-whats-ahead

Elyashiv, T. (2021, October 21). Tal's NFT Take: Discovery and Search is Key to NFT Growth. The Street. https://www.thestreet.com/defi/digital-finance-investing/discovery-and-search-is-key-to-nft-growth

European Central Bank. (2022, November 2). ECB Seeks Scheme Rulebook Manager for the Digital Euro. https://www.ecb.europa.eu/paym/intro/news/html/ecb.mipnews221010.en.html

Jones, Marc. (2022, October 5). SWIFT Sets Out Blueprint for Central Bank Digital Currency Network. Reuters. https://www.reuters.com/technology/swift-sets-out-blueprint-central-bank-digital-currency-network-2022-10-05/

Otieno, N. (2021, September 13). Swiss SIX Receives Regulatory Approval to Launch Digital Token Exchange. Blockchain News. https://blockchain.news/news/Swiss-SIX-Receives-Regulatory-Approval-to-Launch-Digital-Token-Exchange-534fb312-2b8b-4c10-80be-00cb2921be15

Quarmby, B. (2021, October 14). Almost 1.1 million People Have Already Signed up for Coinbase NFT Waitlist. Coin Telegraph. https://cointelegraph.com/news/almost-1-1-million-people-have-already-signed-up-for-coinbase-nft-waitlist

Seward, Z. (2022, January 4). NFT Marketplace OpenSea Valued at $13.3B in $300M Funding Round. Coin Desk. https://www.coindesk.com/business/2022/01/05/nft-marketplace-opensea-valued-at-133b-in-300m-funding-round-report/